JONATHAN POND'S GUIDE TO INVESTMENT AND FINANCIAL PLANNING:

A Timely Reference for Improving Your Financial Life

Jonathan Pond

New York Institute of Finance
New York   London   Toronto   Sydney   Tokyo   Singapore

Library of Congress Cataloging-in-Publication Data

Pond, Jonathan D.
  [Guide to investment and financial planning]
  Jonathan Pond's guide to investment and financial planning : a
timely reference for improving your financial life / Jonathan Pond.
    p. cm.
  ISBN 0-13-156324-6
  1. Finance, Personal. 2. Investments. 3. Estate planning.
  I. Title.
  HG179.P5555 1991
  332.024'01—dc20   91-6559
                                                                    CIP

This publication is designed to provide accurate and
authoritative information in regard to the subject matter
covered. It is sold with the understanding that the publisher
is not engaged in rendering legal, accounting, or other
professional service. If legal advice or other expert
assistance is required, the services of a competent professional
person should be sought.

From a Declaration of Principles
Jointly Adopted by
a Committee of the American Bar Association
and a Committee of Publishers and Associations

© 1991 by NYIF Corp.
Simon & Schuster
A Paramount Communications Company

Printed in the United States of America
10 9 8 7 6 5 4 3 2

Preface

This Guide will enable you to take advantage of the many opportunities that are available to improve your financial condition. In addition, it will answer the questions that arise in your day-to-day financial planning. The first 12 chapters cover all areas of personal financial planning including:

Investing to achieve financial security

Assuring complete insurance coverage

Managing credit wisely

Minimizing income taxes

Meeting education costs

Funding a comfortable retirement

Planning your estate

Additional chapters provide information on the economy in general as well as the economic outlook for major U.S. industries. Finally, worksheets, checklists, and financial tables help you evaluate your current financial situation and plan your financial future.

Personal financial planning is an important subject for everyone. After all, you work hard for your money, and you want to enjoy a comfortable retirement. Unfortunately, achieving financial security is no easy task, and it's made even more intimidating by the supposed complexity of personal finance and by our being bombarded, day in and day out, with conflicting, often biased financial advice. This Guide will help you take more control over your financial future. Successful personal financial planning need not be complicated.

HOW TO USE THIS GUIDE

This book serves three purposes. First, it is a helpful guide to the complicated world of personal finance. By perusing its pages, you can uncover a wealth of ideas that you can use in your personal financial planning. Each chapter begins with an introduction and outlook that summarizes current issues and trends in a particular area of personal finance. Within each chapter you will find timely suggestions and techniques that you can use to improve your own financial situation.

The second use of the book is as a convenient reference to answer the many questions that you are likely to encounter whenever you are about to make a financial decision. Perhaps the biggest obstacle people encounter in their planning is gaining access to timely and objective information. You will want to refer to this source many times throughout the year for unbiased, down-to-earth answers and suggestions.

Finally, the last chapter of this guide contains a variety of worksheets and checklists that you can use to evaluate your financial situation and determine what action you need to take to assure your financial security. They will help you identify what you are doing well and what you need to do in the future. After all, successful personal financial planning is really based on identifying strengths and weaknesses and taking action to correct any weaknesses. It cannot be done overnight. But, if you begin gradually to make some changes, you will soon find that you are well on your way to achieving financial security.

Acknowledgments

Several people were instrumental in assisting in the preparation of this guide, including Lisa Schkolnick, Marla Brill, Viveca Gardiner, and Ivan Kreilkamp. Their suggestions and contributions are much appreciated. The superb editorial support at the New York Institute of Finance, particularly Philip Ruppel, Sheck Cho, and Susan Barry, is also gratefully acknowledged. Finally, I would like to thank my family for their support during the preparation of this guide.

Contents

1

Successful Investing

Saving regularly and investing these savings wisely are the central purposes of personal financial planning, and they are essential to achieving financial security. One of the major tasks that you confront on the way to financial independence, therefore, is learning how to invest successfully; that is, to find the right balance of stock, interest-earning, and, perhaps, real estate investments that will provide growth and, at the same time, preserve your hard-earned savings.

The importance of proper diversification in achieving these goals on a long-term basis is immeasurable. Consider that between August and October of 1987 the stock market lost almost 28 percent of its value. While the market subsequently regained that drop, anyone who had all of his or her money in stocks during that period would have lost a tremendous amount of savings if, for some reason, that investor was forced to sell the holdings shortly after the downturn. However, people who have restricted their investments to safer money market funds and certificates of deposit (CDs) are barely keeping up with inflation—hardly a successful investment result.

Determining an appropriate investment allocation requires an evaluation and periodic review of your personal and financial situation, including age, family status, income, income prospects, objectives, and personal preferences. Generally, the younger you are, the greater the investment risk you can afford to take in exchange for potentially achieving greater investment returns. A retiree, however, should generally opt for a less aggressive investment approach.

Of course, other matters may also influence your investment strategy. A retiree who has substantial income from a pension and Social Security can afford to take a greater degree of investment risk than someone who depends largely on personal savings for income. People who are uncomfortable with investment risk may be better suited for a relatively conservative portfolio, even though it offers less potential for growth than a more aggressive one.

Another factor that must be considered in the investment allocation and selection process is the relative attractiveness of various types of investments. This does not mean that you must shift your investments frequently to achieve financial success. In fact, it is usually the opposite: Buying and holding is a better course. However, you should periodically review your portfolio to ensure that your current investment mix is appropriate in light of prevailing market conditions as well as your personal situation.

Since it appears that the investment markets will not rise as much in the 1990s as they did in the 1980s, investors will have to spend more time evaluating their portfolios and analyzing investment alternatives if they are going to outpace inflation. To help accomplish this, diversification into international securities will become increasingly common even for the average investor. These investments, however, should generally be sought through worldwide diversification rather than concentrating on a single country or region.

SUMMARY OF INVESTMENT ALTERNATIVES

Table 1-1 describes the various commonly used investment alternatives and their advantages and disadvantages. It is divided into three sections, representing the three investment categories: stock investments, interest-earning (including cash equivalent) investments,

Table 1-1. Commonly Used Investment Alternatives

Investment	Description	Advantages	Possible Disadvantages
Stock Investments			
Common stock	Security that represents ownership in a company	Potential for high rate of return through capital gains; many pay dividends	Risk of market decline; not protected by government; value fluctuates daily
Convertible preferred stock	Preferred stock that may be exchanged by owner for common stock	Combines usually attractive dividend payout with potential of capital appreciation of common stock	Lower yield than bonds; sells at a premium to conversion value of the common stock
Futures contracts	Contracts covering the sale of financial instruments or commodities for future delivery; includes agricultural products, metals, Treasury bills, foreign currencies, and stock index futures (i.e., Standard & Poor's (S&P) 500)	High potential return through use of leverage	Highly speculative and volatile; favorite of investment "scamsters"
Options	The right to buy (call) or sell (put) a stock at a given price (strike price) for a given period of time	Inexpensive way to speculate; possible high return for small investment; covered option writers can add income with low risk	Option buyers usually lose entire investment

Table 1-1. (*continued*)

Investment	Description	Advantages	Possible Disadvantages
Preferred stock	Stock sold with a fixed dividend; if company is liquidated, it has priority over common stock	Fixed rate of return; safer than common stock dividends	Dividend is usually never increased; stock price appreciation potential may be limited
Stock mutual fund	Investment trust in which your money is pooled with those of other investors and invested in stocks by professional managers	Professional management; diversification reduces risk; can switch from one fund to another within a family of funds; wide selection; low costs; low investment minimums	Not federally insured; subject to fluctuations in the stock market
Unit investment trust (stocks)	Fixed portfolio of securities deposited with a trustee; offered to public in units	Diversification; professional selection; usually can redeem units	Portfolio is not managed actively; subject to price fluctuation
Warrant	Gives holder right to purchase a given stock at stipulated price over a fixed period of time	If underlying shares rise in value, so will warrant; can exercise warrant at any time	If warrant expires, value of investment is lost
Interest-Earning Investments			
Bond mutual fund	Investment trust in which your dollars are pooled with those of others and	Professional management; diversification reduces risk; can switch from one fund	Not federally insured; subject to fluctuations in interest rates

Investment	Description	Advantages	Disadvantages
	invested by professional managers in various bond issues	to another within a family of funds; wide selection; low costs; low investment minimums	
Certificate of deposit (CD)	Receipt for money left in bank for set period of time at an agreed-upon interest rate; at end of period, bank pays deposit plus interest	Insured up to certain limits by federal government; competitive interest rates	Penalty for early withdrawal; interest rates may rise while your money is locked in
Convertible bond	Bond that may be exchanged by owner for common stock of same company	Combines safety of bonds with potential for capital appreciation of common stock	Lower yield than similar quality nonconvertibles; sell at premiums to the conversion value of the common stock
Corporate bond	Debt obligation of corporation	Receive fixed return over specified time; assured return; low risk with highly rated bond issues	May be called prior to maturity, particularly if interest rates decline
Money market deposit account	A type of money market fund at a bank or savings and loan association; has limited checking privileges	No federal regulation of rates: banks set their own rates; insured by federal government up to certain limits; no withdrawal penalties	Minimum balance required; limited check writing; rates often lower than money market mutual funds

Table 1-1. (*continued*)

Investment	Description	Advantages	Possible Disadvantages
Money market mutual fund	An investment company which buys short-term money market instruments	High short-term interest rates; no withdrawal penalties; handled by professional money managers; check-writing privileges	Usually not insured; no capital growth potential
Mortgage-backed securities	Securities representing a shared ownership in pools of mortgages; backed by federal, state, or local governments; include Ginnie Maes, Fannie Maes, Freddie Macs, etc.	Backed by government or government agencies; high yields; liquidity; receive regular monthly income	Prices decline if interest rates increase; payments dwindle as mortgages are paid off
Municipal bond	Debt obligation of state, city, town, or their agencies	Interest earned is tax-free at federal level and in state and city where issued	Subject to price fluctuations; after-tax return may be lower than other bonds
NOW account	Negotiable order of withdrawal; interest-bearing checking account	Funds in account earn interest; unlimited checking; federally insured up to certain limits	Interest rates are low; must maintain minimum balance
Savings account	Account in which money deposited earns interest	Federally insured up to certain limits; guaranteed	Low interest rates

	yield; can be used as collateral	
Treasury bills	Short-term U.S. Treasury securities; maturities: 13, 16, and 52 weeks	Rates often lower than other short-term investments
Treasury bonds	Long-term U.S. Treasury securities; maturities: 10 years or more	Value declines if interest rates rise
Treasury notes	Medium-term securities of U.S. Treasury; maturities: not less than 1 year and not more than 10 years	Value declines if interest rates rise
	Backed by U.S. government; interest earned is exempt from state and local taxes	
Unit investment trust (bonds)	Fixed portfolio of securities deposited with a trustee; offered to public in units; categories include municipal bonds, corporate bonds, public utility common stocks, etc.	Portfolio is not managed; most have 25–30 year maturities
	Diversification; professional selection; usually can redeem units; available in small dollar amounts	
U.S. savings bonds	Debt obligation of U.S. Treasury	Generally lower rate of interest than available elsewhere
	Backed by U.S. government; if held 5 years, return is 85% of the average yield on 5-year Treasury security with a 6% minimum guar-	

Table 1-1. (*continued*)

Investment	Description	Advantages	Possible Disadvantages
		anteed; exempt from state and local income taxes; may defer federal tax; registered, so it can be replaced if lost or stolen	
Zero-coupon bonds	Debt instrument; sold at discount from face value with no (zero) annual interest paid out; capital appreciation realized upon maturity	Low initial expenditure leads to balloon payment upon maturity; you know exact amount you will receive	Yields lower than for regular bonds; must pay taxes annually as though you received interest unless invested in tax-deferred account
Real estate investments			
Income-producing real estate	Do-it-yourself real estate investing involving the purchase and management of properties ranging from apartments to commercial and industrial buildings	Total control over the acquisition, management, and sale of the property; opportunity for significant tax-favored wealth accumulation	Expensive to get into; risk of loss through vacancies or declining prices; management of property can be a hassle

Real estate investment trust (REIT)	REITs invest in or finance real estate projects including offices, shopping centers, apartments, hotels, and so on; REITs are sold as stock and trade on the stock exchanges	Provides participation in real estate with small amount of money	Subject to fluctuations of real estate and the stock market
Real estate limited partnership	A real estate ownership arrangement involving one or more general partners and limited partners; liability is generally limited to the extent of actual investment; can invest in all kinds of real estate	Provides participation in real estate with small investment; limited partners are relieved of chore of managing the property	Potential for profits is limited vs. buying property yourself; many deals have soured over past years
Undeveloped property	Do-it-yourself investment in raw land that, hopefully, will eventually be developed	Well-situated property can appreciate a great deal; minimal management responsibility	Good raw land is very expensive and difficult to finance long term; lack of income requires ability to commit money over a long period of time

and real estate investments. For more detailed information on each of these investment categories see Chapters 2 through 6.

SETTING INVESTMENT OBJECTIVES

Many people invest without considering what they want to accomplish with their investments. You probably have several financial goals, such as buying a home (or second home), educating your children, or, most important, accumulating sufficient investments to assure a comfortable retirement. This section will help you establish a realistic target return for your investments so that you can invest more wisely, thereby achieving your goals more easily.

The key to successful investing is beating the rate of inflation on an after-tax basis over the long term. An after-tax return on investment that exceeds the inflation rate by 3 percent is an appropriate objective for most investors. Exceeding inflation by 4 percent over the long term is considered very good. Beating long-term inflation is easier said than done, however. As the example in Table 1-2 indicates, an investor with a combined federal and state tax rate of 33 percent would have to earn a 12 percent return on a taxable interest-earning investment (e.g., a corporate bond) in order to beat an assumed 5 percent rate of inflation by 3 percent after taxes.

Table 1-2. Example: A $10,000 Taxable Investment

	Annual Rate of Return	
	10%	12%
Income before taxes	$1000	$1200
Federal income tax (28%)	(280)	(336)
State income tax (5%)	(50)	(60)
Total tax	(330)	(396)
Income after taxes	$ 670	$ 804
After-tax return on investment	6.7%	8.0%
After-tax return in excess of inflation (assuming 5% rate of inflation)	1.7%	3.0%

Most investors don't pay sufficient attention to the impact of taxes and will think they have died and gone to heaven when CD rates reach 10 percent. Yet, as Table 1-2 shows, a 10 percent CD rate keeps an investor just ahead of inflation on an after-tax basis. These rates, however, are very attractive for retirement-oriented accounts since income on these funds is not taxed until the money is withdrawn at retirement. The lesson: Put as much of your retirement-earmarked savings as possible into retirement-oriented accounts such as IRAs (whether deductible or not), 401(k) plans, Keogh plans (if you are self-employed), deferred annuities, and so forth. It's quite easy to beat inflation by 3 percent after taxes when no taxes are being taken out along the way.

Successful investors are inevitably those who take a patient, prudent view of investment selection and allocation. Just because a particular investment doesn't offer an attractive after-tax return doesn't mean it should be avoided. Lower risk investments generally offer lower returns. The key, therefore, is to *balance* your investments with a combination of lower return, lower risk securities and higher risk, higher return potential securities. This is discussed in the following section.

Finally, recognize that investing is almost invariably a long-term process. The only exceptions to this are if you are going to need the money soon (perhaps for a home or to meet college tuition bills), or you are very old or ill and have a short life expectancy. Otherwise, don't fret if you cannot achieve your investment return target over a given year. This happens to everyone, and you have plenty of time to make up for the shortfall.

ALLOCATING INVESTMENTS ACCORDING TO INVESTOR NEEDS

Allocating investments is on one hand an overused and abused excuse to encourage investors to change their investments frequently, and, on the other hand, a very important concept to understand in order to achieve long-term investment success. The following section describes how you can begin to take control of your investments by allocating them according to your needs, not according to what some-

one else says you should be doing in response to market conditions and forecasts.

Most people tend to invest in extremes. Many invest too conservatively, restricting their investments to low-risk interest-earning securities such as CDs and money market funds. Other investors speculate too much by investing their hard-earned money on high-risk stocks or so-called get rich quick investments. Successful long term investors, however, usually take a middle-of-the-road approach to investing by allocating their money among stocks, interest-earning securities, and, perhaps, real estate investments. When speculating on high-risk investments, these investors risk only a small portion of their portfolio, perhaps 5 percent.

In order to be a successful long-term investor, you need to regularly review the allocation of your investments, no matter how small or large they might be. This is a particularly challenging task since the so-called asset allocation decision hinges on so many diverse and rapidly changing factors, including stock market conditions, interest rates, economic prospects, and tax regulations, not to mention your own financial status, objectives, and preferences. Unfortunately, many investors often do not pay sufficient attention to asset allocation. It is easier to focus on individual investments such as a stock mutual fund, municipal bond, or real estate limited partnership rather than step back and look at your present and future investments in their totality.

The Four Steps of Investment Allocation

Many people simply make an investment when they have the money available to do so. However, before making a specific investment, you should review how it will fit into your total portfolio. Therefore, if you haven't done so already, you probably need to review the four-step investment allocation process, culminating in actually selecting specific investments.

Step One. First, you must determine the appropriate percentage of total funds that you have available for investment in each of the three major investment categories: stock invest-

ments, interest-earning investments, and real estate investments. You may not be interested in making or may not be able
to afford to make real estate investments, in which case the
allocation decision is between stock investments and interest-
earning investments. The following tips will help you make
this critical decision.

If you are younger or middle-aged, you should generally
have a considerable portion of your investments in stock,
and, if you are so inclined, income-producing real estate.
Over the long term, these investments have performed very
well, particularly in comparison with interest-earning investments. However, some of your portfolio should remain conservatively invested. A typical portfolio allocation may be 40
percent stocks, 30 percent real estate, and 30 percent interest-earning for those who opt for real estate investments. For
those who do not, 60 percent stocks and 40 percent interest-
earning is widely considered to be a desirable allocation.
Fifty percent of each isn't a bad allocation either, and is a lot
easier to remember.

If your are a preretiree within, say, 10 years of retirement or
if you are retired, your investment allocation should be
somewhat more conservative. This tactic minimizes the possible adverse effects of being caught in a protracted downturn in the stock or real estate market when you don't have a
long time to make up for it. An appropriate allocation depends on many factors, of course, but a typical preretiree or
retiree who, like most of us, will need to rely on his or her
personal investments to help pay living expenses might consider an appropriate portfolio balance to be 40 percent stocks
and 60 percent interest-earning. If the preretiree or retiree
has real estate investments, a good balance would be 30
percent stocks, 20 percent real estate, and 50 percent
interest-earning investments. Note that even retirees need
stocks in their personal portfolios because stocks have pretty
consistently provided an inflation-beating return, which retirees, most of whom have long life expectancies, still need.

Step Two. The second step involves evaluating the general kinds of investments within each of the two or three invest-

ment categories that are suitable for you, for example, "direct" ownership of stocks, interest-earning and real estate, and/or "indirect" ownership via mutual funds or limited partnerships. Most often, the appropriate course is one of diversifying across investment vehicles. For example, with respect to stock investments, you may be best served by having some of your portfolio invested in specific company shares and some in mutual fund shares.

If your portfolio is relatively small, say under $10,000, you should probably stick to mutual funds that offer a lot of advantages for a relatively small investment, such as diversification, low cost (particularly if you buy no-load, meaning no commission funds), and professional management. As your portfolio gets up to the $20,000 and above range, you can start making direct investments, for example, buying stock in particular companies and corporate or municipal bonds.

Deciding how much to place in indirect as opposed to direct investments also requires a great deal of judgment. If you want to keep things simple, the following could be a perfectly good way to split up your investments in order to maintain a 50/50 percent split between total stocks and total interest-earning securities:

	25%	in directly owned common stocks
	25%	in stock mutual funds
Subtotal	50%	in stock investments
	25%	in directly owned, interest-earning investments
	25%	in interest-earning mutual funds
Subtotal	50%	in interest-earning investments
Total	100%	

Step Three. The third step in the investment allocation process further breaks down the general categories of investment into specific industry, market, or fund categories. Appropriate directly owned, interest-earning investments might consist of short-term investments (money market accounts, certificates of deposit), municipal bonds, corporate bonds, and Treasury bonds. Assuming you should also invest in interest-earning mutual funds, you might consider, for example, intermediate-term municipal bond funds, long-term corporate bond funds, and convertible bond funds.

If you are like most people, you are unfamiliar with many kinds of investments that may be worthwhile additions to your portfolio. This doesn't mean you should be involved in some of the unusual investments that have been concocted by the investment community, such as "unbundled stock units" or "Nikkei put options." But, you should strive to become familiar with the many excellent investment securities that are available to individual investors.

Just as you shouldn't place too much of your investment money in one category of investment (interest-earning securities, for example), you should also never place too much money in one single type of investment. A few years ago, many people put too much money into junk bond mutual funds. They suffered greatly when the market for these securities collapsed. So be sure to spread your investments among several categories of interest-earning securities and stocks.

Step Four. The final step consists of selecting specific investments within each of the industry or fund categories that you identified in Step Three—a particular bond or stock issue or mutual fund, for example.

Perhaps the most important ingredient to successful investing is to be your own boss; don't let someone else make your investment decisions for you. It is certainly acceptable for others to make suggestions, but you should make the final decisions. Moreover, by devoting a little time to familiarizing yourself with investments, you can become an excellent investor yourself.

Always buy an investment with the expectation of holding onto it forever. While following this literally may be too extreme, the point is that for the vast majority of people, a buy and hold strategy performs much better than a strategy that involves trading investments frequently. Buy high quality investments and hold onto them.

DEVELOPING YOUR OWN "PERMANENT PORTFOLIO STRUCTURE"

Figure 1-1 depicts the investment allocation process, including common types of investments that might be included in each investment category. Use it to decide how you want to allocate your investments. Finally, view your allocation as a "Permanent Portfolio Structure," which you will not alter significantly in the face of market uncertainty or, worse, the opinions of experts who are wrong at least as often as they are right. Successful investors establish reasonable investment allocation parameters—and stick to them.

COPING WITH MARKET VOLATILITY AND INVESTMENT UNCERTAINTY

Beginning in the latter half of the 1980s, the markets for both stock and interest-earning investments became increasingly volatile and uncertain, frightening experienced and novice investors alike. The 1990s have started out in the same manner, so you should probably resign yourself to the fact that volatile stock and interest-rate markets are becoming the norm. Successful investors will continue to maintain a steady, consistent course, as they should under any market conditions. Nevertheless, there are several important matters that need to be kept in mind in learning to cope with market volatility and investment uncertainty.

If you are like most investors, you have been adversely affected from time to time by large, often sudden declines in stock prices and rapidly rising or declining interest rates. Many investors are prone to act rashly as a result of unexpected (aren't they all?) market fluctuations. Some bail out of most or all of their stock and bond investments, retreating to the safety

Figure 1-1. Investment Allocation

Form of Ownership	Investment Category		
	Equity	Fixed Income	Real Estate
Direct	Common stocks	Bonds, Treasury securities, etc.	Directly owned real estate
Mutual fund/ Partnership	Stock mutual funds	Fixed-income mutual funds	Limited partnerships

and flexibility of short-term investments such as money market funds. Yet, the yield on these investments barely keeps pace with inflation after taxes have been paid on the interest. There are several important things to remember about investing, particularly in the face of market uncertainty.

Maintain a Balanced Portfolio. Your investment portfolio should consist not only of common stock investments, but also fixed-income investments and, perhaps, real estate. Otherwise, you will always risk having a substantial portion of your assets eroded by unfavorable market conditions.

Diversify. Many people have too much of their portfolio invested in the stock of one or a very few companies or a single mutual fund. Lack of diversification is often the result of an individual's participation in his or her employer's stock option or stock purchase plans. Although such participation is usually advisable, there is always a danger that the price of the particular shares will collapse. If you can't afford the risk (and most people can't), liquidate some of your single-issue portfolio.

Buy Quality. Shares of quality, dividend-paying companies are favored during volatile markets. Investors realize that these companies have more staying power if, in fact, market conditions continue to deteriorate.

"Ladder" the Maturities of Your Interest-Earning Investments. Pick interest-earning investments with varying maturities so that if interest rates rise or fall, you won't be stuck with most of your interest-bearing investments maturing at the same time. It is better to have them mature periodically so that you can insulate your investments somewhat from the effects of fluctuating interest rates.

Opt for Mutual Funds That Have Superior Long-Term Track Records. Stock mutual funds have typically performed abysmally during bear markets. Similarly, investors are often surprised to discover that the value of most bond mutual funds declines when interest rates rise. Nevertheless, some funds, usually those that have been in existence for a long time and have produced strong long-term performance records (in comparison with similar funds), are consistently better at handling adverse market conditions than other funds. Conversely, today's high flier is often tomorrow's crash victim.

Use Stop Loss Orders on Stocks. A stop loss order will protect your stocks somewhat against a sharply and rapidly declining market. They are not foolproof, however. For example, in a volatile market, you may be sold out of a stock that subsequently rebounds in price.

When in Doubt, Seek Safe Havens. If you are totally confused, if not frightened, by market conditions, park at least some of your money in safe, short-term investments such as money market funds, Treasury bills, and short-term certificates of deposit. While you may not be earning a particularly attractive return, at least you are protecting some of your assets until the dust settles.

Doing Nothing is Often the Best Response to Crisis. Most investors who react to suddenly adverse market conditions almost always do the wrong thing. They are selling when they should be holding, if not buying. In general, you should not sell into weakness. Wait until things settle down. Also, be very wary of the opinions of experts immediately after the crisis. Ask yourself, "If they're such experts, why didn't they predict this situation in the first place?"

Avoid Investing with Borrowed Money. The investors who were really hurt by the 1987, 1989, and 1990 market downturns were generally those who had invested on margin, in other words, used borrowed money to invest. The only way for them to cover their margin calls was to sell their stock holdings at an inopportune time. Margin can be an effective means of leveraging a stock portfolio, but fully margined investors expose themselves to considerable risk.

Take a Long-Term Investment Perspective. The 500-point, single-day drop in the Dow Jones Index (Dow) on October 19, 1987 was a heartstopper for all of us. Although it seemed the world was coming to an end, the total decline during the awful October 1987 market wiped out only one year's gain on the Dow. Flat (if not down) 12-month stock markets are not that uncommon, yet few people remembered that fact amidst the hysteria. Invest for the long haul and you'll fret less over shorter-term market vacillations.

We were intoxicated by the bull market of the 1980s, which many seers thought would continue unabated. Of course, we all want to participate in these great markets, but we also must realize that they do come to an end, at times, abruptly. By heeding the above suggestions you will be better prepared to weather whatever storms await, not only in stocks, but also with respect to your interest-earning investments.

DECIDING HOW TO INVEST "NEW" MONEY

If you have already begun an investment program or when you do so, you will frequently have the pleasure and dilemma of deciding how to invest "new" money. The following simple rules will help you make these often-perplexing decisions.

Sources of "new" money, in other words money that becomes available to invest, are numerous. Some of these sources include dividend and interest income that is not automatically reinvested, your regular savings, maturing CDs and other interest-earning securities, and, perhaps, bonuses or other periodic windfalls. As new money becomes available to you, you have to choose among the three basic investment categories of stock investments, real estate investments, and interest-earning investments. Interest-earning investments are frequently further broken down into long-term investments and short-term investments (also known as cash equivalent investments).

The following general guidelines may help you determine which of the investment categories is attractive at any given time. Note that you may want to modify these rules somewhat or develop your own so that you can become more comfortable making investment decisions.

Stock Investments

Stock investments are best made when stock prices in general are depressed or at least are not unusually high. One measure of relative stock market prices is the price to earnings (P/E) ratio of a major stock market index such as the Dow Jones Industrial Average (DJIA). P/E ratios are derived by dividing the price of a stock or index of stocks by the earnings per share of a stock or index of stocks. A P/E ratio well above the historical average for the index may be indicative of an overpriced stock market. For example, The Dow Industrial P/E exceeded 20 shortly before the October 1987 stock market crash. By way of comparison, the Dow Industrial P/E ratio over the preceding decade had generally been in the 11 to 15 range. Investors with new money, therefore, may want to consider the current market index P/E ratios in deciding whether or not to invest in stocks. If the DJIA P/E ratio is in the low to mid-teens, stocks are certainly not bargains, but may be trading at reasonable prices. If the index is above that level, new stock investments should be avoided. If below, stocks should be considered. The Dow Industrial P/E ratio is listed in the *Wall Street Journal* and *Barron's*.

Real Estate Investments

Real estate investments are particularly difficult to evaluate. There are a couple of rules of thumb that can help you assess the financial viability of an investment in income-producing real estate, whether you are buying it yourself or through a real estate limited partnership. The simpler one involves comparing the total selling price with the current gross annual rental. A property that is selling for much more than 7 or 8 times gross annual rental is likely to yield a negative cash flow, and should therefore be avoided.

A second real estate rule of thumb is the capitalization rate, usually referred to as the "cap rate." The cap rate is determined as follows:

$$\text{Capitalization rate} = \frac{\text{Net operating income}}{\text{Total amount invested}}$$

For example, a limited partnership in an apartment building requiring a total investment of $3,500,000 has an estimated net operating income of $300,000. The cap rate is $300,000/$3,500,000 or 8.6 percent. A cap rate of 8 or greater is considered desirable.

Undeveloped land is particularly difficult to evaluate. Generally, land with significant appreciation potential is well situated and, therefore, very expensive. Cheap land usually remains cheap.

Interest-Earning Investments

Interest-earning investments consist of both investments with a long-term maturity and investments with a short maturity or no maturity like a money market fund.

Long-Term, Interest-Earning Securities. The bellwether yield on long-term Treasury bonds is an easy-to-obtain indicator of relative yields on interest-earning securities. Yields on most longer-term securities tend to move in tandem with the long-term Treasury yield. In recent years, long-term Treasury yields over 9 percent have often signaled attractive returns from many interest-earning securities as they did during the 1990 Iraqi crisis. When the long Treasury yield is between 8 and 9 percent, you may still be able to find decent returns on them as well. The interest rates on long Treasuries, as well as other interest-earning securities, are commonly available in the financial press, including the *Wall Street Journal.*

Short-Term, Interest-Earning Securities. Short-term, interest-earning securities should generally be viewed as a temporary place to invest your money when you cannot confidently identify attractive stock, real estate, or long-term, interest-earning investments. These securities consist of money market funds, Treasury bills, savings accounts, and short-term CDs. The reason they should be viewed only as temporary (except, perhaps, for some emergency funds that you may need to access quickly) is that they rarely offer any hope of providing a return that beats inflation by very much after taxes are paid on the interest. Nevertheless, there are times when short-term interest earning securities should be the investment of choice until stock market, interest-rate, and real estate conditions become more favorable.

INTERPRETING THE MAJOR STOCK AND BOND INDEXES

You've probably heard and read the names many times: the Dow Industrials, the S&P 500, the Wilshire 5000, the Salomon Brothers Index. You probably also know that they are stock or bond indexes, but what do they tell us? The following section describes the composition of the major stock and bond indexes.

Stock Indexes

Dow Jones Industrial Average (DJIA). This most often used index consists of the following 30 blue chip stocks, whose prices are averaged (after adjustment for stock splits) to make up the DJIA:

Allied Sig.	Chevron	Gen Motors
Alum Co	Coca-Cola	Goodyear
Amer Exp	Du Pont	IBM
AT&T	Eastman	Int'l Paper
Beth Steel	Exxon	McDonald's
Boeing	Gen Electric	Merck

Minn M&M	Proc Gamb	USX Corp.
Navistar	Sears	United Tech
Phillip Morris	Texaco	Westinghouse
Primerica	Union Carbide	Woolworth

Because the DJIA focuses only on 30 large companies, it can be misleading. For example, from mid-1989 to mid-1990, the DJIA showed a modest gain while the broader indexes, described below, all showed rather substantial declines. Two other Dow Jones averages are the Dow Jones Utilities Average, consisting of 15 major utilities, and the Dow Jones Transportation Average, which consists of 20 major transportation companies, including trucking companies, railroads, and airlines.

The Standard and Poor's 500-Stock Index (S&P 500). This measure is more representative of market performance than the DJIA and is used by most individual investors. This index consists of the average of prices for 500 corporations listed on the New York Stock Exchange, including 425 industrials, 20 railroads, and 55 utilities.

The New York Stock Exchange (NYSE) Index. This index includes all of the stocks listed on the NYSE.

The American Stock Exchange (AMEX) Index. The AMEX Index consists of the stocks listed on the American Stock Exchange, most of which are smaller than those listed on the NYSE.

National Association of Securities Dealers Automated Quotations (NASDAQ) Index. This index includes over 2000 stocks traded over the counter; these are generally smaller companies than those listed on the NYSE or the AMEX.

Wilshire 5000 Index. This average is produced by Wilshire Associates and is a blend of NYSE, AMEX, and most active, over-the-counter issues. It consists of 5000 stocks. As the broadest index, it is more representative of the overall stock market.

Bond Indexes

Dow Jones 20-Bond Index. This index is computed by averaging the prices of 10 utility and 10 industrial bonds.

Dow Jones Municipal Bond Yield Average. This average shows the yields of low-coupon bonds in five states and 15 major cities.

Figure 1-2. Cumulative Growth of Stocks and Treasury Securities: 1926-1989

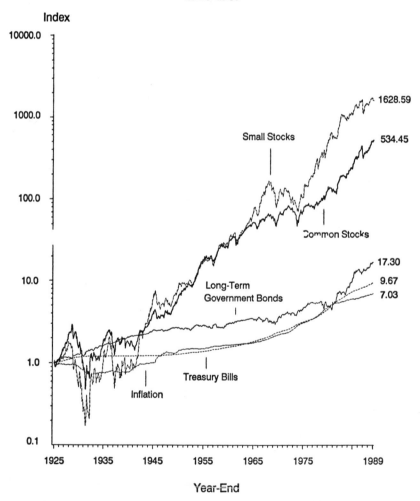

Salomon Brothers Corporate Bond Index. This index is comprised of a portfolio of approximately 4000 corporate bond issues, including utilities, industrials, finance companies, and banks.

GROWTH OF STOCKS AND TREASURY SECURITIES

Figure 1-2 depicts the cumulative growth of a dollar invested in common stocks, small company stocks, long-term government bonds, and Treasury bills from the end of 1925 to the end of 1989. The cumulative increase in the consumer price index is also presented.

AVERAGE ANNUAL RETURNS OF STOCKS, BONDS, AND TREASURY SECURITIES FOR THE DECADES

Table 1-3 lists the compound annual returns of stocks, bonds, and Treasury securities for the last six decades and for the period 1926 to 1929. Inflation figures over similar periods are also presented. Note that over most of the decades surveyed, stocks provided superior returns than the interest-earning security categories.

Table 1-3. Average Annual Returns for the Decades

	1920s*	1930s	1940s	1950s	1960s	1970s	1980s
S&P 500	19.2%	0.0%	9.2%	19.4%	7.8%	5.9%	17.5%
Small company	−4.5	1.4	20.7	16.9	15.5	11.5	15.8
Long-term government	5.0	4.9	3.2	−0.1	1.4	5.5	12.6
Long-term corporation	5.2	6.9	2.7	1.0	1.7	6.2	13.0
Treasury bills	3.7	0.6	0.4	1.9	3.9	6.3	8.9
Inflation	−1.1	−2.0	5.4	2.2	2.5	7.4	5.1

*Based on the period from 1926 to 1929.

Source: © 1990. Ibbotson, Roger G., and Rex A. Sinquefield, *Stocks, Bonds, Bills, and Inflation*, (SBBI), 1982, updated in *1990 Yearbook*™. Ibbotson Associates, Chicago. All rights reserved.

2

Short-Term Investments

It was not too long ago that the only place for investors to earn interest on funds they wanted to keep relatively liquid was a low-yielding passbook savings account. Today, there is a very broad range of more appealing choices of short-term, interest-earning investments, commonly referred to as cash equivalents. The following list explains some of these options.

Money market mutual funds invest in short-term debt, such as commercial paper, Treasury bills, and certificates of deposit. Shares are generally redeemable at any time, either through the mail or by telephone.

There are a variety of money market mutual funds, including tax-exempt funds that invest solely in short-term municipal debt, and U.S. government money market funds, which invest in Treasury bills and government-guaranteed securities.

Money market deposit accounts, offered by banks and other savings institutions, have liquidity features similar to money market mutual funds, although they may require higher investment minimums and have more stringent restrictions on withdrawals. Their rates tend to be lower than money market mutual funds.

Certificates of deposit, also offered by banks, can offer competitive yields. Maturities range from 90 days to 10 years, although investors who may need access to their money should limit themselves to maturities of 1 year or less. There is usually an early withdrawal penalty if a certificate of deposit is withdrawn before its stated maturity.

Treasury bills, along with U.S. savings bonds, are the only debt instruments guaranteed directly by the full faith and credit of the U.S. government. For investors seeking liquidity, maturities of under 1 year, which require a minimum investment of $10,000, are most appropriate.

Investors may use these cash equivalent investments for a variety of purposes. Often, they serve as a "parking place" for money awaiting a more attractive investment opportunity. During times of high short-term interest rates, cash equivalents can be attractive investments themselves. In addition, liquid savings accounts may be used for emergency funds to help meet living expenses if regular sources of income are unexpectedly reduced or suspended, or if unexpected expenses crop up.

Since there may be substantial differences in yield among short-term investments, particularly on an after-tax basis, it is advisable to check prevailing rates on a regular basis to achieve the highest possible returns. On the other hand, you should keep in mind that short-term investments will, at best, barely beat inflation on an after-tax basis. For this reason, they should generally be viewed as a temporary parking place for money pending more attractive investment alternatives.

SHORT-TERM INVESTMENT ALTERNATIVES

Investors have a smorgasboard of short-term investment alternatives from which to choose. This section describes the most commonly used short-term, or cash equivalent, investments.

Certificates of Deposit

A certificate of deposit (CD) is a receipt for funds deposited in a financial institution at a specified interest rate for a specified period of time. Some institutions offer a minimum deposit of as little as $500; time of maturity ranges from 3 months to 10 years. Short-term CDs, however, generally have maturities of 1 year or less. There are a variety of CDs designed for individual investors with varying interest rates, maturities, and minimum deposits.

Accounts of depository institutions offering CDs may be insured by either a private insurance company, a state insurance fund, or a federal agency. Federal agency-insured institutions are far safer than other kinds, and a prudent investor will limit investment to these. Federal deposit insurance programs make a deposit a riskless investment up to a certain amount. The Federal Deposit Insurance Corporation (FDIC), a corporation of the federal government, insures the deposits of most banks. Deposits of most savings and loan institutions and credit unions are similarly insured under other government-backed deposit insurance corporations. The federal deposit insurance limit is currently $100,000 of a depositor's principal and interest (for all kinds of deposits—savings and checking accounts, NOW accounts, money market deposit accounts, and CDs). Higher limits can be achieved with multiple accounts using different family members as owners or co-owners. Be sure to check on current federal deposit insurance regulations, because Congress has been considering limitations on the amount of federal insurance in light of the savings and loan debacle.

Several brokerage firms sell so-called brokered CDs. In essence, they offer a CD shopping service over the phone, which may result in your being able to obtain a better CD rate than you could at a local financial institution.

Money Market Funds

When, in the mid-1970s, money market rates climbed far above the rates offered by banks and thrifts, a new kind of mutual fund, the money market fund, was invented to capitalize on the money market's high return and liquidity. These funds are designed to appeal to the small investor, who may find it difficult to invest directly in money market securities and may often find that substantial funds are required. Transaction costs are very small, and since money market funds are able to buy a broad range of securities, credit risk is relatively low. (Remember, though, that like most investments, money market funds are not riskless.) The three types of money market funds are: general purpose funds, which invest in a wide range of good quality money market instruments and typically have an average maturity of 30 to 40 days; U.S. government short-term funds, which invest solely in U.S. treasury securities and U.S. government agency issues; and tax-exempt money market funds, which invest in short-term municipal securities and are exempt from federal income taxes but, because of their tax deductibility, have a lower yield than the other two types. Most mutual fund companies offer a variety of money market funds.

Money Market Deposit Accounts

Money market deposit accounts (MMDAs) are offered by banks which are free to pay any interest rate they choose. MMDAs, unlike CDs, have no maturity date, and as their interest rate varies, a set yield is not guaranteed. Disadvantages of MMDAs, compared to money market funds, include generally lower interest rates, a generally higher minimum balance, limited checkwriting privileges, and the inconvenience of going to the bank to transfer or withdraw funds. Unlike money market funds, however, money market accounts are insured up to $100,000.

Treasury Bills

Treasury bills, one of the several securities offered by the U.S. government to the investing public, offer investors no risk, very high liquidity, exemption from state and local income taxes, and a wide range of maturities. Treasury bills, or T-bills, are negotiable, non-interest-bearing securities with an original maturity of 1 year or less. Currently, bills are offered in minimum denominations of $10,000 and increments of $5000 thereafter. An investor in a T-bill earns a return by receiving more for the bill at its maturity than he or she paid for it at issue; bills are always issued at a discount from face value, the amount being determined in bill auctions held by the Federal Reserve. T-bills may be purchased directly from the Federal Reserve or, for a nominal charge, through a bank or brokerage firm.

Savings Accounts

Passbook savings accounts are a convenient and liquid short-term investment, but they also pay the lowest interest rate (usually around 5.5 percent). Savings accounts are insured by the FDIC up to $100,000 and can be used as collateral against a bank loan. Negotiable order of withdrawal (NOW) accounts and Super NOW accounts are hybrids of checking and savings accounts that require a minimum deposit and may pay higher interest rates.

Municipal Notes

State and local governments issue interest-bearing municipal notes with maturities ranging from 1 month to 1 year. They are secured by the issuer's pledge of credit, a pledge that does not absolutely remove debt risk, as it is possible that a municipality might default on its securities. Municipal notes' primary attraction is that interest income on them is exempt from federal taxation, and from state taxes as well if you are a resident of the state where the notes are issued. Smaller investors may participate in these securities through a tax-exempt money market fund.

MAKING THE MOST OF SHORT-TERM INVESTMENTS

Many people become accustomed to always making the same kind of short-term investment. By devoting some time to evaluating the various types of short-term investments, you will be able to make the most of the money that you invest in these securities. This section suggests ways to make the most of your short-term investment.

Finding the Highest Rates

Rates on short-term (cash equivalent) investments vary, sometimes considerably. Local and financial newspapers usually provide extensive coverage of rates offered on certificates of deposit, money market accounts, and Treasury bills. Interest rates on certificates of deposit vary not only from one local bank to another, but also from one region to another. CDs are often advertised nationwide, and you can make the purchase by mail. Just be sure the bank or savings institution is federally insured.

Competition for your money is often intense—and you will be the beneficiary. Local banks may engage in a price war to attract money. Many mutual fund companies are temporarily waiving all or part of the fees charged to money market investors in order to attract deposits. So keep abreast of conditions in the short-term investment markets. You may be handsomely rewarded for your efforts.

If you are in one of the higher income tax brackets, be sure to compare the after-tax yields on taxable short-term investments, like CDs and ordinary money market accounts, with yields on tax-exempt money market accounts. Also remember that T-bills are exempt from state and local taxes, so if you live in a high-tax area, you may benefit. It's not very difficult to measure after-tax return; simply deduct any taxes that would be due from the total interest received on any short-term investments that you are considering. The key amounts to compare, of course, are what is left over after you pay Uncle Sam and the state. You may well find that you'll be better off with a tax-exempt money market fund, although conditions do change periodically. So compare rates of return on short-term investments regularly.

Selecting Convenient Features

Short-term investments vary in the number of convenient features they offer. In general, money market mutual funds are the most convenient and flexible, but it is up to you to decide which, if any of the following conveniences will make your financial life a little easier:

Telephone switching between funds

Checkwriting privileges

Immediate confirmations and regular statements

Expedited redemptions

Low investment minimums

Timely resolution of problems

Table 2–1. Average Interest Rates on Short-Term Investment: 1984–1988

Type of Short-Term Investment	Average Interest Rates				
	1984	1985	1986	1987	1988
Taxable money market funds	10.0%	7.7%	6.3%	6.1%	7.1%
Certificates of deposit:					
6-month	10.0	7.8	6.5	6.5	7.2
1-year	10.4	8.3	6.8	6.8	7.5
Treasury bills:					
3-month	9.5	7.5	6.0	5.8	6.7
6-month	9.8	7.7	6.0	6.0	6.9
1-year	9.9	7.8	6.1	6.3	7.1
Municipal notes: 1-year	6.1	5.1	4.3	4.4	5.2

Source: Board of Governors of the Federal Reserve System. *Federal Reserve Bulletin*

Weighing the financial returns against the availability of such features as those listed above, will complete the picture of exactly what your short-term investment can do for you.

COMPARING YIELDS ON SHORT-TERM INVESTMENTS

Table 2-1 is a comparison of average interest rates on various short-term investments for the years 1984 through 1988. Note the significant interest rate variations that occurred during these years as well as often significant variations of yield among various investment categories within the same year. It pays to shop around for the best yields.

3

Stock Market Investments

While the robust performance of the stock market after the October 1987 crash had begun to draw the individual investor back to stocks, the 1990 market decline caused many to abandon them once again. Of course, stock investments have long played a major role in investing, although in recent years, interest-earning investments and real estate investments have become worthy contenders for the investor's dollar. Growth in interest-earning and real estate investments has been aided by the lackluster performance of the stock market from 1965 to 1985 and, of course, the frightening events of October 1987. Individual investors will re-enter or enter the stock markets for the first time, either through individual stock purchases or stock mutual funds, in greater numbers during the 1990s as they note the superior total return performance of stocks versus other investment alternatives. Although there will be more participation in the stock market, individuals still remain skeptical of a market increasingly dominated by institutions and frequently buffetted by market uncertainty. Also, program trading and leveraged buyouts reinforce the individual investor's opinion that he or she is at an unfair disadvantage in the market.

Jittery stock prices seem to be almost an annual phenomenon, so investors will become more uncertain about the short-term prospects for stocks. Concerns over the economy will continue throughout the 1990s as conflicting forecasts by leading market observers exacerbate the uncertainty.

Any changes in the tax laws will most likely be beneficial to stock investors. Lower capital gains rates (possibly tied to length of holding period) and/or indexation of capital gains are receiving support on Capitol Hill. At the same time, more attention will be paid to activity in the international stock markets, particularly with the focus on the removal of European trade barriers culminating in 1992.

Stocks and stock mutual funds (see Chapter 5) will provide investors with above-average long-term investment return opportunities, in spite of the budget and foreign trade deficits, economic uncertainty, and other problems that have always provided the timid with sufficient reason to avoid stocks. Derivative securities, for example, options and futures, should be avoided by individual investors; they are a game for the specialists.

Many people have either not invested in stocks yet or have abandoned the stock market in the face of dramatic declines in stock prices. Nevertheless, in spite of the roller coaster ride of stock prices, most people should have at least some of their money invested in stocks and should take the time to understand the way it all works. After all, if you are fortunate enough to work for a company that has an employee pension plan, chances are that the professionals who manage the pension investments have half or more of the fund invested in stocks.

Fortunately, you don't have to be an expert to be a good stock investor. All it takes is a little time to familiarize yourself with the stock markets and, depending upon whether you want to buy stocks directly or through mutual funds, particular stocks or stock mutual funds. Don't be misled into believing that you have to stay on top of the market or your investments every day. If you buy high-quality stocks and stock mutual funds and hold onto them — through thick and through thin — you will almost always beat your neighbor who spends all sorts of time worrying about and trading his or her stocks.

SUMMARY OF STOCK AND OTHER EQUITY INVESTMENTS

Table 3-1 summarizes the characteristics of the various kinds of stock investments, derivative securities such as options, and other ownership (equity) investments. All of these investments confer on the owner the right to profit from any appreciation in value of the invest-ment or to suffer the effect of any decline in value.

As the table indicates, the categories vary considerably with respect to risk as well as other characteristics. Many are very risky and, therefore, are usually appropriate only for investors with the resources and expertise to manage the risk effectively. Note also that the capital gain tax implications of equity investments may change in 1990 as a result of initiatives under Congressional and White House consideration.

STOCK INVESTMENT STRATEGIES

The following well-respected strategies are among the most com-monly used for investing in stock. This is not a compendium of esoteric or high-risk investment techniques; instead, this section summarizes basic strategies for achieving long-term stock investment success. You should always keep these strategies in mind, not only when making new investments but also when evaluating your stock portfolio and when contemplating a change in overall investment strategy.

1. **Never buy stocks indiscriminately**. Many investors buy stocks haphazardly simply because they have money to spend. Investments should be made only when you have a good reason to buy a particular stock. If possible, you should keep some cash available to take advantage of new opportunities as they arise.

2. **Select a promising industry**. At any given time, most in-dustries in the economy are either on the upswing or the downswing with respect to earnings potential. When choosing a stock to buy, the investor should start by select-ing a promising industry. He or she should have a good reason for selecting an industry and a company within it whose future looks promising.

3. **Diversify**. Investors should try to own stocks in several different industries. Overdiversification on a small amount of money is unwise, however, because the investor may have difficulty keeping track of individual stock holdings. Mutual funds should be considered by investors of any size

Table 3-1. Characteristics of Stock Investments, Derivative Securities, and Other Equity Investments

Instrument	Role in Portfolio	Liquidity	Price Volatility	Leverage Available	Investing Strategies Available	Tax Comments	General Comments
Common stock	Inflation hedge	High	Varies	Buying on margin	Stop-loss orders and/or dollar-cost averaging		Reinvestment plans available for many companies
Preferred stock	Stable income	High	Lower	Buying on margin	Dividend reinvestment		Features are important considerations
Mutual funds	Inflation hedge and/or instant diversificaton	High	Medium[1]	No	Dividend reinvestment and/or dollar-cost averaging		"Families" allow flexibility
Options	Portfolio insurance and/or speculative instrument	High	Higher	Margin available under limited conditions	Can provide downside price protection	Tax liability depends on exercise date	Covered option writing can add income to investment portfolio
Commodity futures	Speculative instrument	High	High	Buying on margin	Selling short	Trading not allowed on IRAs, Keogh plans	Speculative
Stock-index futures	Speculative instrument and/or portfolio insurance	High	High	Buying on margin	Hedge against downside risk of overall portfolio	Considered capital asset by IRS	Speculative

New issues	Growth or speculative instrument	Medium[2]	Higher	No margin on primary issue	Possibility for speculative gains		No commissions in primary market
Foreign equities	Global diversification and/or inflation hedge	Medium[3]	Varies[4]			Some countries impose local taxes	American depositary receipts remove custodial and trading inconveniences
Warrants	Speculative and/or portfolio hedge	High	Higher	Yes[5]	Warrant hedging	Considered capital asset by IRS	
Precious metals	Inflation hedge	High[6]	Higher	No		Considered capital asset by IRS	Investor should trade only with established dealer
Collectibles	Growth and/or value stability	Low	Varies	No	Significant appreciation probably only with high-priced items		Significant upkeep expenses usually required

[1]Specialty or sector funds could have a less stable value than fully diversified stock mutual funds.

[2]Liquidity of a new issue in the secondary market depends on the number of shares offered, the underwriters' active marketing, and whether the issue is listed. These factors are not usually considerations for market-established instruments.

[3]Low turnover on smaller foreign exchanges—other than British, Canadian, and Japanese stock markets—could result in liquidity limitations.

[4]The combination of currency exchange and price fluctuations generally makes the value of foreign equities less stable than that of their U.S. counterparts.

[5]Transactions with overseas brokerage firms could result in time lags between order and execution, or order and delivery, in sales of securities.

[6]Platinum is much less liquid than gold or silver.

portfolio as a convenient way to achieve broad diversification.

4. **Buy low and sell high.** Investors should condition themselves to buy stocks when business is down and sell them when business is up. Stocks can gain when prices are low, and major selling opportunities come when stocks are hot and prices are high.

5. **Stay abreast of market trends.** It is always important to look at general trends in the market. A stock that has already risen in value might be a good candidate for continued gains if the market is still rising. Conversely, a stock that does not respond to a general market rise might be a poor investment.

6. **Use stop loss orders to protect against loss.** Potential losses can be limited by using stop loss orders, which "fence in" gains by restricting the effects of a market downturn on an investor's stocks. Stop loss orders can also be used to force investors to sell. For example, if an investor buys a stock at $12 per share and it rises to $18 per share, he or she might put a stop loss order in at $15 per share to lock in a gain. The risk of this strategy is that the investor might get left behind at $15 per share by a volatile stock price, but this is often preferable to a larger loss due to plummeting stock prices.

7. **Maintain long holding periods.** The buy-and-hold strategy of investing usually works for high-quality stocks because the general market gains ground over time, and thus the value of most holding increases. Only more experienced investors who can devote considerable time to managing their portfolios are consistently successful with a trading strategy. Studies have shown that over most holding periods of 10 years or longer, investors have enjoyed returns well in excess of inflation; shorter holding periods generally produce much lower returns.

8. **Use dividend reinvestment programs.** Dividend reinvestment programs (DRPs) are a useful way for investors to begin a stock accumulation program. Investors purchase modest amounts of stock in companies that they intend to hold onto and have all their dividends reinvested to pur-

chase additional shares regularly. Investors may also want to augment their holdings by making additional optional purchases through the DRP.

9. **Buy good performers.** Investors should try to buy value. Companies with strong balance sheets and solid earnings growth are consistently better long-run performers.

10. **Look for regular small stock dividends.** Investors may want to consider buying stock in companies that habitually pay regular small stock dividends. A small stock dividend (20 percent or less) often does not result in a lower stock price consistent with the dilution of ownership. This strategy therefore allows investors to increase the value of their holdings with no current tax effect.

11. **Buy low P/E, high-dividend stocks.** Many successful long-term investors use the investment strategy of purchasing common stocks of companies with low P/E ratios and high dividend yields. A "7 and 7" strategy, for example, involves buying stock in companies with a P/E ratio of less than 7 and a dividend yield of greater than 7. The logic behind this is that the stock price is depressed (a low P/E ratio) and, hence, the stock is being purchased when no one else wants it, which in itself is often a good strategy. As long as the company is fundamentally sound, the dividend yield of such stocks is relatively attractive, and the investor is betting that when the P/E ratio returns to normal (perhaps 12), the company will eventually increase its dividend to maintain an attractive yield.

12. **Know the risks of short selling.** Short selling is a very risky approach to playing bear markets; most investors are usually wrong in predicting them. In fact, the odd-lot short sale index has been one of the most consistent contrary indicators of future market performance. In other words, an increase in odd-lot short-selling activity almost certainly means a bull market. For most bearish investors, buying put options is preferable to short selling.

13. **Write covered call options.** Writing call options on stocks in the portfolio provides additional income from the premiums received. A conservative covered call-writing program can be implemented with minimal risk to the investor.

STOCK RANKING INDEXES

Tables 3-2 and 3-3 explain the stock rating symbols used by Standard & Poor's and Value Line. You may find these rating indexes useful if you or someone who advises you use the Value Line or Standard & Poor's services. These ratings can provide a quick appraisal of the relative ranking of a particular stock, but, of course, this represents only one piece of relevant information in the process of evaluating a stock investment. Relative quality of bonds or other debt, that is, degrees of protection for principal and interest, cannot be applied to common stocks, and therefore these rankings should not be confused with bond quality ratings.

Standard & Poor's Ratings

Growth and stability of earnings and dividends are deemed key elements in establishing Standard & Poor's earnings and dividend rankings for common stocks, which are designed to capsulize the nature of this record in a single symbol. These rankings are based upon a computerized scoring system that considers per-share earnings and dividend records from the most recent 10 years. Basic scores computed for earnings and dividends are adjusted for growth, stability within the long-term trend, and cyclicality. A Standard & Poor's common stock ranking is not a forecast of future market price performance, but is basically an appraisal of past performance and relative current standing. The S&P preferred stock

Table 3-2. Standard & Poor's Stock Rating Symbols

Common Stocks		Preferred Stocks	
A+	= Highest	AAA	= Prime
A	= High	AA	= High grade
A−	= Good	A	= Sound
B+	= Medium	BBB	= Medium grade
B	= Speculative	BB	= Lower grade
B−	= Highly Speculative	B	= Speculative
C	= Marginal	C	= Nonpaying
D	= In reorganization	NR	= No rating
NR	= No ranking		

Table 3-3. Value Line Stock Rating Symbols

Common Stock: Timeliness Rank

Rank 1 (highest). Expect this stock to be one of the best price performers during the next 12 months.
Rank 2 (above average). Expect better-than-average price performance.
Rank 3 (average). Expect price performance in line with market.
Rank 4 (below average). Expect below-average price performance.
Rank 5 (lowest). Expect poorest price performance relative to that of other stocks.

Common Stock: Safety Rank

Rank 1 (highest). This is probably one of the safest, most stable, and least risky stocks.
Rank 2 (above average). This stock is probably safer and less risky than most stocks.
Rank 3 (average). This stock is probably an average safety and risk stock.
Rank 4 (below average). This stock is probably riskier and less safe than most stocks.
Rank 5 (lowest). This stock is probably one of the riskiest, least safe stocks.

---

rating is an assessment of the capacity and willingness of an issuer to pay preferred stock dividends and any applicable sinking fund obligations.

Value Line Rankings

The Value Line Investment Survey ranks each of the 1700 stocks that it monitors according to timeliness and safety. These ranks are updated every week. The timeliness rank indicates the probable relative price performance of a stock within the next 12 months and is based upon such measures as current earnings and stock price in relation to the past 10 years' experience, earnings momentum, and the past deviation between actual and estimated quarterly earnings. The safety rank is a measure of risk avoidance. It is based mainly on the company's relative financial strength and the stock's price stability. The safety rank changes infrequently.

HOW TO INTERPRET A VALUE LINE REPORT

Figure 3-1 illustrates a typical Value Line report and provides explanations of the information contained therein. The Value Line Investment Survey provides quarterly one-page reports on each of 1700 stock issues, and can be conveniently found in most libraries.

Figure 3-1. Value Line Report and Description

Ratings & Reports   A   B   BB   C   D

PHILIP MORRIS NYSE-MO   RECENT PRICE **85**   P/E RATIO **8.4** (Trailing: 9.6 / Median: 9.5)   RELATIVE P/E RATIO **0.73**   DIV'D YLD **5.1%**   343

High	17.8	29.6	34.2	30.7	29.6	31.6	32.4	38.4	38.6	48.5	55.1	67.8	72.4	83.3	95.1
Low	11.7	16.9	24.4	17.0	20.4	24.9	25.8	27.9	31.1	29.1	42.0	44.1	54.0	62.1	79.0

BUSINESS: Philip Morris Inc. is the nation's largest cigarette producer (estimated 35% of domestic consumption) and exporter. Major brands: Marlboro, Benson & Hedges, Parliament, Merit, Virginia Slims, Players. Acquired Miller, second largest beer manufacturer in U.S., in 1970. Sells High Life, Lite and Lowenbrau. Acquired Seven-Up, third leading soft drink co. in '78. Owns Mission Viejo, West Coast real estate developer. '84 depreciation rate 6.7%. Estimated plant age: 5 yrs. Insiders own about 1.5% of common shares. Has 60,000 employees, 30,300 common stockholders. Chairman & C.E.O.: H. Maxwell. President: & C.O.O: J.A. Murphy. Inc: Virginia. Address: 120 Park Avenue, New York, NY 10017.

We look for Philip Morris to generate a huge amount of excess cash over the next three to five years. The company's core domestic tobacco business throws off an awesome level of profits—$1.7 billion in 1984 and an estimated $2.0 billion this year. Since capital requirements for this operation are relatively modest (and declining), much of these funds are available for other investment purposes. Indeed, our cash flow analysis suggests that through the end of this decade, PM's "free" cash flow will average about $1 billion annually and could be much more if the company decides to scuttle the Miller and/or Seven Up divisions, neither of which have lived up to expectations.

How will management utilize these monies? Completion of an announced share buyback program, coupled with a steady paring of the debt load and regular, double-digit dividend increases through the 1988-90 period, seem all but assured; such moves, however, would "sop up" only a portion of the excess cash flow. Further share repurchases could be undertaken, but we think the acquisition of a major consumer products outfit remains an intriguing possibility. Though

We won't factor the benefits from acquisitions into our estimates and projections until any deals are finalized, success in this regard could greatly enhance PM's earnings growth prospects—and stock price appreciation potential—to the 1988-90 period. As it is, based on current operations alone, we look for PM's share profits to grow at about a 15% rate, compounded annually, over the next three to five years.

These timely shares have been under pressure of late, as Wall Street struggled to determine the possible effect of pending product liability litigation against cigarette manufacturers, a very complicated and difficult to assess situation. Though PM does not expect any cases in which it is directly involved to go to trial this year and although to date the tobacco industry has *never* lost a

(Continued on page 389)

(Continued on page 389)

A Recent price—nine days prior to delivery date.

AA Here is the core of Value Line's advice—the rank for Timeliness; the rank for Safety; Beta—the stock's sensitivity to fluctuations of the market as a whole.

B P/E ratio—the most recent price divided by the latest six months' earnings per share plus earnings estimated for the next six months.

BB P/E Median—a rounded average of four middle values of the range of average annual price-earnings ratios over the past 10 years.

C Relative P/E Ratio—the stock's current P/E divided by the median P/E for all stocks under Value Line review.

D Dividend Yield—cash dividends *estimated to be declared in the next 12 months* divided by the recent price.

E The 3-5 year target price range, estimated. The range is placed in proper position on the price chart, and is shown numerically in the "1988-90 Projections" box in the lower right-hand corner of the price chart.

F The date of delivery to the subscribers. The survey is mailed on a schedule that aims for delivery to every subscriber on Friday afternoon.

G Annual Total Return—the estimated future average annual growth plus current dividend yield—plus possible annualized change in the trend of the price-earnings ratio.

H The stock's **highest and lowest price** of the year.

I The **Value Line**—reported earnings plus depreciation ("cash flow") multiplied by a number selected to correlate the stock's 3- to 5-year projected target price with "cash flow" projected out to 1988-90.

J Monthly price ranges of the stock—plotted on a ratio (logarithmic) grid to show percentage changes in true proportion. For example, a ratio chart equalizes the move of a $10 stock that rises to $11 with a $100 stock that rises to $110. Both have advanced 10% and over the same space on a ratio grid.

K Relative price strength—describes the stock's past price performance relative to the Value Line Composite Average of 1700 stocks. The Timeliness Rank usually predicts the future direction of this line.

L The number of shares traded monthly as a percentage of the total outstanding.

M Statistical milestones that reveal significant long-term trends. The statistics are presented in two ways: 1) The upper series records results on a per-share basis; 2) the lower records results on a

company basis. On pages 30 to 33, you will find conclusions that might be drawn from an inspection of these milestones. Note that the statistics for the year 1985 are estimated, as are the figures for the average of the years 1988-90. The estimates would be revised, if necessary, should future evidence require. The weekly *Summary & Index* would promptly call attention to such revisions.

N A condensed summary of the **business.**

O A 400-word **report on recent developments and prospects**—issued once every three months on a preset schedule.

P Most large corporations engage in several lines of business. Hence sales and profit margins are shown by **lines of business.**

Q Value Line indexes of **financial strength, price stability, price growth persistence,** and **earnings predictability.**

R Footnotes explain a number of things, such as the way earnings are reported, whether "fully diluted," on a "primary" basis, or on an "average shares outstanding" basis.

S Quarterly dividends paid are actual payments. The total of dividends paid in four quarters may not equal the figure shown in the annual series on dividends declared. (Sometimes a dividend declared at the end of the year will be paid in the first quarter of the following year.)

T Quarterly earnings are shown on a **per share** basis (estimates in bold type). Quarterly sales on a gross basis.

U Annual rates of change (on a per share basis). Actual past, estimated future.

V Current position—current assets, current liabilities, and other components of working capital.

W The **capital structure** as of recent date showing the percentage of capital in long-term debt (33%), and in common stock (67%); the number of times that total interest charges were earned (7.0 in 1984).

X A record of **the decisions taken by the biggest institutions** (over $70 million in equity holdings)—including banks, insurance companies, mutual funds, investment advisers, internally managed endowments, and pension funds—to buy or sell during the past five quarters and how many shares were involved, and the total number of shares they hold.

Y The **record of insider decisions**—decisions by officers and directors to buy or sell as reported to the SEC a month or more after execution.

Z Options patch—indicates listed options are available on the stock, and on what exchange they are most actively traded.

Source: Value Line Inc., *How to Use the Value Line Investment Survey* (New York, 1985).

Many individual investors rely on this well-regarded service to assist them in stock selection and review. In evaluating a single stock, Value Line suggests first identifying stocks ranked 1 (highest) or 2 (above average) for timeliness (see "Stock Ranking Indexes" for a further explanation of the rankings). Second, from the list of timely stocks, pick those that are in the industries also shown to be most timely. The weekly Value Line "Summary and Index" section ranks industries in order of timeliness. The third step is to pick from the list of most timely stocks in the most timely industries those that also conform to your safety constraints. Conservative investors should usually give preference to stocks ranked 1 or 2 for safety. Those seeking more volatile stocks might opt for lower rankings. Fourth, investors seeking dividend yield can find the estimated dividend yield of each stock in the weekly Value Line "Summary and Index."

THE YEARLY DOW JONES INDUSTRIAL AVERAGES

Table 3-4 is a summary of year-to-year performance data for the Dow Jones Industrial Average over the last 27 years. Although there have been turbulent periods in the stock market, the DJIA rose 19 out of the 27 years shown. During the 1980s, the stock market increased in eight years of the decade — including 1987, when the infamous October 19 stock market crash occurred.

HISTORICAL PERFORMANCE OF COMMON STOCK INVESTMENTS

Figure 3-2 shows the cumulative total returns and capital appreciation of common stocks from 1926 to 1989, total annual returns in percent, and dividend yields in percent. As the graph depicts, a dollar invested in common stocks at year-end 1925, with dividends reinvested, grew to $534.46 at year-end 1989, a compound annual growth rate of 10.3 percent. The basis of this data is common stocks represented by the Standard & Poor's 500 Stock Composite Index. (Prior to March 1957, the S&P Composite consisted of 90 stocks.)

Table 3-4. Year-to-Year Performance of the Dow Jones Industrial Average: 1963–1990

Year	High	Date	Low	Date	Close	% Change for the Year	P/E[1] Ratio	% Yield
1990[2]	2999.75	July 16	2543.24	Jan. 30				
1989	2791.41	Oct. 9	2144.64	Jan. 3	2753.20	+27.0	12.4	3.74%
1988	2183.50	Oct. 21	1879.14	Jan. 20	2168.57	+11.85	10.1	3.67
1987	2722.42	Aug. 25	1738.74	Oct. 19	1938.83	+ 2.26	14.6	3.67
1986	1955.57	Dec. 2	1502.29	Jan. 22	1895.95	+22.58	16.4	3.54
1985	1553.10	Dec. 16	1184.96	Jan. 4	1546.67	+27.66	16.1	4.01
1984	1286.64	Jan. 6	1086.57	July 24	1211.57	− 3.74	10.7	5.00
1983	1287.20	Nov. 29	1027.04	Jan. 3	1258.64	+20.27	17.4	4.47
1982	1070.55	Dec. 27	776.92	Aug. 12	1046.54	+19.60	114.4	5.17
1981	1024.05	Apr. 27	824.01	Sept. 25	875.00	− 9.23	7.7	6.42
1980	1000.17	Nov. 20	759.13	Apr. 21	963.99	+14.93	7.9	5.64
1979	897.61	Oct. 5	796.67	Nov. 7	838.74	+ 4.19	6.7	6.08
1978	907.74	Sept. 8	742.12	Feb. 28	805.01	− 3.15	7.1	6.03
1977	1014.79	Jan. 3	800.85	Nov. 2	831.17	−17.27	9.3	5.51
1976	1014.79	Sept. 21	858.71	Jan. 2	1004.65	+17.86	10.4	4.12
1975	881.81	July 15	632.04	Jan. 2	852.41	+38.32	11.3	4.39
1974	891.66	Mar. 13	577.60	Dec. 6	616.24	−27.57	6.2	6.12
1973	1051.70	Jan. 11	788.31	Dec. 5	850.86	−16.58	9.9	4.15
1972	1036.27	Dec. 11	889.15	Jan. 26	1020.02	+14.58	15.2	3.16
1971	950.82	Apr. 28	797.97	Nov. 23	890.20	+ 6.11	16.2	3.47
1970	842.00	Dec. 29	631.15	May 26	838.92	+ 4.82	16.4	3.76
1969	968.85	May 14	769.93	Dec. 17	800.36	−15.19	14.0	4.24
1968	985.21	Dec. 3	825.13	Mar. 21	943.75	+ 4.27	16.3	3.32
1967	943.08	Sept. 25	786.41	Jan. 3	905.11	+15.20	16.8	3.33
1966	995.15	Feb. 9	744.32	Oct. 7	785.69	−18.94	13.6	4.06
1965	969.26	Dec. 31	840.59	June 28	969.26	+10.88	18.1	2.95
1964	891.71	Nov. 18	766.08	Jan. 2	874.13	+14.57	18.8	3.57
1963	767.21	Dec. 18	646.79	Jan. 2	762.95	+17.00	18.5	3.07

[1]Price/earnings ratio as of year end.
[2]Through August 17, 1990.

STOCKS WITH A HISTORY OF STEADILY INCREASING DIVIDENDS

Many conservative long-term investors like to invest in financially solid companies that have a history of steadily increasing dividends. Figure 3-3, a reprint of data prepared by Value Line, is but one list of companies meeting these criteria. At the time the list was prepared, all had a minimum dividend yield of 3 percent as well as an average growth in dividend payout of 10 percent per year over the last five years. Finally, all have strong balance sheets which should provide

Figure 3.2. Common Stock Returns and Yields: 1926–1989

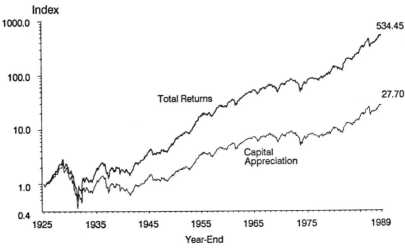

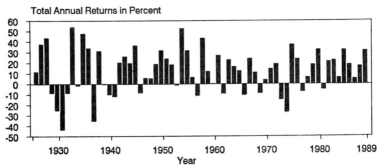

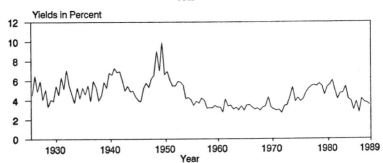

Source: *Stocks, Bonds, Bills, and Inflation, 1990 Yearbook*. Ibbotson Associates, Chicago.

Figure 3-3. Thirty Financially Solid Companies
with Steadily Increasing Dividends

Banc One Corp.	Genuine Parts	National Presto Ind.
Borden, Inc.	Hanson PLC (ADR)	National Service Ind.
Clorox Co.	Harland (John H.)	Penney (J.C.)
Consol. Papers	Imasco Ltd.	Philip Morris
Deluxe Corp.	Jefferson-Pilot Corp.	Royal Trustco Ltd.
Fifth Third Bancorp	K mart Corp.	UST Inc.
First Wachovia Corp.	Kimberly-Clark	Unilever PLC (ADR)
Gannett Co.	Marsh & McLennan	Unilever NV (NY Shs)
General Mills	NBD Bancorp	Wells Fargo & Co.
General Motors	National City Corp.	Westinghouse Electric

*the companies with the capacity to continue paying dividends at
increasing levels.*

BUILDING A PORTFOLIO WITH DIVIDEND REINVESTMENT PROGRAMS

*Dividend reinvestment programs are a wonderful way for aver-
age investors to build up their portfolios of high-quality stocks at little
or no cost. There are drawbacks, but on balance they make sense for
many people. Most larger dividend-paying companies offer these
plans.*

The dividend reinvestment programs offered by some companies allow shareholders to have dividends automatically reinvested in additional shares of the same stock without added
commissions. Some companies will even discount the market
price of their stock for shares purchased through such a program.

Because the dividends are reinvested at regular intervals,
these plans are one way to use dollar cost averaging by buying
more shares when prices are low and fewer when they are
high. In addition, reinvesting dividends can dramatically boost
long-term returns. To illustrate, consider that the Standard &
Poor's 500 Index has risen 415 percent over the last 15 years. If
the dividends of the stocks in the index had been reinvested,
however, the total return would be 905 percent.

One drawback of dividend reinvestment plans is that you

must pay taxes on the reinvested dividends even though they are not received in cash. In addition, you'll need to keep track of reinvested dividends so you can include them in your cost basis when you sell your shares.

Another potential drawback is that dividend reinvestment accounts can take more time to get into or out of than stocks purchased through traditional means. To be certain of the rules, contact the investor relations department of the company sponsoring the plan in which you plan to invest.

INVESTING IN FOREIGN STOCKS

There is always a bull market somewhere in the world, but usually it is not in the United States. Investing in foreign stocks has already proven profitable to many investors. If you haven't invested in them already, you should consider adding foreign shares to your stock portfolio.

Anyone who has driven a car, microwaved a frozen dinner, listened to the radio, or watched television has probably come into contact with products made outside of the United States. Yet until recently, investing in foreign companies was truly foreign to many people.

But the abundance of foreign securities and investment products that have appeared in the United States in the last few years has succeeded in bringing both Main Street and Wall Street dollars to Paris, Tokyo, London, and Malaysia—and that participation has helped tip the scales of world stock market dominance in favor of companies based abroad. Today, foreign companies account for over 70 percent of the world's stock market capitalization, compared with 50 percent just 10 years ago.

Investors find foreign stocks appealing because they often perform better than U.S. issues. According to Frank Russell Company, the U.S. stock market had an average annualized return of 15.4 percent between 1979 and 1988, ranking it *only* thirteenth among nations with established stock markets.

The direction of the U.S. dollar has a substantial impact on how foreign securities perform. When the dollar rises against foreign currencies, earnings of overseas companies translate into fewer U.S. dollars and overseas holdings are worth less to U.S. investors. On the other hand, when the dollar declines, foreign earnings are enhanced when translated into U.S. currency and foreign holdings are worth more to U.S. investors.

International Mutual Funds

Because foreign stocks can buffer losses in the American stock market and provide a hedge against currency swings, it is generally a good idea to keep 5 to 10 percent of your money in international stocks. There are many mutual funds that specialize in investing in foreign stocks. Funds with the word global in their names have the option of investing in both the United States and abroad. International or foreign funds usually have no investments in U.S. securities. Global funds may be advantageous if you want a portfolio manager to shift among foreign and domestic companies based on currency fluctuations and the outlooks for various markets. Single country and single region international funds have become very popular, although the investor is usually better advised to opt for a broad-based international fund which lets the portfolio manager decide which countries offer the best investment opportunities.

American Depository Receipts

If you prefer to own individual foreign stocks, you may want to consider American Depository Receipts (ADRs). While a few foreign companies trade directly on the stock exchange, hundreds of others are available via ADRs. An ADR is a negotiable receipt issued by a U.S. bank that represents the holder's interest in the underlying foreign shares. All transactions, including dividends, are made in U.S. dollars. ADRs are traded on the New York and American Stock Exchanges and on the over-the-counter market.

4

Interest-Earning Investments

While the attention of many investors was riveted to the stock market during the latter half of the 1980s, bonds and other interest-earning investments were undergoing revolutionary changes that would make them more complex, more volatile, and at the same time, more attractive as investment vehicles. Today, investors can choose from a wide array of taxable, tax-exempt, and tax-deferred bonds, as well as a variety of other interest-earning (often referred to as fixed-income) investment securities, such as fixed-income mutual funds, unit trusts, and mortgage-backed securities. A separate classification of short-term interest-earning investments, known as cash equivalents were discussed in Chapter 2.

Common stocks, of course, have long been viewed as one of the better hedges against inflation. Yet, interest-earning investments also have a place in the portfolios of investors who are seeking attractive, inflation-beating rates of return with moderate risk. Despite the dramatic descent in interest rates since the early 1980s, bond yields after inflation is taken into account are actually more attractive now than they were during that period.

With the attractive interest rates available today, however, comes increased volatility in the prices of most interest-earning securities. Until the 1970s, when interest rates moved at a snail's pace, bonds were considered a safe, stable haven for income-oriented investors. Today, when interest rates can fluctuate several percentage points within the course of a year, price volatility is a factor that must be taken into account in planning and selecting these investments.

You need to evaluate how interest-earning investments fit into your overall investment portfolio (including your retirement account investments) and then decide the kinds of interest-earning securities that are most suitable. It is safe to say that interest-earning investments belong in every portfolio. However, the proportion as well as the type of investment vehicles will vary considerably among investors. For example, someone who is retired or is nearing retirement will in all likelihood require a larger proportion of interest-earning investments in his or her portfolio than a younger individual.

Many considerations must be taken into account when selecting an appropriate interest-earning security. One of the most important is the tax treatment of interest and capital gains or losses, particularly if you live in a state which levies a high tax on interest income. The lowering of federal income tax rates as well as the inclusion of some tax-exempt interest in the alternative minimum tax, are relatively new developments that must be kept in mind. Maturity, quality, relative yield, liquidity, and call features are other important factors in the selection process.

Interest-earning investing will almost certainly continue to be a somewhat complex, yet potentially rewarding, investment arena throughout the 1990s. The popularity of the myriad of interest-earning investments which have come on the scene in the last decade will prompt a new, even more diverse crop of products. Changes in tax laws will continue to play a major role in evaluating the relative attractiveness of tax-exempt and tax-favored securities as investment vehicles.

Interest-earning securities, for the most part, should be purchased when you think interest rates are high and with the expectation that they will be held until maturity or call. You should leave the chore of predicting interest rate trends up to the mutual fund managers. Indeed, bond mutual funds should be a significant component of most investors' portfolios. Municipal bonds will probably continue to offer more attractive after-tax returns to most taxable interest-earning investments. Investments in newer types of securities, such as foreign bonds, should be accomplished through professionally managed mutual funds with proven expertise in these areas.

INTEREST-EARNING INVESTMENT STRATEGIES

Volatile interest rates combined with the proliferation of many different kinds of interest-earning securities have discouraged many investors from taking the plunge into these investments. Instead, they are content with short-term securities such as money market funds and savings accounts. Yet, with a little effort, you can increase your investment returns by taking advantage of the many attractive interest-earning investment vehicles that are available to average investors. The following suggestions will help you become a better investor in interest-earning securities.

1. **Become familiar with the many interest-earning securities that are currently available.** Many people don't realize how many longer-term interest earning investment alternatives are available. The following is a list of many of the commonly available securities. Most can be purchased either directly or through a mutual fund for as little as $1000.

   U.S. Treasury Notes
   U.S. Treasury Bonds
   U.S. Savings Bonds
   U.S. Government Agency Debt
   Mortgage-Backed (Pass-Through) Certificates
   Municipal Notes
   Uninsured Municipal Bonds
   Insured Municipal Bonds
   Certificates of Deposit
   Zero Coupon Bonds—Corporate
   Zero Coupon Bonds—Municipal
   Zero Coupon Bonds—U.S. Treasury
   High-Grade Corporate Bonds

Medium-Grade Corporate Bonds
High-Yield (Junk) Bonds
Convertible Bonds
Foreign Bonds
U.S. Government Bond Mutual Fund—Long Term
U.S. Government Bond Mutual Fund—Intermediate Term
Ginnie Mae Mutual Fund
Investment-Grade Corporate Bond Fund
High-Yield (Junk) Corporate Bond Fund
Uninsured Municipal Bond Fund
Insured Municipal Bond Fund
International Bond Mutual Fund
Unit Investment Trust
Closed-End Bond Fund

Chances are that some of the above securities can benefit you now or some time in the future. Be aware, however, that some of these securities may have various risks that make them inappropriate for your needs.

2. **Monitor prevailing interest rates.** You should also become familiar with prevailing interest rates. Develop some rules of thumb that help you decide when you consider interest rates to be high. For example, you may find that interest-earning securities are attractive when they pay a rate of interest that beats inflation by a couple of percentage points after taxes are taken out. Many individual investors monitor the yield on long-term Treasury bonds to get an idea of the level of interest rates.

The key to investing successfully in interest-earning investments is to purchase longer maturity securities when you think interest rates are high and are likely to fall in order to lock in high returns. Conversely, you should purchase shorter maturity securities (or cash equivalent investments) if you think prevailing interest rates are likely to rise.

3. **Don't speculate on interest rate changes.** Many investors don't understand the volatility of interest-earning investments until they find that their bond or bond mutual fund, for example, has lost value. Fixed income security prices can, in fact, be more volatile than stock prices. This risk,

which is shared by all long-term fixed income securities, is called interest rate risk. Simply stated, interest rate risk means that the principal value of a fixed income investment will decline if interest rates in general rise. Fixed-income mutual funds have this risk, although many fund managers are pretty adept at handling interest rate risk over the long run. Some individual investors perceive themselves as experts in predicting the direction of interest rates and, therefore, buy individual interest-earning securities with the intention of selling them before they mature. Many such armchair speculators end up losing a great deal of money on a supposedly safe investment. The only way to avoid this risk is to hold onto these securities until they mature. So, you are better off buying with the intention of holding to maturity, even though you may end up selling them early anyway to meet living expenses or to take advantage of an increase in the value of your investments caused by a decline in interest rates. The lesson here is to leave interest rate speculation to the professionals.

4. **Ladder the maturities of your interest-earning investments**. Smart investors do what is known as laddering or staggering the maturities of their interest-earning investments. Rather than investing a substantial amount of money in a single issue or in several issues with roughly the same maturity, you should opt for a variety of maturities—some short term, some intermediate term, and some long term. That way, if there is a significant change in interest rates, you will not have placed a heavy, and perhaps incorrect, bet on a single maturity. Simply stated, laddering maturities minimizes the risk in your interest-earning security portfolio. Don't forget to time some of the maturities to coincide with times when you may need the money, for instance to meet college tuition bills or to provide money during your first few years of retirement.

5. **Compare interest rates on various types of securities.** You'll probably be amazed at how different interest rates are on various interest-earning securities. For example, over the past several years, interest rates on tax-exempt bonds have been very attractive compared with the after-

tax returns on Treasury securities and corporate bonds. Rates on medium-grade bonds are sometimes much higher than on high-grade bonds even though the risk of default on medium-grade bonds is not much higher than the blue chips, i.e., high quality issues of financially strong companies or municipalities. So before making an investment, compare returns. You're efforts will be well rewarded.

6. **Make mutual funds a part of your interest-earning investment portfolio.** Fixed-income mutual funds are an excellent way to participate in the many attractive interest-earning investment opportunities. Most investors are not aware of the wide variety of mutual funds that are available, including Treasury funds, mortgage-backed securities funds, tax-exempt bond funds, corporate bond funds, and even foreign bond funds. Within most of those categories you can select funds that invest in high-quality issues, medium-quality issues, or low-quality issues. Finally, you can often select funds that concentrate on long-duration securities or intermediate- or shorter-duration securities.

7. **Consider the tax effects of each investment.** You can probably increase your investment returns by carefully examining the tax effects of alternative interest-earning investments. Some are fully taxable, Treasury securities are federally taxable but exempt from state taxes, and municipal obligations are usually exempt from federal taxes and may be exempt from state taxes. It is important to keep in mind that the most heavily taxed (and usually higher yielding) securities should be placed in your tax-deferred retirement accounts. On the other hand, tax-favored investments should be placed in your taxable portfolio.

8. **Don't chase yield.** An interest-earning investment that pays 14 percent interest when prevailing rates are 9 percent is trying to tell you something. This is a junk bond. Yet, many investors erroneously think that the higher the yield, the more attractive the investment. This is not so. As many junk bond junkies found out to their dismay, some of these bonds went down the tubes. While it may be appropriate to allocate a very small proportion of your portfolio to a more speculative investment, be sure not to bet the ranch on it.

9. **Make interest-earning investments one part of a well-balanced portfolio.** Some people invest too much money in fixed-income investments because they are afraid of stocks. Others think stocks are the ultimate investment and have too little money in interest-earning securities. What everyone needs is balance, and a well-balanced portfolio consists of approximately equal portions of stocks, interest-earning investments, and, if you are so-inclined, income-producing real estate.

INVESTING IN U.S. TREASURY SECURITIES

High interest from the federal government! Great tax breaks! No commission charges!

No, this isn't a pitch for another new and improved investment product. But if the U.S. government ever decided to create a hard-sell ad for Treasury securities, it would probably read something like this. While other investments may earn better returns at times, Treasury securities consistently appear in a wide variety of investment portfolios.

U.S. Treasury issues—which, along with U.S. savings bonds, are the only types of securities that are direct obligations of Uncle Sam—have long been classic, bread-and-butter investments. Their appealing features include:

High Liquidity. Individual investors must often pay higher fees when buying municipal and taxable bonds because the market for small blocks of securities is limited. But the Treasury arena is so huge that an investor with $1000 is on the same footing as someone with $100,000.

Noncallability. Many investors who think they've locked in high yields for decades get a rude awakening when an issuer redeems its bonds after 5 or 10 years. This won't happen with Treasuries, though, since most of them cannot be called.

Freedom. These issues are free from state and local taxes.

Low or No Sales Commissions. It costs nothing to purchase bonds through a local branch of the Federal Reserve
Bank. You can also pay a small sales charge when you buy
them through a bank or a broker. It may be worthwhile to buy
through a broker, since you can purchase issues on the secondary market rather than waiting for federal auctions. In addition,
because brokers maintain an active secondary market in Treasury issues, they are easier to sell before maturity than if you
purchase them directly from the Fed.

There are several species of Treasury issues from which to
choose. Treasury bills come in minimum denominations of
$10,000 and mature in 1 year or less. Treasury notes mature in 1
to 10 years and have a minimum purchase requirement of
$1000 (except for 2- and 3-year notes, which require a minimum
investment of $5000). Treasury bonds have a $1000 minimum
and mature in over 10 years. Zero-coupon Treasuries have a
face value of $1000; unlike traditional Treasury issues, zero-
coupon Treasuries must be purchased from a dealer, who sets
the minimum investment requirement. You can also invest in
U.S. Treasury issues through a U.S. government-only mutual
fund. However, the interest may be subject to state and local
taxes, depending on the investment policy and structure of the
fund.

TREASURY SECURITY ISSUE DATE CALENDAR

*Table 4-1 summarizes the customary issue dates for various
maturities of Treasury bills, notes, and bonds. The exact dates for each
issue are announced in the financial press approximately one week in
advance. Each Monday issue of the* Wall Street Journal *summarizes
U.S. Treasury (as well as corporate and municipal) offerings. These
dates will be useful if you plan to buy these securities when they are
issued. They may be purchased directly from the Federal Reserve or
through your bank or broker.*

INVESTING IN U.S. SAVINGS BONDS

*Some investors look at U.S. savings bonds like a mid-size Chevy
sedan: boring but dependable. Series EE bonds, which are issued and*

Table 4–1. Maturity Dates of Treasury Bills, Notes, and Bonds

Treasury Bills	
13-week	Every Monday
26-week	Every Monday
52-week	Every fourth Thursday
Treasury Notes	
2-year	Monthly; on a Wednesday late in the month
3-year	Quarterly; on the 15th day of February, May, August, and November
4-year	Quarterly; late in March, June, September, and December
7-year	Quarterly; early in January, April, July, and October
10-year	Quarterly; on the 15th day of February, May, August, and November
Treasury Bonds	
30-year	Quarterly; on the 15th day of February, May, August, and November

backed by the Federal government, sell for half their face or redemption value, which ranges from $50 to $10,000. The annual rate of interest changes twice a year, and is pegged at 85 percent of the yield on 5-year Treasury bills or 6 percent, whichever is greater. Bonds purchased before November 1986 have a minimum rate of 7.5 percent. The bonds must be held for at least 5 years to receive these rates. Accrued interest is subject to federal, but not state and local taxes.

The College Break

Interest on bonds purchased in January 1990 and after may be free of taxes when they are used to pay for college tuition and educational fees for a dependent child, spouse, or self. However, the tax break is phased out gradually for families with adjusted gross incomes of $60,000 to $90,000 ($40,000 to $55,000 for single filers) when the bonds are redeemed. These income levels are adjusted for inflation, and parents earning over the maximum adjusted gross income when the bonds are redeemed will be ineligible for this favorable tax treatment. The bonds must be purchased by the parents and held in one or both of their names to qualify.

Even parents who don't qualify for the tax break because their income is too high, however, can still reap tax benefits from Series EE bonds. The so-called kiddie tax imposed by the Tax Reform Act of 1986 makes all net unearned income over $1000 taxable at the parents' rate if a child is under age 14. After age 14, all income, regardless of the amount, is taxable at the child's generally lower rate. Because taxes on accrued interest need not be paid until redemption, Series EE bonds can help parents circumvent the kiddie tax if they hold off cashing in the bonds until the child reaches age 14.

Transaction Tips

Keep copies of the issue dates and serial numbers in a safe place separate from your bonds. This will make it easier to replace them if they are lost or stolen.

Make large purchases in small denominations so you have the option of gradually redeeming a large purchase at your local bank. It is possible to redeem part of a Series EE bond with a denomination of $100 or more, but the transaction will have to be handled through your local branch of the Federal Reserve Bank.

To avoid a heavy tax bill at redemption, you may want to consider rolling U.S. savings bonds over into Series HH bonds. Because these are taxed on the basis of their current, semiannual interest payments, you can receive current income from your bonds and continue to avoid further taxes until redemption. The main drawback of this is the low interest rate, which has remained at 6 percent for several years.

Even though you may purchase your bonds at a bank, you should direct important questions elsewhere, since bank personnel are often not well versed on the particulars of U.S. savings bonds. It is safer to get your information from the Savings Bond Division of your local branch of the Federal Reserve Bank.

Since bonds are credited with interest for the entire month in which they are bought, it is best to purchase them at the end of the month. Before redeeming a bond, you should find out when the interest is credited. Older savings bonds are credited only once every 6 months, and if you cash in a bond a day early, you will lose 6 months' interest.

Perhaps the easiest way to purchase savings bonds is by telephone. They are available 24 hours a day and can be charged to VISA or Mastercard. Simply call 1-800-US BONDS and be prepared to provide the bondowners name, address, and Social Security number, and the denomination desired.

SAVINGS BOND MATURITY TABLES

Table 4-2 provides information on the length of time Series E and Series H U.S. savings bonds and U.S. savings notes of varying issue dates will continue to earn interest. If you have old savings bonds, you should check them against this table to make sure they are still producing interest income.

Table 4–2. Timetable of Savings Bond and Savings Note Interest Earnings

Series E Bond Extended Maturities

Date of Issue	Date of Maturity	Term of Bond
May 1941–Apr. 1952	May 1981–Apr. 1992	40 years*
May 1952–Jan. 1957	Jan. 1992–Sept. 1996	39 years, 8 months
Feb. 1957–May 1959	Jan. 1996–Apr. 1998	38 years, 11 months
June 1959–Nov. 1965	Mar. 1997–Aug. 2003	37 years, 9 months
Dec. 1965–May 1969	Dec. 1992–May 1996	27 years
June 1969–Nov. 1973	Apr. 1995–Sept. 1999	25 years, 10 months
Dec. 1973–June 1980	Dec. 1998–June 2005	25 years

Series H Extended Maturities

Date of Issue	Date of Maturity	Term of Bond
June 1952–Jan. 1957	Feb. 1982–Sept. 1986	29 years, 8 months*
Feb. 1957–May 1959	Feb. 1987–May 1989	30 years*
June 1959–Dec. 1979	June 1989–Dec. 2009	30 years

Savings Notes Extended Maturities

Date of Issue	Date of Maturity	Term of Bond
May 1967–Oct. 1970	Nov. 1991–Apr. 1995	24 years, 6 months

*Maturity dates of these Bonds will not be extended further.

FIGURING OUT SAVINGS BOND
REDEMPTION VALUES

Tables 4-3 and 4-4 are reprints of U.S. Treasury tables showing the redemption values of Series E and Series EE U.S. savings bonds as of April 1991. These tables can be used to approximate the redemption value and accrued interest on savings bonds that you own. If exact redemption values are needed, most banks can provide this information or monthly tables may be purchased from the Department of the Treasury.

HISTORICAL RETURNS ON GOVERNMENT
AND CORPORATE BONDS

Figures 4-1 and 4-2 show the cumulative annual total returns of long-term government bonds and long-term corporate bonds from 1926 to 1989. One dollar invested in long-term government bonds at year-end 1925 grew to $17.30 at year-end 1990. Over a similar period, long-term corporate bonds grew to $25.45.

COMPARING TAXABLE INVESTMENTS
WITH FEDERALLY TAX-EXEMPT INVESTMENTS

Table 4-5 shows the taxable yield required to equal the yield on a federally tax-exempt investment. For example, a taxable security would have to yield 11.11 percent to equal an 8 percent tax-exempt yield for a taxpayer in the 28 percent tax bracket. Note that some tax-exempt investments may be subject to the alternative minimum tax. Table 4-6 illustrates how to compute taxable equivalent yields on investments whose interest is exempt from both federal and state income taxes.

COMPARING TAXABLE INVESTMENTS
WITH INVESTMENTS THAT ARE EXEMPT
FROM BOTH FEDERAL AND STATE TAXES

Table 4-6 can be used to determine whether you are better off investing in a given taxable interest-earning security or in a single

Table 4-3. U.S. Savings Bonds, Series EE Redemption Values and Interest Earned.

U.S. SAVINGS BONDS, SERIES EE-REDEMPTION VALUES AND INTEREST EARNED AMOUNTS BY DENOMINATION-SEPTEMBER 1990

ISSUE YEAR	ISSUE MONTHS	$50		$75		$100		$200		$500		$1,000		$5,000		$10,000	
		REDEMP. VALUE	INTEREST EARNED	REDEMP. VALUE	INTEREST EARNED	REDEMP. VALUE	INTEREST EARNED	REDEMP. VALUE	INTEREST EARNED	REDEMP. VALUE	INTEREST EARNED	REDEMP. VALUE	INTEREST EARNED	REDEMP. VALUE	INTEREST EARNED	REDEMP. VALUE	INTEREST EARNED
1990	Apr. thru Sep.	Not eligible for payment															
	Mar.	25.52	.52	38.28	.78	51.04	1.04	102.08	2.08	255.20	5.20	510.40	10.40	2,552.00	52.00	5,104.00	104.00
	Feb.	25.60	.60	38.40	.90	51.20	1.20	102.40	2.40	256.00	6.00	512.00	12.00	2,560.00	60.00	5,120.00	120.00
	Jan.	25.70	.70	38.55	1.05	51.40	1.40	102.80	2.80	257.00	7.00	514.00	14.00	2,570.00	70.00	5,140.00	140.00
		PROCEEDS FROM SERIES EE SAVINGS BONDS WITH ISSUE DATES BEGINNING JANUARY 1990 MAY BE ELIGIBLE FOR SPECIAL TAX EXEMPTION WHEN USED FOR POST SECONDARY EDUCATION — SEE INSIDE FRONT COVER															
1989	Dec.	25.78	.78	38.67	1.17	51.56	1.56	103.12	3.12	257.80	7.80	515.60	15.60	2,578.00	78.00	5,156.00	156.00
	Nov.	25.88	.88	38.82	1.32	51.76	1.76	103.52	3.52	258.80	8.80	517.60	17.60	2,588.00	88.00	5,176.00	176.00
	Oct.	25.98	.98	38.97	1.47	51.96	1.96	103.92	3.92	259.80	9.80	519.60	19.60	2,598.00	98.00	5,196.00	196.00
	Sep.	26.08	1.08	39.12	1.62	52.16	2.16	104.32	4.32	260.80	10.80	521.60	21.60	2,608.00	108.00	5,216.00	216.00
	Aug.	26.18	1.18	39.27	1.77	52.36	2.36	104.72	4.72	261.80	11.80	523.60	23.60	2,618.00	118.00	5,226.00	236.00
	July	26.28	1.28	39.42	1.92	52.56	2.56	105.12	5.12	262.80	12.80	525.60	25.60	2,628.00	128.00	5,256.00	256.00
	June	26.38	1.38	39.57	2.07	52.76	2.76	105.52	5.52	263.80	13.80	527.60	27.60	2,638.00	138.00	5,276.00	276.00
	May	26.48	1.48	39.72	2.22	52.96	2.96	105.92	5.92	264.80	14.80	529.60	29.60	2,648.00	148.00	5,296.00	296.00
	Apr.	26.58	1.58	39.87	2.37	53.16	3.16	106.32	6.32	265.80	15.80	531.60	31.60	2,658.00	158.00	5,316.00	316.00
	Mar.	26.70	1.70	40.05	2.55	53.40	3.40	106.80	6.80	267.00	17.00	534.00	34.00	2,670.00	170.00	5,340.00	340.00
	Feb.	26.80	1.80	40.20	2.70	53.60	3.60	107.20	7.20	268.00	18.00	536.00	36.00	2,680.00	180.00	5,360.00	360.00
	Jan.	26.92	1.92	40.38	2.88	53.84	3.84	107.68	7.68	269.20	19.20	538.40	38.40	2,692.00	192.00	5,384.00	384.00
1988	Dec.	27.04	2.04	40.56	3.06	54.08	4.08	108.16	8.16	270.40	20.40	540.80	40.80	2,704.00	204.00	5,408.00	408.00
	Nov.	27.16	2.16	40.74	3.24	54.32	4.32	108.64	8.64	271.60	21.60	543.20	43.20	2,716.00	216.00	5,432.00	432.00
	Oct.	27.28	2.28	40.92	3.42	54.56	4.56	109.12	9.12	272.80	22.80	545.60	45.60	2,728.00	228.00	5,456.00	456.00
	Sep.	27.40	2.40	41.10	3.60	54.80	4.80	109.60	9.60	274.00	24.00	548.00	48.00	2,740.00	240.00	5,480.00	480.00
	Aug.	27.52	2.52	41.28	3.78	55.04	5.04	110.08	10.08	275.20	25.20	550.40	50.40	2,752.00	252.00	5,504.00	504.00
	July	27.64	2.64	41.46	3.96	55.28	5.28	110.56	10.56	276.40	26.40	552.80	52.80	2,764.00	264.00	5,528.00	528.00
	June	27.76	2.76	41.64	4.14	55.52	5.52	111.04	11.04	277.60	27.60	555.20	55.20	2,776.00	276.00	5,552.00	552.00
	May	27.90	2.90	41.85	4.35	55.80	5.80	111.60	11.60	279.00	29.00	558.00	58.00	2,790.00	290.00	5,580.00	580.00
	Apr.	28.02	3.02	42.03	4.53	56.04	6.04	112.08	12.08	280.20	30.20	560.40	60.40	2,802.00	302.00	5,604.00	604.00
	Jan. thru Mar.	28.16	3.16	42.24	4.74	56.32	6.32	112.64	12.64	281.60	31.60	563.20	63.20	2,816.00	316.00	5,632.00	632.00
1987	Oct. thru Dec.	28.16	3.16	42.24	4.74	56.32	6.32	112.64	12.64	281.60	31.60	563.20	63.20	2,816.00	316.00	5,632.00	632.00
	Apr. thru Sep.	29.00	4.00	43.50	6.00	58.00	8.00	116.00	16.00	290.00	40.00	580.00	80.00	2,900.00	400.00	5,800.00	800.00
	Jan. thru Mar.	29.98	4.98	44.97	7.47	59.96	9.96	119.92	19.92	299.80	49.80	599.60	99.60	2,998.00	498.00	5,996.00	996.00
1986	Nov. thru Dec.	29.98	4.98	44.97	7.47	59.96	9.96	119.92	19.92	299.80	49.80	599.60	99.60	2,998.00	498.00	5,996.00	996.00
	Oct.	31.54	6.54	47.31	9.81	63.08	13.08	126.16	26.16	315.40	65.40	630.80	130.80	3,154.00	654.00	6,308.00	1,308.00
	Apr. thru Sep.	32.94	7.94	49.41	11.91	65.88	15.88	131.76	31.76	329.40	79.40	658.80	158.80	3,294.00	794.00	6,588.00	1,588.00
	Jan. thru Mar.	34.46	9.46	51.69	14.19	68.92	18.92	137.84	37.84	344.60	94.60	689.20	189.20	3,446.00	946.00	6,892.00	1,892.00

SEPTEMBER 1990

Table 4-3. U.S. Savings Bonds, Series EE Redemption Values and Interest Earned. (*Cont.*)

ISSUE YEAR	ISSUE MONTHS	$50 REDEMP. VALUE	$50 INTEREST EARNED	$75 REDEMP. VALUE	$75 INTEREST EARNED	$100 REDEMP. VALUE	$100 INTEREST EARNED	$200 REDEMP. VALUE	$200 INTEREST EARNED	$500 REDEMP. VALUE	$500 INTEREST EARNED	$1,000 REDEMP. VALUE	$1,000 INTEREST EARNED	$5,000 REDEMP. VALUE	$5,000 INTEREST EARNED	$10,000 REDEMP. VALUE	$10,000 INTEREST EARNED
1985	Oct. thru Dec.	34.46	9.46	51.69	14.19	68.92	18.92	137.84	37.84	344.60	94.60	689.20	189.20	3,446.00	946.00	6,892.00	1,892.00
	May thru Sep.	36.14	11.14	54.21	16.71	72.28	22.28	144.56	44.56	361.40	111.40	722.80	222.80	3,614.00	1,114.00	7,228.00	2,228.00
	Apr.	36.58	11.58	54.87	17.37	73.16	23.16	146.32	46.32	365.80	115.80	731.60	231.60	3,658.00	1,158.00	7,316.00	2,316.00
	Jan. thru Mar.	38.00	13.00	57.00	19.50	76.00	26.00	152.00	52.00	380.00	130.00	760.00	260.00	3,800.00	1,300.00	7,600.00	2,600.00
1984	Nov. thru Dec.	38.00	13.00	57.00	19.50	76.00	26.00	152.00	52.00	380.00	130.00	760.00	260.00	3,800.00	1,300.00	7,600.00	2,600.00
	Oct.	38.50	13.50	57.75	20.25	77.00	27.00	154.00	54.00	385.00	135.00	770.00	270.00	3,850.00	1,350.00	7,700.00	2,700.00
	May thru Sep.	39.46	14.46	59.19	21.69	78.92	28.92	157.84	57.84	394.60	144.60	789.20	289.20	3,946.00	1,446.00	7,892.00	2,892.00
	Apr.	40.04	15.04	60.06	22.56	80.08	30.08	160.16	60.16	400.40	150.40	800.80	300.80	4,004.00	1,504.00	8,008.00	3,008.00
	Jan. thru Mar.	41.64	16.64	62.46	24.96	83.28	33.28	166.56	66.56	416.40	166.40	832.80	332.80	4,164.00	1,664.00	8,328.00	3,328.00
1983	Oct. thru Dec.	41.64	16.64	62.46	24.96	83.28	33.28	166.56	66.56	416.40	166.40	832.80	332.80	4,164.00	1,664.00	8,328.00	3,328.00
	May thru Sep.	43.30	18.30	64.95	27.45	86.60	36.60	173.20	73.20	433.00	183.00	866.00	366.00	4,330.00	1,830.00	8,660.00	3,660.00
	Apr.	44.04	19.04	66.06	28.56	88.08	38.08	176.16	76.16	440.40	190.40	880.80	380.80	4,404.00	1,904.00	8,808.00	3,808.00
	Jan. thru Mar.	45.86	20.86	68.79	31.29	91.72	41.72	183.44	83.44	458.60	208.60	917.20	417.20	4,586.00	2,086.00	9,172.00	4,172.00
1982	Nov. thru Dec.	45.86	20.86	68.79	31.29	91.72	41.72	183.44	83.44	458.60	208.60	917.20	417.20	4,586.00	2,086.00	9,172.00	4,172.00
	Oct.	48.14	23.14	72.21	34.71	96.28	46.28	192.56	92.56	481.40	231.40	962.80	462.80	4,814.00	2,314.00	9,628.00	4,628.00
	Apr. thru Sep.	50.56	25.56	75.84	38.34	101.12	51.12	202.24	102.24	505.60	255.60	1,011.20	511.20	5,056.00	2,556.00	10,112.00	5,112.00
	Jan. thru Mar.	52.08	27.08	78.12	40.62	104.16	54.16	208.32	108.32	520.80	270.80	1,041.60	541.60	5,208.00	2,708.00	10,416.00	5,416.00
1981	Oct. thru Dec.	52.08	27.08	78.12	40.62	104.16	54.16	208.32	108.32	520.80	270.80	1,041.60	541.60	5,208.00	2,708.00	10,416.00	5,416.00
	May thru Sep.	53.64	28.64	80.46	42.96	107.28	57.28	214.56	114.56	536.40	286.40	1,072.80	572.80	5,364.00	2,864.00	10,728.00	5,728.00
	Apr.	54.94	29.94	82.41	44.91	109.88	59.88	219.76	119.76	549.40	299.40	1,098.80	598.80	5,494.00	2,994.00	10,988.00	5,988.00
	Jan. thru Mar.	56.60	31.60	84.90	47.40	113.20	63.20	226.40	126.40	566.00	316.00	1,132.00	632.00	5,660.00	3,160.00	11,320.00	6,320.00
1980	Nov. thru Dec.	56.60	31.60	84.90	47.40	113.20	63.20	226.40	126.40	566.00	316.00	1,132.00	632.00	5,660.00	3,160.00	11,320.00	6,320.00
	Oct.	56.86	31.86	85.29	47.79	113.72	63.72	227.44	127.44	568.60	318.60	1,137.20	637.20	5,686.00	3,186.00	11,372.00	6,372.00
	May thru Sep.	59.42	34.42	89.13	51.63	118.84	68.84	237.68	137.68	594.20	344.20	1,188.40	688.40	5,942.00	3,442.00	11,884.00	6,884.00
	Apr.	58.82	33.82	88.23	50.73	117.64	67.64	235.28	135.28	588.20	338.20	1,176.40	676.40	5,882.00	3,382.00	11,764.00	6,764.00
	Jan. thru Mar.	61.48	36.48	92.22	54.72	122.96	72.96	245.92	145.92	614.80	364.80	1,229.60	729.60	6,148.00	3,648.00	12,296.00	7,296.00

SEPTEMBER 1990

Table 4-4. U.S. Savings Bonds, Series EE Redemption Values and Interest Earned.

ISSUE YEAR	ISSUE MONTHS	$10		$25		$50		$75		$100		$200		$500		$1,000	
		REDEMP. VALUE	INTEREST EARNED	REDEMP. VALUE	INTEREST EARNED	REDEMP. VALUE	INTEREST EARNED	REDEMP. VALUE	INTEREST EARNED	REDEMP. VALUE	INTEREST EARNED	REDEMP. VALUE	INTEREST EARNED	REDEMP. VALUE	INTEREST EARNED	REDEMP. VALUE	INTEREST EARNED
1980	May thru June			40.49	21.74	80.98	43.48	121.47	65.22	161.96	86.96	323.92	173.92	809.80	434.80	1,619.60	869.60
	Apr.			40.09	21.34	80.18	42.68	120.27	64.02	160.36	85.36	320.72	170.72	801.80	426.80	1,603.60	853.60
	Jan. thru Mar.			41.59	22.84	83.18	45.68	124.77	68.52	166.36	91.36	332.72	182.72	831.80	456.80	1,663.60	913.60
1979	Nov. thru Dec.			41.59	22.84	83.18	45.68	124.77	68.52	166.36	91.36	332.72	182.72	831.80	456.80	1,663.60	913.60
	Oct.			41.20	22.45	82.40	44.90	123.60	67.35	164.80	89.80	329.60	179.60	824.00	449.00	1,648.00	898.00
	June thru Sep.			42.74	23.99	85.48	47.98	128.22	71.97	170.96	95.96	341.92	191.92	854.80	479.80	1,709.60	959.60
	May			42.65	23.90	85.30	47.80	127.95	71.70	170.60	95.60	341.20	191.20	853.00	478.00	1,706.00	956.00
	Apr.			42.23	23.48	84.46	46.96	126.69	70.44	168.92	93.92	337.84	187.84	844.60	469.60	1,689.20	939.20
	Jan. thru Mar.			43.81	25.06	87.62	50.12	131.43	75.18	175.24	100.24	350.48	200.48	876.20	501.20	1,752.40	1,002.40
1978	Dec.			43.70	24.95	87.40	49.90	131.10	74.85	174.80	99.80	349.60	199.60	874.00	499.00	1,748.00	998.00
	Nov.			43.28	24.53	86.56	49.06	129.84	73.59	173.12	98.12	346.24	196.24	865.60	490.60	1,731.20	981.20
	Oct.			44.90	26.15	89.80	52.30	134.70	78.45	179.60	104.60	359.20	209.20	898.00	523.00	1,796.00	1,046.00
	June thru Sep.			44.89	26.14	89.78	52.28	134.67	78.42	179.56	104.56	359.12	209.12	897.80	522.80	1,795.60	1,045.60
	May			46.67	27.92	93.34	55.84	140.01	83.76	186.68	111.68	373.36	223.36	933.40	558.40	1,866.80	1,116.80
	Apr.			48.59	29.84	97.18	59.68	145.77	89.52	194.36	119.36	388.72	238.72	971.80	596.80	1,943.60	1,193.60
	Jan. thru Mar.			48.59	29.84	97.18	59.68	145.77	89.52	194.36	119.36	388.72	238.72	971.80	596.80	1,943.60	1,193.60
1977	Dec.			48.46	29.71	96.92	59.42	145.38	89.13	193.84	118.84	387.68	237.68	969.20	594.20	1,938.40	1,188.40
	Nov.			48.90	30.15	97.80	60.30	146.70	90.45	195.60	120.60	391.20	241.20	978.00	603.00	1,956.00	1,206.00
	Oct.			50.97	32.22	101.94	64.44	152.91	96.66	203.88	128.88	407.76	257.76	1,019.40	644.40	2,038.80	1,288.80
	June thru Sep.			50.84	32.09	101.68	64.18	152.52	96.27	203.36	128.36	406.72	256.72	1,016.80	641.80	2,033.60	1,283.60
	May			50.35	31.60	100.70	63.20	151.05	94.80	201.40	126.40	402.80	252.80	1,007.00	632.00	2,014.00	1,264.00
	Apr.			52.49	33.74	104.98	67.48	157.47	101.22	209.96	134.96	419.92	269.92	1,049.80	674.80	2,099.60	1,349.60
	Jan. thru Mar.			52.49	33.74	104.98	67.48	157.47	101.22	209.96	134.96	419.92	269.92	1,049.80	674.80	2,099.60	1,349.60
1976	Dec.			52.35	33.60	104.70	67.20	157.05	100.80	209.40	134.40	418.80	268.80	1,047.00	672.00	2,094.00	1,344.00
	Nov.			51.86	33.11	103.72	66.22	155.58	99.33	207.44	132.44	414.88	264.88	1,037.20	662.20	2,074.40	1,324.40
	Oct.			54.06	35.31	108.12	70.62	162.18	105.93	216.24	141.24	432.48	282.48	1,081.20	706.20	2,162.40	1,412.40
	June thru Sep.			53.94	35.19	107.88	70.38	161.82	105.57	215.76	140.76	431.52	281.52	1,078.80	703.80	2,157.60	1,407.60
	May			53.42	34.67	106.84	69.34	160.26	104.01	213.68	138.68	427.36	277.36	1,068.40	693.40	2,136.80	1,386.80
	Apr.			55.70	36.95	111.40	73.90	167.10	110.85	222.80	147.80	445.60	295.60	1,114.00	739.00	2,228.00	1,478.00
	Jan. thru Mar.			55.70	36.95	111.40	73.90	167.10	110.85	222.80	147.80	445.60	295.60	1,114.00	739.00	2,228.00	1,478.00
1975	Dec.			55.70	36.95	111.40	73.90	167.10	110.85	222.80	147.80	445.60	295.60	1,114.00	739.00	2,228.00	1,478.00
	Nov.			55.57	36.82	111.14	73.64	166.71	110.46	222.28	147.28	444.56	294.56	1,111.40	736.40	2,222.80	1,472.80
	Oct.			55.03	36.28	110.06	72.56	165.09	108.84	220.12	145.12	440.24	290.24	1,100.60	725.60	2,201.20	1,451.20
	June thru Sep.			57.37	38.62	114.74	77.24	172.11	115.86	229.48	154.48	458.96	308.96	1,147.40	772.40	2,294.80	1,544.80
	May			57.23	38.48	114.46	76.96	171.69	115.44	228.92	153.92	457.84	307.84	1,144.60	769.60	2,289.20	1,539.20
	Apr.			56.69	37.94	113.38	75.88	170.07	113.82	226.76	151.76	453.52	303.52	1,133.80	758.80	2,267.60	1,517.60
	Jan. thru Mar.			58.39	39.64	116.78	79.28	175.17	118.92	233.56	158.56	467.12	317.12	1,167.80	792.80	2,335.60	1,585.60

SEPTEMBER 1990

67

Table 4-4. U.S. Savings Bonds, Series EE Redemption Values and Interest Earned. *(Cont.)*

ISSUE YEAR	ISSUE MONTHS	$10		$25		$50		$75		$100		$200		$500		$1,000	
		REDEMP. VALUE	INTEREST EARNED	REDEMP. VALUE	INTEREST EARNED	REDEMP. VALUE	INTEREST EARNED	REDEMP. VALUE	INTEREST EARNED	REDEMP. VALUE	INTEREST EARNED	REDEMP. VALUE	INTEREST EARNED	REDEMP. VALUE	INTEREST EARNED	REDEMP. VALUE	INTEREST EARNED
1974	Dec.			58.39	39.64	116.78	79.28	175.17	118.92	233.56	158.58	467.12	317.12	1,167.80	792.80	2,335.60	1,585.60
	Nov.			58.26	39.51	116.52	79.02	174.78	118.53	233.04	158.04	466.08	316.08	1,165.20	790.20	2,330.40	1,580.40
	Oct.			57.70	38.95	115.40	77.90	173.10	116.85	230.80	155.80	461.60	311.60	1,154.00	779.00	2,308.00	1,558.00
	June thru Sep.			59.58	40.83	119.16	81.66	178.74	122.49	238.32	163.32	476.64	326.64	1,191.60	816.60	2,383.20	1,633.20
	May			59.44	40.69	118.88	81.38	178.32	122.07	237.76	162.76	475.52	325.52	1,188.80	813.80	2,377.60	1,627.60
	Apr.			59.14	40.39	118.28	80.78	177.42	121.17	236.56	161.56	473.12	323.12	1,182.80	807.80	2,365.60	1,615.60
	Jan. thru Mar.			61.58	42.83	123.16	85.66	184.74	128.49	246.32	171.32	492.64	342.64	1,231.60	856.60	2,463.20	1,713.20
1973	Dec.			61.58	42.83	123.16	85.66	184.74	128.49	246.32	171.32	492.64	342.64	1,231.60	856.60	2,463.20	1,713.20
	Aug. thru Nov.			62.40	43.65	124.80	87.30	187.20	130.95	249.60	174.60	499.20	349.20	1,248.00	873.00	2,496.00	1,746.00
	July			62.25	43.50	124.50	87.00	186.75	130.50	249.00	174.00	498.00	348.00	1,245.00	870.00	2,490.00	1,740.00
	June			61.94	43.19	123.88	86.38	185.82	129.57	247.76	172.76	495.52	345.52	1,238.80	863.80	2,477.60	1,727.60
	Feb. thru May			64.36	45.61	128.72	91.22	193.08	136.83	257.44	182.44	514.88	364.88	1,287.20	912.20	2,574.40	1,824.40
	Jan.			64.20	45.45	128.40	90.90	192.60	136.35	256.80	181.80	513.60	363.60	1,284.00	909.00	2,568.00	1,818.00
1972	Dec.			63.66	44.91	127.32	89.82	190.98	134.73	254.64	179.64	509.28	359.28	1,273.20	898.20	2,546.40	1,796.40
	Aug. thru Nov.			66.16	47.41	132.32	94.82	198.48	142.23	264.64	189.64	529.28	379.28	1,323.20	948.20	2,646.40	1,896.40
	July			66.01	47.26	132.02	94.52	198.03	141.78	264.04	189.04	528.08	378.08	1,320.20	945.20	2,640.40	1,890.40
	June			65.44	46.69	130.88	93.38	196.32	140.07	261.76	186.76	523.52	373.52	1,308.80	933.80	2,617.60	1,867.60
	Feb. thru May			67.96	49.21	135.92	98.42	203.88	147.63	271.84	196.84	543.68	393.68	1,359.20	984.20	2,718.40	1,968.40
	Jan.			67.79	49.04	135.58	98.08	203.37	147.12	271.16	196.16	542.32	392.32	1,355.80	980.80	2,711.60	1,961.60
1971	Dec.			67.22	48.47	134.44	96.94	201.66	145.41	268.88	193.88	537.76	387.76	1,344.40	969.40	2,688.80	1,938.80
	Aug. thru Nov.			69.83	51.08	139.66	102.16	209.49	153.24	279.32	204.32	558.64	408.64	1,396.60	1,021.60	2,793.20	2,043.20
	July			69.66	50.91	139.32	101.82	208.98	152.73	278.64	203.64	557.28	407.28	1,393.20	1,018.20	2,786.40	2,036.40
	June			69.09	50.34	138.18	100.68	207.27	151.02	276.36	201.36	552.72	402.72	1,381.80	1,006.80	2,763.60	2,013.60
	Feb. thru May			71.73	52.98	143.46	105.96	215.19	158.94	286.92	211.92	573.84	423.84	1,434.60	1,059.60	2,869.20	2,119.20
	Jan.			71.57	52.82	143.14	105.64	214.71	158.46	286.28	211.28	572.56	422.56	1,431.40	1,056.40	2,862.80	2,112.80
1970	Dec.			70.95	52.20	141.90	104.40	212.85	156.60	283.80	208.80	567.60	417.60	1,419.00	1,044.00	2,838.00	2,088.00
	Aug. thru Nov.			73.73	54.98	147.46	109.96	221.19	164.94	294.92	219.92	589.84	439.84	1,474.60	1,099.60	2,949.20	2,199.20
	July			73.53	54.78	147.06	109.56	220.59	164.34	294.12	219.12	588.24	438.24	1,470.60	1,095.60	2,941.20	2,191.20
	June			72.91	54.16	145.82	108.32	218.73	162.48	291.64	216.64	583.28	433.28	1,458.20	1,083.20	2,916.40	2,166.40
	Feb. thru May			75.57	56.82	151.14	113.64	226.71	170.46	302.28	227.28	604.56	454.56	1,511.40	1,136.40	3,022.80	2,272.80
	Jan.			75.40	56.65	150.80	113.30	226.20	169.95	301.60	226.60	603.20	453.20	1,508.00	1,133.00	3,016.00	2,266.00
1969	Dec.			74.76	56.01	149.52	112.02	224.28	168.03	299.04	224.04	598.08	448.08	1,495.20	1,120.20	2,990.40	2,240.40
	Aug. thru Nov.			77.44	58.69	154.88	117.38	232.32	176.07	309.76	234.76	619.52	469.52	1,548.80	1,173.80	3,097.60	2,347.60
	July			77.23	58.48	154.46	116.96	231.69	175.44	308.92	233.92	617.84	467.84	1,544.60	1,169.60	3,089.20	2,339.20
	May thru June			76.61	57.86	153.22	115.72	229.83	173.58	306.44	231.44	612.88	462.88	1,532.20	1,157.20	3,064.40	2,314.40
	Apr.			75.97	57.22	151.94	114.44	227.91	171.66	303.88	228.88	607.76	457.76	1,519.40	1,144.40	3,038.80	2,288.80
	Jan. thru Mar.			79.11	60.36	158.22	120.72	237.33	181.08	316.44	241.44	632.88	482.88	1,582.20	1,207.20	3,164.40	2,414.40

SEPTEMBER 1990

Table 4-4. U.S. Savings Bonds, Series EE Redemption Values and Interest Earned. (Cont.)

U.S. SAVINGS BONDS, SERIES E-REDEMPTION VALUES AND INTEREST EARNED AMOUNTS BY DENOMINATION-SEPTEMBER 1990

ISSUE YEAR	ISSUE MONTHS	$10		$25		$50		$75		$100		$200		$500		$1,000	
		REDEMP. VALUE	INTEREST EARNED	REDEMP. VALUE	INTEREST EARNED	REDEMP. VALUE	INTEREST EARNED	REDEMP. VALUE	INTEREST EARNED	REDEMP. VALUE	INTEREST EARNED	REDEMP. VALUE	INTEREST EARNED	REDEMP. VALUE	INTEREST EARNED	REDEMP. VALUE	INTEREST EARNED
1968	Dec.			79.11	60.36	158.22	120.72	237.33	181.08	316.44	241.44	632.88	482.88	1,582.20	1,207.20	3,164.40	2,414.40
	Nov.			78.02	59.27	156.04	118.54	234.06	177.81	312.08	237.08	624.16	474.16	1,560.40	1,185.40	3,120.80	2,370.80
	Oct.			77.38	58.63	154.76	117.26	232.14	175.89	309.52	234.52	619.04	469.04	1,547.60	1,172.60	3,095.20	2,345.20
	June thru Sep.			80.57	61.82	161.14	123.64	241.71	185.46	322.28	247.28	644.56	494.56	1,611.40	1,236.40	3,222.80	2,472.80
	May			79.62	60.87	159.24	121.74	238.86	182.61	318.48	243.48	636.96	486.96	1,592.40	1,217.40	3,184.80	2,434.80
	Apr.			78.95	60.20	157.90	120.40	236.85	180.60	315.80	240.80	631.60	481.60	1,579.00	1,204.00	3,158.00	2,408.00
	Jan. thru Mar.			82.20	63.45	164.40	126.90	246.60	190.35	328.80	253.80	657.60	507.60	1,644.00	1,269.00	3,288.00	2,538.00
1967	Dec.			82.20	63.45	164.40	126.90	246.60	190.35	328.80	253.80	657.60	507.60	1,644.00	1,269.00	3,288.00	2,538.00
	Nov.			81.23	62.48	162.46	124.96	243.69	187.44	324.92	249.92	649.84	499.84	1,624.60	1,249.60	3,249.20	2,499.20
	Oct.			80.53	61.78	161.06	123.56	241.59	185.34	322.12	247.12	644.24	494.24	1,610.60	1,235.60	3,221.20	2,471.20
	June thru Sep.			83.85	65.10	167.70	130.20	251.55	195.30	335.40	260.40	670.80	520.80	1,677.00	1,302.00	3,354.00	2,604.00
	May			82.92	64.17	165.84	128.34	248.76	192.51	331.68	256.68	663.36	513.36	1,658.40	1,283.40	3,316.80	2,566.80
	Apr.			82.24	63.49	164.48	126.98	246.72	190.47	328.96	253.96	657.92	507.92	1,644.80	1,269.80	3,289.60	2,539.60
	Jan. thru Mar.			85.63	66.88	171.26	133.76	256.89	200.64	342.52	267.52	685.04	535.04	1,712.60	1,337.60	3,425.20	2,675.20
1966	Dec.			85.63	66.88	171.26	133.76	256.89	200.64	342.52	267.52	685.04	535.04	1,712.60	1,337.60	3,425.20	2,675.20
	Nov.			84.70	65.95	169.40	131.90	254.10	197.85	338.80	263.80	677.60	527.60	1,694.00	1,319.00	3,388.00	2,638.00
	Oct.			83.98	65.23	167.96	130.46	251.94	195.69	335.92	260.92	671.84	521.84	1,679.60	1,304.60	3,359.20	2,609.20
	June thru Sep.			87.45	68.70	174.90	137.40	262.35	206.10	349.80	274.80	699.60	549.60	1,749.00	1,374.00	3,498.00	2,748.00
	May			86.57	67.82	173.14	135.64	259.71	203.46	346.28	271.28	692.56	542.56	1,731.40	1,356.40	3,462.80	2,712.80
	Apr.			85.83	67.08	171.66	134.16	257.49	201.24	343.32	268.32	686.64	536.64	1,716.60	1,341.60	3,433.20	2,683.20
	Jan. thru Mar.			89.37	70.62	178.74	141.24	268.11	211.86	357.48	282.48	714.96	564.96	1,787.40	1,412.40	3,574.80	2,824.80
1965	Dec.			89.37	70.62	178.74	141.24	268.11	211.86	357.48	282.48	714.96	564.96	1,787.40	1,412.40	3,574.80	2,824.80
	Sep. thru Nov.			89.10	70.35	178.20	140.70	267.30	211.05	356.40	281.40	712.80	562.80	1,782.00	1,407.00	3,564.00	2,814.00
	Aug.			88.64	69.89	177.28	139.78	265.92	209.67	354.56	279.56	709.12	559.12	1,772.80	1,397.80	3,545.60	2,795.60
	July			87.89	69.14	175.78	138.28	263.67	207.42	351.56	276.56	703.12	553.12	1,757.80	1,382.80	3,515.60	2,765.60
	June			91.52	72.77	183.04	145.54	274.56	218.31	366.08	291.08	732.16	582.16	1,830.40	1,455.40	3,660.80	2,910.80
	Mar. thru May			91.02	72.27	182.04	144.54	273.06	216.81	364.08	289.08	728.16	578.16	1,820.40	1,445.40	3,640.80	2,890.80
	Feb.			90.58	71.83	181.16	143.66	271.74	215.49	362.32	287.32	724.64	574.64	1,811.60	1,436.60	3,623.20	2,873.20
	Jan.			91.35	72.60	182.70	145.20	274.05	217.80	365.40	290.40	730.80	580.80	1,827.00	1,452.00	3,654.00	2,904.00
1964	Dec.			95.23	76.48	190.46	152.96	285.69	229.44	380.92	305.92	761.84	611.84	1,904.60	1,529.60	3,809.20	3,059.20
	Sep. thru Nov.			94.63	75.88	189.26	151.76	283.89	227.64	378.52	303.52	757.04	607.04	1,892.60	1,517.60	3,785.20	3,035.20
	Aug.			94.16	75.41	188.32	150.82	282.48	226.23	376.64	301.64	753.28	603.28	1,883.20	1,508.20	3,766.40	3,016.40
	July			93.27	74.52	186.54	149.04	279.81	223.56	373.08	298.08	746.16	596.16	1,865.40	1,490.40	3,730.80	2,980.80
	June			97.23	78.48	194.46	156.96	291.69	235.44	388.92	313.92	777.84	627.84	1,944.60	1,569.60	3,889.20	3,139.20
	Mar. thru May			96.60	77.85	193.20	155.70	289.80	233.55	386.40	311.40	772.80	622.80	1,932.00	1,557.00	3,864.00	3,114.00
	Feb.			96.14	77.39	192.28	154.78			384.56	309.56	769.12	619.12	1,922.80	1,547.80	3,845.60	3,095.60
	Jan.			95.22	76.47	190.44	152.94			380.88	305.88	761.76	611.76	1,904.40	1,529.40	3,808.80	3,058.80

SEPTEMBER 1990

Table 4-4. U.S. Savings Bonds, Series EE Redemption Values and Interest Earned. (Cont.)

ISSUE YEAR	ISSUE MONTHS	$10 REDEMP. VALUE	$10 INTEREST EARNED	$25 REDEMP. VALUE	$25 INTEREST EARNED	$50 REDEMP. VALUE	$50 INTEREST EARNED	$75 REDEMP. VALUE	$75 INTEREST EARNED	$100 REDEMP. VALUE	$100 INTEREST EARNED	$200 REDEMP. VALUE	$200 INTEREST EARNED	$500 REDEMP. VALUE	$500 INTEREST EARNED	$1,000 REDEMP. VALUE	$1,000 INTEREST EARNED
1963	Dec.			99.27	80.52	198.54	161.04			397.08	322.08	794.16	644.16	1,985.40	1,610.40	3,970.80	3,220.80
	Sep. thru Nov.			98.64	79.89	197.28	159.78			394.56	319.56	789.12	639.12	1,972.80	1,597.80	3,945.60	3,195.60
	Aug.			98.17	79.42	196.34	158.84			392.68	317.68	785.36	635.36	1,963.40	1,588.40	3,926.80	3,176.80
	July			97.23	78.48	194.46	156.96			388.92	313.92	777.84	627.84	1,944.60	1,569.60	3,889.20	3,139.20
	June			101.36	82.61	202.72	165.22			405.44	330.44	810.88	660.88	2,027.20	1,652.20	4,054.40	3,304.40
	Mar. thru May			100.60	81.85	201.20	163.70			402.40	327.40	804.80	654.80	2,012.00	1,637.00	4,024.00	3,274.00
	Feb.			100.13	81.38	200.26	162.76			400.52	325.52	801.04	651.04	2,002.60	1,627.60	4,005.20	3,255.20
	Jan.			99.17	80.42	198.34	160.84			396.68	321.68	793.36	643.36	1,983.40	1,608.40	3,966.80	3,216.80
1962	Dec.			103.40	84.65	206.80	169.30			413.60	338.60	827.20	677.20	2,068.00	1,693.00	4,136.00	3,386.00
	Sep. thru Nov.			102.97	84.22	205.94	168.44			411.88	336.88	823.76	673.76	2,059.40	1,684.40	4,118.80	3,368.80
	Aug.			102.24	83.49	204.48	166.98			408.96	333.96	817.92	667.92	2,044.80	1,669.80	4,089.60	3,339.60
	July			101.26	82.51	202.52	165.02			405.04	330.04	810.08	660.08	2,025.20	1,650.20	4,050.40	3,300.40
	June			104.30	85.55	208.60	171.10			417.20	342.20	834.40	684.40	2,086.00	1,711.00	4,172.00	3,422.00
	Mar. thru May			104.04	85.29	208.08	170.58			416.16	341.16	832.32	682.32	2,080.80	1,705.80	4,161.60	3,411.60
	Feb.			103.30	84.55	206.60	169.10			413.20	338.20	826.40	676.40	2,066.00	1,691.00	4,132.00	3,382.00
	Jan.			102.30	83.55	204.60	167.10			409.20	334.20	818.40	668.40	2,046.00	1,671.00	4,092.00	3,342.00
1961	Dec.			105.64	86.89	211.28	173.78			422.56	347.56	845.12	695.12	2,112.80	1,737.80	4,225.60	3,475.60
	Sep. thru Nov.			105.35	86.60	210.70	173.20			421.40	346.40	842.80	692.80	2,107.00	1,732.00	4,214.00	3,464.00
	Aug.			104.20	85.45	208.40	170.90			416.80	341.80	833.60	683.60	2,084.00	1,709.00	4,168.00	3,418.00
	July			103.67	84.92	207.34	169.84			414.68	339.68	829.36	679.36	2,073.40	1,698.40	4,146.80	3,396.80
	June			107.95	89.20	215.90	178.40			431.80	356.80	863.60	713.60	2,159.00	1,784.00	4,318.00	3,568.00
	Mar. thru May			107.64	88.89	215.28	177.78			430.56	355.56	861.12	711.12	2,152.80	1,777.80	4,305.60	3,555.60
	Feb.			106.41	87.66	212.82	175.32			425.64	350.64	851.28	701.28	2,128.20	1,753.20	4,256.40	3,506.40
	Jan.			105.52	86.77	211.04	173.54			422.08	347.08	844.16	694.16	2,110.40	1,735.40	4,220.80	3,470.80
1960	Dec.			109.87	91.12	219.74	182.24			439.48	364.48	878.96	728.96	2,197.40	1,822.40	4,394.80	3,644.80
	Sep. thru Nov.			109.67	90.92	219.34	181.84			438.68	363.68	877.36	727.36	2,193.40	1,818.40	4,386.80	3,636.80
	Aug.			108.43	89.68	216.86	179.36			433.72	358.72	867.44	717.44	2,168.60	1,793.60	4,337.20	3,587.20
	July			107.49	88.74	214.98	177.48			429.96	354.96	859.92	709.92	2,149.80	1,774.80	4,299.60	3,549.60
	June			111.93	93.18	223.86	186.36			447.72	372.72	895.44	745.44	2,238.60	1,863.60	4,477.20	3,727.20
	Mar. thru May			111.74	92.99	223.48	185.98			446.96	371.96	893.92	743.92	2,234.80	1,859.80	4,469.60	3,719.60
	Feb.			110.48	91.73	220.96	183.46			441.92	366.92	883.84	733.84	2,209.60	1,834.60	4,419.20	3,669.20
	Jan.			109.54	90.79	219.08	181.58			438.16	363.16	876.32	726.32	2,190.80	1,815.80	4,381.60	3,631.60
1959	Dec.			114.06	95.31	228.12	190.62			456.24	381.24	912.48	762.48	2,281.20	1,906.20	4,562.40	3,812.40
	Sep. thru Nov.			113.82	95.07	227.64	190.14			455.28	380.28	910.56	760.56	2,276.40	1,901.40	4,552.80	3,802.80
	Aug.			112.55	93.80	225.10	187.60			450.20	375.20	900.40	750.40	2,251.00	1,876.00	4,502.00	3,752.00
	July			111.61	92.86	223.22	185.72			446.44	371.44	892.88	742.88	2,232.20	1,857.20	4,464.40	3,714.40
	June			116.22	97.47	232.44	194.94			464.88	389.88	929.76	779.76	2,324.40	1,949.40	4,648.80	3,898.80
	May			111.93	93.18	223.86	186.36			447.72	372.72	895.44	745.44	2,238.60	1,863.60	4,477.20	3,727.20
	Jan. thru Apr.			116.55	97.80	233.10	195.60			466.20	391.20	932.40	782.40	2,331.00	1,956.00	4,662.00	3,912.00

SEPTEMBER 1990

Table 4-4. U.S. Savings Bonds, Series EE Redemption Values and Interest Earned. (Cont.)

ISSUE YEAR	ISSUE MONTHS	$10 REDEMP. VALUE	$10 INTEREST EARNED	$25 REDEMP. VALUE	$25 INTEREST EARNED	$50 REDEMP. VALUE	$50 INTEREST EARNED	$75 REDEMP. VALUE	$75 INTEREST EARNED	$100 REDEMP. VALUE	$100 INTEREST EARNED	$200 REDEMP. VALUE	$200 INTEREST EARNED	$500 REDEMP. VALUE	$500 INTEREST EARNED	$1,000 REDEMP. VALUE	$1,000 INTEREST EARNED
1958	Dec.			115.17	96.42	230.34	192.84			460.68	385.66	921.36	771.36	2,303.40	1,928.40	4,606.80	3,856.80
	Nov.			113.71	94.96	227.42	189.92			454.84	379.84	909.68	769.68	2,274.20	1,899.20	4,548.40	3,798.40
	July thru Oct.			118.40	99.65	236.80	199.30			473.60	398.60	947.20	797.20	2,368.00	1,993.00	4,736.00	3,986.00
	June			117.04	98.29	234.08	196.58			468.16	393.16	936.32	786.32	2,340.80	1,965.80	4,681.60	3,931.60
	May			115.58	96.83	231.16	193.66			462.32	387.32	924.64	774.64	2,311.60	1,936.60	4,623.20	3,873.20
	Jan. thru Apr.			120.34	101.59	240.68	203.18			481.36	406.36	962.72	812.72	2,406.80	2,031.80	4,813.60	4,063.60
1957	Dec.			118.93	100.18	237.86	200.36			475.72	400.72	951.44	801.44	2,378.60	2,003.60	4,757.20	4,007.20
	Nov.			117.43	98.68	234.86	197.36			469.72	394.72	939.44	789.44	2,348.60	1,973.60	4,697.20	3,947.20
	July thru Oct.			122.27	103.52	244.54	207.04			489.08	414.08	978.16	828.16	2,445.40	2,070.40	4,890.80	4,140.80
	June			120.88	102.13	241.76	204.26			483.52	408.52	967.04	817.04	2,417.60	2,042.60	4,835.20	4,085.20
	May			119.35	100.60	238.70	201.20			477.40	402.40	954.80	804.80	2,387.00	2,012.00	4,774.00	4,024.00
	Feb. thru Apr.			124.27	105.52	248.54	211.04			497.08	422.08	994.16	844.16	2,485.40	2,110.40	4,970.80	4,220.80
	Jan.			122.60	103.85	245.20	207.70			490.40	415.40	980.80	830.80	2,452.00	2,077.00	4,904.00	4,154.00
1956	Dec.			121.89	103.14	243.78	206.28			487.56	412.56	975.12	825.12	2,437.80	2,062.80	4,875.60	4,125.60
	Oct. thru Nov.			120.49	101.74	240.98	203.48			481.96	406.96	963.92	813.92	2,409.80	2,034.80	4,819.60	4,069.60
	Sep.			119.49	100.74	238.98	201.48			477.96	402.96	955.92	805.92	2,389.80	2,014.80	4,779.60	4,029.60
	Aug.			124.42	105.67	248.84	211.34			497.68	422.68	995.36	845.36	2,488.40	2,113.40	4,976.80	4,226.80
	June thru July			124.14	105.39	248.28	210.78			496.56	421.56	993.12	843.12	2,482.80	2,107.80	4,965.60	4,215.60
	Apr. thru May			120.75	102.00	241.50	204.00			483.00	408.00	966.00	816.00	2,415.00	2,040.00	4,830.00	4,080.00
	Mar.			119.73	100.98	239.46	201.96			478.92	403.92	957.84	807.84	2,394.60	2,019.60	4,789.20	4,039.20
	Feb.			124.67	105.92	249.34	211.84			498.68	423.68	997.36	847.36	2,493.40	2,118.40	4,986.80	4,236.80
	Jan.			124.36	105.61	248.72	211.22			497.44	422.44	994.88	844.88	2,487.20	2,112.20	4,974.40	4,224.40
1955	Dec.			122.71	103.96	245.42	207.92			490.84	415.84	981.68	831.68	2,454.20	2,079.20	4,908.40	4,158.40
	Oct. thru Nov.			121.67	102.92	243.34	205.84			486.68	411.68	973.36	823.36	2,433.40	2,058.40	4,866.80	4,116.80
	Sep.			126.69	107.94	253.38	215.88			506.76	431.76	1,013.52	863.52	2,533.80	2,158.80	5,067.60	4,317.60
	Aug.			126.36	107.61	252.72	215.22			505.44	430.44	1,010.88	860.88	2,527.20	2,152.20	5,054.40	4,304.40
	June thru July			124.73	105.98	249.46	211.96			498.92	423.92	997.84	847.84	2,494.60	2,119.60	4,989.20	4,239.20
	Apr. thru May			123.71	104.96	247.42	209.92			494.84	419.84	989.68	839.68	2,474.20	2,099.20	4,948.40	4,198.40
1954	Dec.			128.82	110.07	257.64	220.14			515.28	440.28	1,030.56	880.56	2,576.40	2,201.40	5,152.80	4,402.80
	Oct. thru Nov.			128.50	109.75	257.00	219.50			514.00	439.00	1,028.00	878.00	2,570.00	2,195.00	5,140.00	4,390.00
	Sep.			126.82	108.07	253.64	216.14			507.28	432.28	1,014.56	864.56	2,536.40	2,161.40	5,072.80	4,322.80
	Aug.			125.76	107.01	251.52	214.02			503.04	428.04	1,006.08	856.08	2,515.20	2,140.20	5,030.40	4,280.40
	June thru July			130.94	112.19	261.88	224.38			523.76	448.76	1,047.52	897.52	2,618.80	2,243.80	5,237.60	4,487.60
	Apr. thru May			130.60	111.85	261.20	223.70			522.40	447.40	1,044.80	894.80	2,612.00	2,237.00	5,224.00	4,474.00
	Mar.			128.96	110.21	257.92	220.42			515.84	440.84	1,031.68	881.68	2,579.20	2,204.20	5,158.40	4,408.40
	Feb.			127.87	109.12	255.74	218.24			511.48	436.48	1,022.96	872.96	2,557.40	2,182.40	5,114.80	4,364.80
	Jan.			133.14	114.80	266.28	228.78			532.56	457.56	1,065.12	915.12	2,662.80	2,287.80	5,325.60	4,575.60

SEPTEMBER 1990

Table 4-4. U.S. Savings Bonds, Series EE Redemption Values and Interest Earned. (Cont.)

ISSUE YEAR	ISSUE MONTHS		$10 REDEMP. VALUE	$10 INTEREST EARNED	$25 REDEMP. VALUE	$25 INTEREST EARNED	$50 REDEMP. VALUE	$50 INTEREST EARNED	$75 REDEMP. VALUE	$75 INTEREST EARNED	$100 REDEMP. VALUE	$100 INTEREST EARNED	$200 REDEMP. VALUE	$200 INTEREST EARNED	$500 REDEMP. VALUE	$500 INTEREST EARNED	$1,000 REDEMP. VALUE	$1,000 INTEREST EARNED
1953	Dec.				133.14	114.39	266.28	228.78			532.56	457.56	1,065.12	915.12	2,662.80	2,287.80	5,325.60	4,575.60
	Oct. thru Nov.				132.80	114.05	265.60	228.10			531.20	456.20	1,062.40	912.40	2,656.00	2,281.00	5,312.00	4,562.00
	Sep.				131.13	112.38	262.26	224.76			524.52	449.52	1,049.04	899.04	2,622.60	2,247.60	5,245.20	4,495.20
	Aug.				130.04	111.29	260.08	222.58			520.16	445.16	1,040.32	890.32	2,600.80	2,225.80	5,201.60	4,451.60
	June thru July				135.40	116.65	270.80	233.30			541.60	466.60	1,083.20	933.20	2,708.00	2,333.00	5,416.00	4,666.00
	Apr. thru May				135.07	116.32	270.14	232.64			540.28	465.28	1,080.56	930.56	2,701.40	2,326.40	5,402.80	4,652.80
	Mar.				133.42	114.67	266.84	229.34			533.68	458.68	1,067.36	917.36	2,668.40	2,293.40	5,336.80	4,586.80
	Feb.				134.55	115.80	269.10	231.60			538.20	463.20	1,076.40	926.40	2,691.00	2,316.00	5,382.00	4,632.00
	Jan.				140.27	121.52	280.54	243.04			561.08	486.08	1,122.16	972.16	2,805.40	2,430.40	5,610.80	4,860.80
1952	Dec.				140.27	121.52	280.54	243.04			561.08	486.08	1,122.16	972.16	2,805.40	2,430.40	5,610.80	4,860.80
	Oct. thru Nov.				139.90	121.15	279.80	242.30			559.60	484.60	1,119.20	969.20	2,798.00	2,423.00	5,596.00	4,846.00
	Sep.				138.17	119.42	276.34	238.84			552.68	477.68	1,105.36	955.36	2,763.40	2,388.40	5,526.80	4,776.80
	Aug.				136.85	118.10	273.70	236.20			547.40	472.40	1,094.80	944.80	2,737.00	2,362.00	5,474.00	4,724.00
	June thru July				142.66	123.91	285.32	247.82			570.64	495.64	1,141.28	991.28	2,853.20	2,478.20	5,706.40	4,956.40
	May				142.34	123.59	284.68	247.18			569.36	494.36	1,138.72	988.72	2,846.80	2,471.80	5,693.60	4,943.60
	Apr.				137.06	118.31	274.12	236.62			548.24	473.24	1,096.48	946.48	2,741.20	2,366.20	5,482.40	4,732.40
	Jan. thru Mar.				142.89	124.14	285.78	248.28			571.56	496.56	1,143.12	993.12	2,857.80	2,482.80	5,715.60	4,965.60
1951	Dec.				142.89	124.14	285.78	248.28			571.56	496.56	1,143.12	993.12	2,857.80	2,482.80	5,715.60	4,965.60
	Nov.				140.84	122.09	281.68	244.18			563.36	488.36	1,126.72	976.72	2,816.80	2,441.80	5,633.60	4,883.60
	Oct.				139.50	120.75	279.00	241.50			558.00	483.00	1,116.00	966.00	2,790.00	2,415.00	5,580.00	4,830.00
	June thru Sep.				145.43	126.68	290.86	253.36			581.72	506.72	1,163.44	1,013.44	2,908.60	2,533.60	5,817.20	5,067.20
	May				143.31	124.56	286.62	249.12			573.24	498.24	1,146.48	996.48	2,866.20	2,491.20	5,732.40	4,982.40
	Apr.				141.93	123.18	283.86	246.36			567.72	492.72	1,135.44	985.44	2,838.60	2,463.60	5,677.20	4,927.20
	Jan. thru Mar.				147.96	129.21	295.92	258.42			591.84	516.84	1,183.68	1,033.68	2,959.20	2,584.20	5,918.40	5,168.40
1950	Dec.				147.96	129.21	295.92	258.42			591.84	516.84	1,183.68	1,033.68	2,959.20	2,584.20	5,918.40	5,168.40
	Nov.				145.80	127.05	291.60	254.10			583.20	508.20	1,166.40	1,016.40	2,916.00	2,541.00	5,832.00	5,082.00
	Oct.				144.39	125.64	288.78	251.28			577.56	502.56	1,155.12	1,005.12	2,887.80	2,512.80	5,775.60	5,025.60
	June thru Sep.	A			150.53	131.78	301.06	263.56			602.12	527.12	1,204.24	1,054.24	3,010.60	2,635.60	6,021.20	5,271.20
	Jan. thru Apr.	A	58.82	51.32	148.48	129.73	296.96	259.46			593.92	518.92	1,187.84	1,037.84	2,969.60	2,594.60	5,939.20	5,189.20
1949 A	Dec.		58.82	51.32	147.06	128.31	294.12	256.62			588.24	513.24	1,176.48	1,026.48	2,941.20	2,566.20	5,882.40	5,132.40
	Nov.		58.09	50.59	145.23	126.48	290.46	252.96			580.92	505.92	1,161.84	1,011.84	2,904.60	2,529.60	5,809.20	5,059.20
	June thru Oct.	A B	57.53	50.03	143.83	125.08	287.66	250.16			575.32	500.32	1,150.64	1,000.64	2,876.60	2,501.60	5,753.20	5,003.20
	May	A B	55.21	47.71	138.02	119.27	276.04	238.54			552.08	477.08	1,104.16	954.16	2,760.40	2,385.40	5,520.80	4,770.80
	Jan. thru Apr.	A B	54.68	47.18	136.69	117.94	273.38	235.88			546.76	471.76	1,093.52	943.52	2,733.80	2,358.80	5,467.60	4,717.60
1948 A B	Dec.		54.68	47.18	136.69	117.94	273.38	235.88			546.76	471.76	1,093.52	943.52	2,733.80	2,358.80	5,467.60	4,717.60
	Nov.	A B	53.80	46.30	134.51	115.76	269.02	231.52			538.04	463.04	1,076.08	926.08	2,690.20	2,315.20	5,380.40	4,630.40
	June thru Oct.	A B	53.29	45.79	133.23	114.48	266.46	228.96			532.92	457.92	1,065.84	915.84	2,664.60	2,289.60	5,329.20	4,579.20
	May	A B	52.44	44.94	131.09	112.34	262.18	224.68			524.36	449.36	1,048.72	898.72	2,621.80	2,246.80	5,243.60	4,493.60
	Jan. thru Apr.	A B	52.56	45.06	131.41	112.66	262.82	225.32			525.64	450.64	1,051.28	901.28	2,628.20	2,253.20	5,256.40	4,506.40

SEPTEMBER 1990

72

Table 4-4. U.S. Savings Bonds, Series EE Redemption Values and Interest Earned. (Cont.)

ISSUE YEAR	ISSUE MONTHS	$10 REDEMP. VALUE	$10 INTEREST EARNED	$25 REDEMP. VALUE	$25 INTEREST EARNED	$50 REDEMP. VALUE	$50 INTEREST EARNED	$75 REDEMP. VALUE	$75 INTEREST EARNED	$100 REDEMP. VALUE	$100 INTEREST EARNED	$200 REDEMP. VALUE	$200 INTEREST EARNED	$500 REDEMP. VALUE	$500 INTEREST EARNED	$1,000 REDEMP. VALUE	$1,000 INTEREST EARNED
1947 A B	Dec.	52.56	45.06	131.41	112.66	262.82	225.32			525.64	450.64	1,051.28	901.28	2,628.20	2,253.20	5,256.40	4,506.40
A B	Nov.	51.74	44.24	129.34	110.59	258.68	221.18			517.36	442.36	1,034.72	884.72	2,586.80	2,211.80	5,173.60	4,423.60
A B	June thru Oct.	50.63	43.13	126.57	107.82	253.14	215.64			506.28	431.28	1,012.56	862.56	2,531.40	2,156.40	5,062.80	4,312.80
A B	May	49.83	42.33	124.57	105.82	249.14	211.64			498.28	423.28	996.56	846.56	2,491.40	2,116.40	4,982.80	4,232.80
A B	Jan. thru Apr.	49.35	41.85	123.38	104.63	246.76	209.26			493.52	418.52	987.04	837.04	2,467.60	2,092.60	4,935.20	4,185.20
1946 A B	Dec.	49.35	41.85	123.38	104.63	246.76	209.26			493.52	418.52	987.04	837.04	2,467.60	2,092.60	4,935.20	4,185.20
A B	Nov.	48.57	41.07	121.42	102.67	242.84	205.34			485.68	410.68	971.36	821.36	2,428.40	2,053.40	4,856.80	4,106.80
A B	June thru Oct.	48.10	40.60	120.25	101.50	240.50	203.00			481.00	406.00	962.00	812.00	2,405.00	2,030.00	4,810.00	4,060.00
A B	May	47.36	39.86	118.41	99.66	236.82	199.32			473.64	398.64	947.28	797.28	2,368.20	1,993.20	4,736.40	3,996.40
A B	Jan. thru Apr.	46.91	39.41	117.28	98.53	234.56	197.06			469.12	394.12	938.24	788.24	2,345.60	1,970.60	4,691.20	3,941.20
1945 A B	Dec.	46.91	39.41	117.28	98.53	234.56	197.06			469.12	394.12	938.24	788.24	2,345.60	1,970.60	4,691.20	3,941.20
A B	Nov.	45.77	38.27	114.43	95.68	228.86	191.36			457.72	382.72	915.44	765.44	2,288.60	1,913.60	4,577.20	3,827.20
A B	June thru Oct.	45.33	37.83	113.33	94.58	226.66	189.16			453.32	378.32	906.64	756.64	2,266.60	1,891.60	4,533.20	3,783.20
A B	May	44.62	37.12	111.54	92.79	223.08	185.58			446.16	371.16			2,230.80	1,855.80	4,461.60	3,711.60
A B	Jan. thru Apr.	44.19	36.69	110.47	91.72	220.94	183.44			441.88	366.88			2,209.40	1,834.40	4,418.80	3,668.80
1944 A B	Dec.	44.19	36.69	110.47	91.72	220.94	183.44			441.88	366.88			2,209.40	1,834.40	4,418.80	3,668.80
A B	Nov.	43.50	36.00	108.75	90.00	217.50	180.00			435.00	360.00			2,175.00	1,800.00	4,350.00	3,600.00
A B	June thru Oct.	43.08	35.58	107.70	88.95	215.40	177.90			430.80	355.80			2,154.00	1,779.00	4,308.00	3,558.00
A B	May			106.11	87.36	212.22	174.72			424.44	349.44			2,122.20	1,747.20	4,244.40	3,494.40
A B	Jan. thru Apr.			105.09	86.34	210.18	172.68			420.36	345.36			2,101.80	1,726.80	4,203.60	3,453.60
1943 A B	Dec.			105.09	86.34	210.18	172.68			420.36	345.36			2,101.80	1,726.80	4,203.60	3,453.60
A B	Nov.			103.48	84.73	206.96	169.46			413.92	338.92			2,069.60	1,694.60	4,139.20	3,389.20
A B	June thru Oct.			102.48	83.73	204.96	167.46			409.92	334.92			2,049.60	1,674.60	4,099.20	3,349.20
A B	May			100.91	82.16	201.82	164.32			403.64	328.64			2,018.20	1,643.20	4,036.40	3,286.40
A B	Jan. thru Apr.			99.95	81.20	199.90	162.40			399.80	324.80			1,999.00	1,624.00	3,998.00	3,248.00
1942 A B	Dec.			99.95	81.20	199.90	162.40			399.80	324.80			1,999.00	1,624.00	3,998.00	3,248.00
A B	Nov.			98.40	79.65	196.80	159.30			393.60	318.60			1,968.00	1,593.00	3,936.00	3,186.00
A B	June thru Oct.			97.45	78.70	194.90	157.40			389.80	314.80			1,949.00	1,574.00	3,898.00	3,148.00
A B	May			96.00	77.25	192.00	154.50			384.00	309.00			1,920.00	1,545.00	3,840.00	3,090.00
A B	Jan. thru Apr.			94.35	75.60	188.70	151.20			377.40	302.40			1,887.00	1,512.00	3,774.00	3,024.00
1941 A B	Dec.			94.35	75.60	188.70	151.20			377.40	302.40			1,887.00	1,512.00	3,774.00	3,024.00
A B	Nov.			92.86	74.11	185.72	148.22			371.44	296.44			1,857.20	1,482.20	3,714.40	2,964.40
A B	June thru Oct.			91.96	73.21	183.92	146.42			367.84	292.84			1,839.20	1,464.20	3,678.40	2,928.40
A B	May			90.59	71.84	181.18	143.68			362.36	287.36			1,811.80	1,436.80	3,623.60	2,873.60

A. BONDS WITH THESE ISSUE DATES HAVE REACHED FINAL MATURITY AND WILL EARN NO ADDITIONAL INTEREST.
B. BONDS WITH ISSUE DATES OF AUGUST 1949 AND PRIOR ARE NOT ELIGIBLE FOR EXCHANGE TO SERIES HH BONDS.

SEPTEMBER 1990

Figure 4-1. Long-Term Government Bonds.
Rates of Return: 1926-1989

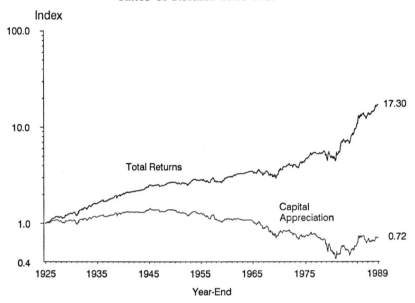

Index

Total Returns

Capital
Appreciation

17.30

0.72

Year-End

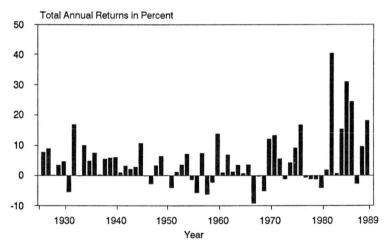

Total Annual Returns in Percent

Year

Source: *Stocks, Bonds, Bills, and Inflation, 1990 Yearbook.* Ibbotson Associates, Chicago.

Figure 4-2. Long-Term Corporate Bonds. Rates of Return: 1926-1989

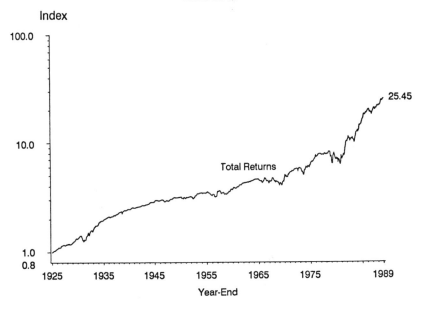

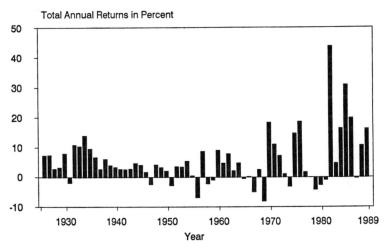

Source: *Stocks, Bonds, Bills, and Inflation, 1990 Yearbook*. Ibbotson Associates, Chicago.

Table 4–5. Taxable Yield Equivalents
to Federally Tax-Exempt Yields

	Federal Income Tax Bracket		
Tax Exempt Yield*	15%	28%	31%
	Approximate Equivalent Taxable Yield		
5.00	5.88	6.94	7.25
5.25	6.18	7.29	7.61
5.50	6.47	7.64	7.97
5.75	6.76	7.99	8.33
6.00	7.06	8.33	8.70
6.10	7.18	8.47	8.84
6.20	7.29	8.61	8.99
6.25	7.35	8.68	9.06
6.30	7.41	8.75	9.13
6.40	7.53	8.89	9.28
6.50	7.65	9.03	9.42
6.60	7.76	9.17	9.57
6.70	7.88	9.31	9.71
6.75	7.94	9.38	9.78
6.80	8.00	9.44	9.86
6.90	8.12	9.58	10.00
7.00	8.24	9.72	10.14
7.10	8.35	9.86	10.29
7.20	8.47	10.00	10.43
7.25	8.53	10.07	10.51
7.30	8.59	10.14	10.58
7.40	8.71	10.28	10.72
7.50	8.82	10.42	10.87
7.60	8.94	10.56	11.01
7.70	9.06	10.69	11.16
7.75	9.12	10.76	11.23
7.80	9.18	10.83	11.30
7.90	9.29	10.97	11.45
8.00	9.41	11.11	11.59
8.10	9.53	11.25	11.74

Table 4–5. (*Cont.*)

Tax Exempt Yield*	Federal Income Tax Bracket		
	15%	28%	31%
	Approximate Equivalent Taxable Yield		
8.20	9.65	11.39	11.88
8.25	9.71	11.46	11.96
8.30	9.76	11.53	12.03
8.40	9.88	11.67	12.17
8.50	10.00	11.81	12.32
8.60	10.12	11.94	12.46
8.70	10.24	12.08	12.61
8.75	10.29	12.15	12.68
8.80	10.35	12.22	12.75
8.90	10.47	12.36	12.90
9.00	10.59	12.50	13.04
9.10	10.71	12.64	13.19
9.20	10.82	12.78	13.33
9.25	10.88	12.85	13.41
9.30	10.94	12.92	13.48
9.40	11.06	13.06	13.62
9.50	11.18	13.19	13.77
9.60	11.29	13.33	13.91
9.70	11.41	13.47	13.06
9.75	11.47	13.54	14.13
9.80	11.53	13.61	14.20
9.90	11.65	13.75	14.35
10.00	11.76	13.89	14.49

*The yield on purchases of tax-exempt securities made at par or above par.

state municipal bond or bond fund that is exempt from both federal and state taxes. In spite of their apparent lower yields, you may actually be better off investing in municipal securities in your resident state after taxes are computed.

To make an approximate comparison between a taxable investment and a double tax-free investment, multiply the yield you

Table 4-6. Comparison Between a Taxable Investment
and a Double Tax-Free Investment

State Tax Rate For Your Locale	Multiplier For Investor In:	
	28% bracket	31% bracket
2%	1.42	1.48
3	1.43	1.49
4	1.45	1.51
5	1.46	1.53
6	1.48	1.54
7	1.49	1.56
8	1.51	1.58
9	1.53	1.59
10	1.54	1.61
11	1.56	1.68
12	1.58	1.70
20% of Federal Tax Liability	1.47	1.61
25% of Federal Tax Liability	1.49	1.63

can receive on a double tax-free security by the following multiplier reflecting your applicable state tax rate on interest income. The result is the equivalent taxable yield. The factor that you use depends upon whether you are in the 28 percent or 31 percent federal tax bracket. For example, a 7 percent federal and state tax-free yield would be the equivalent of a 10.2 percent fully taxable yield for an investor in the 28 percent federal tax bracket whose state tax rate on interest income is 5 percent (7% × 1.46). For a 31 percent federal tax bracket investor, the equivalent fully taxable yield would be 11.0 percent (7% × 1.53).

The multipliers apply only to yields, not to total returns. Capital gains realized from the sales of bonds or bond fund shares are taxable. To calculate the equivalent taxable yield on out-of-state municipals, which avoid federal taxation but are subject to state and local taxes, the multipliers are 1.39 for investors in the 28 percent federal bracket and 1.45 for investors in the 31 percent federal bracket.

5

Mutual Funds

Mutual funds have experienced explosive growth in recent years because they are an excellent financial choice for investors of any size portfolio. Mutual funds offer diversification and professional management to small- and medium-sized portfolios that might not be able to afford them otherwise, as well as alleviating the burden of evaluating and selecting individual securities from wealthier individuals and institutions.

Basically, a mutual fund is a pool of investors' money that is used to purchase a professionally managed, diversified portfolio of stocks, bonds, money market instruments, or other securities. Pooling the money gives each investor the benefit of a greater portfolio than his or her funds alone could purchase. Each share in a mutual fund represents a small slice of the large portfolio pie.

The first open-end mutual fund, the Massachusetts Investors Trust, was started in 1924. Industry growth remained relatively sluggish until the postwar stock market boom of the 1950s and 1960s. Then in the late 1960s and early 1970s, a succession of bear markets caused a decline in their popularity. Sales picked up again in the late 1970s and have flourished in recent years with a bullish stock market and the introduction of a variety of fixed-income and money market funds.

Closed-end fund offerings have also grown rapidly in recent years. Closed-end funds, which also pool investors' money, differ from open-end funds in that they each have a fixed number of shares that are traded on a stock exchange. Open-end funds issue new shares whenever a new investor makes an investment in the fund. Closed-end funds do not issue new shares—holders buy shares in the fund on a stock exchange.

For most investors, the advantages that mutual funds offer outweigh their disadvantages. On the positive side:

Owning mutual fund shares is a low-cost way to diversify your portfolio, thereby reducing investment risk.

Bookkeeping tasks, such as depositing dividend checks and keeping track of a large number of securities, are avoided.

You have access to a number of convenient services, such as an option to automatically reinvest dividends and capital gains and regular, automatic investment plans. These features are useful for individuals who can benefit from a systematic, forced savings plan (which includes almost everybody). Fund companies also often allow you to switch from one type of fund to another with a minimum of paperwork, although many funds now have restrictions on the number of trades you can make during a year.

Readily available current and past performance records are listed in newspapers, magazines, and other publications.

Mutual funds are able to reduce transaction costs because of the large volume they invest.

Your funds are managed by a professional who can monitor them continually.

The main drawback of the funds is that, like the securities they invest in, their value will fluctuate with changing market conditions. Another problem is the increasingly confusing array of fee structures for mutual funds. These include no-loads, which carry no sales commission and are sold directly to the public; load funds, which carry a commission of up to 8.5 percent to invest; and low-load funds, which have a lower commission of 1% to 2%. Some newer funds have contingent deferred sales charges, which are deducted from your account if you redeem your shares within a specified time after buying them. You should ask about a fund's fees before investing. A final drawback of mutual funds is your inability to control the realization of taxable capital gains.

Mutual funds are playing an increasingly important role in individual and institutional investment management, and as mutual funds begin to demonstrate consistency of performance, more investors will see the benefit of this investment method. To capture investment dollars, mutual funds will offer even more attractive and convenient features, as well as a broader range of funds, particularly in the arena of international and global stock or fixed-income funds. The continued proliferation of mutual funds will make fund selection that much more difficult, but a more sophisticated investing public will opt for those funds with superior long-term track records.

MUTUAL FUND SELECTION STRATEGIES

There are literally thousands of mutual funds from which to choose. Once you have invested, however, funds offer the advantage of requiring little further attention. But choosing the right fund to meet your unique needs is crucial. This section will help you make wise fund investment decisions.

Always Keep Your Investment Objectives in Mind

Funds vary significantly in their investment objectives; the best fund to provide income to help with daily living expenses will almost certainly not be the best fund to help save for your children's college tuitions. Certain funds are designed specifically to provide substantial income, while others sacrifice income for capital gains. Funds whose objective aim is growth of capital and future income may be most suitable unless you need present income. If your main wish is to minimize income taxation, you might opt to choose a fund that holds tax-free municipal bonds or one which holds mostly low-yielding growth stocks.

Besides picking specific funds to match specific investment needs, you should make sure that your overall portfolio—the total funds you have invested anywhere—is adequately diversified. Keep this in mind in all your investment decisions. If you know your retirement funds are extremely safe in government securities, for example, you may feel more confident about investing in riskier growth stocks with other funds.

Choose Long-Term High Performers

Unfortunately, there is no way to predict the future performance of any investment; however, there are a number of useful criteria you can use in selecting a fund. The best way to develop a portfolio that will be effective for an extended time is to buy funds that have a proven record of long-term success. People tend to rely too heavily on funds' recent performance. However, any given top performer over the last year may not prove so successful over a longer period of time. Sector funds, for example, whose assets are concentrated in just one industry, will often perform spectacularly in one year and then turn in an incredibly poor performance in the next. It's very hard to tell which funds will be the next quarter's high flyers, but if you're going to trust a fund with your money for any length of time, be sure to pick a fund that has performed well over 5 or 10 years. There will always be relatively new funds that will prove to be successful, but it's wise to restrict your investments to funds that have proven their value over time.

Performance, as an attribute of mutual funds, refers to the fund's total return. This figure is the sum of the increase or decrease of a fund's net asset value (NAV) per share during a given period and the total of dividend distributions per share and capital gains for the same period of time. Many business publications print a wide variety of mutual fund statistics, including the top performing funds in several periods of time. Your first step in selecting a fund should be to check these tables for funds that were among the top 25 performers in both the last 5-year and 10-year periods.

Evaluate Defensive Capabilities

Once you have selected several funds that pass the 5-year and 10-year performance hurdles, consider how well those same funds performed in a down year, a year in which the stock market as a whole declined. Down-year performance is a crucial indicator of the fund's ability to keep your portfolio from being hit too badly when prices are falling. For the same reason that you may wish to stay away from sector funds, which can perform wonderfully in the right circumstances but will probably be disastrous as a long-term investment, you should avoid funds that did not perform adequately in a bad year. In some ways this is the truest test of a fund's overall worth; only the finest fund managers will be able to weather foul investment climates as well as fair ones. The latest down year was 1981, but a fund that did not exist then may be evaluated for its performance in 1984, a year which was in large part flat or down. You may also want to check how the fund pulled through more sudden declines, like the October 1987 crash.

Check the Portfolio Manager's Record

Although a fund's investment policy may be determined by its board of directors, it is a fund's manager who performs the actual operation of the fund. Find out how long the portfolio manager of a fund has been managing it, and whether the present manager may take credit for the fund's past successes. If the manager is new to the fund, try to find out his or her history and how any funds managed by this person in the past have fared. A fund is not required to provide a portfolio manager's identity in its reports, so you may need to ask the fund for this information. A manager determines what sectors of the economy will be most heavily represented in the portfolio and, within these sectors, which companies will be included. You can examine a fund's list of investments, which is included in its annual reports, and check to see how well diversified they are. You should also look at how well the fund's holdings will react to shifts in inflation, interest rates, and other factors. A fund's holdings should not all be in sectors of the economy that rely on the same factors—favorable interest rates, for example.

Other Factors to Consider

Before investing in any fund, carefully read its prospectus, where you can learn the affiliations and aims of the fund's directors, the fund's investment policy, its possible risks, and its potential rewards. Other useful information that might be included in a prospectus (or in supplementary reports) are expense breakdowns, sales and redemptions of fund shares, the extent of portfolio turnover, and the management's view on current and future developments. When narrowing down your fund selection, it is especially important to compare loads (sales charges) and expense ratios. If two funds perform identically, always choose the one with lower expenses. You also may wish to consider a fund's asset size. Small funds may be small for a reason; they also tend to incur higher expenses and are often erratic in performance.

Funds that use leverage—investing with borrowed money—are inherently more volatile and risky, but may be an attractive feature for more aggressive investors. Redemption fees are another minor feature that may nonetheless be a problem if they are too high. Many funds charge a temporary redemption fee of 1 or 2 percent to discourage excessive trading, with the fee reduced or eliminated after a specified period of time. If the fee on a fund is especially high, or if it is permanent and more than minimal, an investor may want to avoid the fund. Finally, read the prospectus to make sure the fund doesn't engage in any activities that make you uncomfortable, such as writing naked options, selling short, or trading index futures.

ASSEMBLING AND EVALUATING A MUTUAL FUND PORTFOLIO

Mutual funds should be an essential investment tool for most investors. As discussed in the previous section, because there are thousands of funds currently available, choosing the right one can be a formidable task; and assembling a well-balanced portfolio of funds can prove to be an even greater challenge. This section will assist you in assembling and evaluating a mutual fund portfolio that will help you achieve financial peace-of-mind.

Assembling a Fund Portfolio

The task of assembling a portfolio of mutual funds may seem daunting at first, given the wide variety of funds that are available. But you will find that with a little effort, you can construct a very suitable group of funds that will help you achieve your financial objectives. Funds have a wide variety of investment objectives, such as maximum capital gains, growth and income, or income. Many investors are well served by investing a part of their money in several different fund categories. There are three levels of analysis that are necessary prior to actually selecting individual funds.

1. **Determine your investment objectives.** Before you can start to acquire appropriate investments, you need to clearly specify your investment objectives. How much risk can you afford to take? What major future financial hurdles, such as college education costs, will you need to overcome and when? What are your future income prospects? By realistically assessing your current situation and future needs, you can begin to identify what you want to accomplish with your investments. From there you can begin to identify the kinds of mutual funds that will help you meet your investment objectives.

2. **Determine an appropriate portfolio allocation.** The portfolio allocation process involves assigning appropriate percentages of your total investment portfolio (no matter how small or large it might be) to interest-earning investments and stock investments. Virtually everyone should have stock investments, and many experts suggest that stocks comprise 50 to 60 percent of a portfolio for younger people and 40 to 50 percent of a portfolio for people who are less than 10 years from retirement.

3. **Identify appropriate categories of mutual funds.** After you
   have decided on your portfolio allocation, the specific categories of investments within the stock portion and interest-
   earning portion must be determined. You need to consider
   several things, including your investment objectives, current financial status, the current investment climate, and
   your familiarity with the various fund categories. Table 5-1
   is an illustration of a typical mutual fund portfolio allocation, based upon a 50-50 split between stock funds and
   interest-earning funds.

Note that the stock fund portion of the portfolio includes speculative funds, but is heavily weighted in favor of more conservative funds. Also, international funds are included. Mutual
funds are an excellent way to participate in the attractive international stock markets. The interest-earning side of the portfolio is broadly diversified among a variety of interest-earning
investment categories. Mutual funds are an excellent way for
investors to assemble an appropriate portfolio with modest
resources.

Table 5–1. Average Mutual Fund Portfolio Allocation

Investment Category	Percentage of Total Portfolio
Stock funds:	
Maximum capital gain	10%
Growth and income	20
Index	10
International	10
Subtotal: Stock funds	50
Interest-earning funds:	
Corporate bond	10
Government bond	15
Municipal bond	15
Money market	10
Subtotal: Interest-earning funds	50
Total fund portfolio	100%

Evaluating a Fund Portfolio

Once you have put together a mutual fund portfolio, you will need to evaluate it periodically both from the standpoint of the allocation of the total portfolio and individual fund performance. With respect to the portfolio as a whole, you will need to determine how the total fund assets are allocated. Is the allocation in line with your parameters? If not, perhaps some reallocation is necessary. In other words, if stock prices have risen sharply, the proportion of stocks in relation to your total portfolio is probably higher than you had originally determined was appropriate. If so, you should sell some of your stock funds and buy additional interest-earning funds. Note that you would do the opposite if stock prices fell. As you may surmise, this disciplined approach to fund evaluation forces you to·sell stock funds when stock prices are high and buy stock funds when stock prices have dropped. This is exactly what most investors should be doing, but few have the discipline, and most do the opposite. How often should you reallocate? Certainly no more frequently than once per quarter and probably less frequently unless there has been a precipitous change in stock or bond prices.

Beyond having to sell certain funds as part of a portfolio reallocation, you also need to periodically make an objective evaluation of each fund in your portfolio. If you selected good funds in the first place, you are probably better off holding onto them even if they disappoint you for a few months or quarters. But if a fund that you own consistently turns in results that are below the average for its fund category, you should consider replacing it with a better performing fund. This shouldn't happen too often, however. Most importantly, don't fret over short-term fluctuations in either market conditions or in performance of funds in your investment "stable."

STANDARD MUTUAL FUND INVESTMENT CATEGORIES

Many investors tend to concentrate their mutual funds in one or very few fund categories. Yet there are many types of mutual funds that are currently available that can help most investors achieve a well-diversified, well-balanced portfolio. Brief descriptions of each of the many categories of mutual funds follow and are organized into four sections: stock funds, bond funds, money market funds, and specialized funds.

Stock Funds

Maximum capital gains funds (also called **aggressive growth funds**) attempt to achieve very high returns by investing in more speculative stocks, maximizing capital gains income at the expense of income from dividends. For these funds, the potential for rapid growth is the primary criterion for investment. In addition, techniques such as leveraged buying, option writing, and short-term trading further increase possible yields. Of course, the potential for greater rewards means that these funds are quite risky; they tend to do very well in bull markets and very poorly in bear markets. **Small company growth funds** (also called **emerging growth funds**) are a type of maximum capital gains funds specializing in stocks of promising small companies.

Long-term growth funds seek capital gains from companies that have realized steady growth in earnings. These companies aim to grow at a steady rate; they generally do not employ speculative investing techniques, and are more stable, less volatile, and more consistent than maximum capital gains funds. Growth funds aim to achieve a rate of growth that beats inflation without taking the risks necessary to achieve occasional spectacular success.

Growth and income funds seek a balanced stock portfolio that will achieve capital appreciation as well as current income from dividends. These funds are less risky than growth funds, because the dividend income may offset at least some of the periodic losses in stock prices. In times of high market volatility—either in an up or down direction—growth and income funds are slower to respond. **Income funds**, or **equity-income funds**, generally invest about half their portfolio in dividend-paying stocks and the rest in convertible securities and straight debt instruments. Income funds may have capital growth as a secondary objective.

International stock funds are a good investment because foreign stock markets have pretty consistently outperformed the U.S. stock market. Moreover, there are many excellent companies that trade only on foreign stock exchanges. Therefore, many investors turn to international investments, which also provide additional diversification to a portfolio. Because American investors will have difficulty finding adequate information on foreign companies, many of which are not governed by the kinds of regulatory bodies that protect American investments, an international fund is the best means for an investor to enter the international market. Some international funds invest only in one country or region. **Global stock funds**, however, differ in that they also invest in U.S. securities.

Bond Funds

For many years, especially during the period of high inflation in the 1970s, bond funds were poor investments; but if inflation stays low, they will continue to be outstanding investments as they have been in recent years. Except for funds that invest solely in government bonds, all bond funds have some degree of risk of default; however, the real risks of holding bonds or bond funds is that high inflation will outpace the returns and/or rising interest rates will reduce the principal value of the investment. You should also note that within each bond fund category, there are usually several funds that specialize in investments of either short-term duration, intermediate-term duration, or long-term duration.

Corporate bond funds seek a high level of income by buying bonds of corporations.

Government bond funds, backed by the full faith and credit of the U.S. government, offer total credit safety, although they do fluctuate with interest rates like all bonds and bond funds. One variety of government bond funds are those which invest a majority of their portfolio in mortgage-backed securities issued by the Government National Mortgage Association, called GNMA or Ginnie Mae funds. Holders of GNMA certificates receive both interest and partial return of principal. A GNMA fund also reinvests the capital distributions. Different kinds of GNMA funds, holding either premium or discount certificates, can vary in their total return according to the stability or volatility of interest rates.

Convertible bond funds. Convertible securities are bonds or preferred stock that can be exchanged for a fixed number of shares in the common stock of the underlying company. The conversion feature is intended to induce investors to accept a lower interest rate in the hopes that the accompanying stock will rise in value and bring up the convertible's value. When stocks rise, convertibles will rise as well—albeit at a slower rate—while when stocks fall, convertibles tend to fall less because of the benefit of their yield. Convertibles thus combine, in diluted form, features of both stocks and bonds.

International bond funds. These funds' returns depend in part on the relative strength of the American dollar. An international bond fund typically invests primarily in high-quality government or corporate bonds, and enters into currency hedges in countries whose currency is expected to appreciate against the dollar. These funds can provide a portfolio with an additional degree of diversification.

Municipal bond funds, introduced in 1976, provide investors with a means for tax-free income with liquidity, convenience, and professional management. Since municipal bond prices do not appear in the daily papers, and have other features making them inconvenient for the individual investor to manage, muni bond funds are a useful way for one to invest in municipal bonds but avoid these problems. Interest earned from bonds not issued in the investor's own state is fully taxable in his or her own state, so in order to produce maximum tax-free income, funds have been developed that hold bonds only from one state. A New York investor owning the New York muni fund will avoid state taxes and increase after-tax return. However, single-state funds generally have slightly lower yields than multistate municipal bond funds.

High-yield bond funds, also called **junk bond funds,** specialize in low-quality, high-yield bonds that may offer substantial profits, but which also carry higher risk. High-yield funds invest either in corporate bonds or municipal bonds. They can be very volatile, and investors in corporate high-yield bond funds in recent years have been surprised to find their principal eroding from time to time, sometimes significantly.

Money Market Funds

Money market funds, first created in 1972, have become the most widely held mutual fund category, holding a variety of short-term money market instruments. Their three main objectives are preservation of capital, liquidity, and as high income as can be achieved without sacrificing the first two. Money market funds offer excellent liquidity: An investor need only write a check to transfer money. These funds are commonly used as an account in which funds can be stored until new stock or bond investment opportunities arise. **U.S. government money market funds** and **tax-exempt money market funds** invest in short-term instruments of the U.S. government and states/municipalities, respectively. As with municipal bond funds, there are also some single-state tax-exempt money funds.

Specialized Funds

Balanced funds maintain a combination of common stocks, bonds, and perhaps preferred stocks. Balanced funds may have income, growth, or growth-income as an objective. They provide diversification between stocks and bonds in the same fund with a low minimum investment, and are thus a good investment for someone with a small amount to invest.

Specialized industry funds, also known as **sector funds**, invest only in the stocks of a single industry, such as bio-technology, waste management, or energy. Sector funds, unlike well-diversified funds, zero in on a particular area of the stock market that may or may not have attractive prospects. The lack of diversity across industries means that sector funds can rapidly switch from excellent to abysmal performance. Sector funds behave more like individual stocks than diversified funds, and their erratic behavior cannot be predicted by the same criteria (such as past track record and management skill) that usually guide purchase of funds.

Asset allocation funds are the opposite extreme, providing extremely broad diversification. They generally invest in up to five or six different markets, so that any one market's losses may be offset by another's gain. Variable funds, commonly referred to as **market timing funds**, may shift allocation according to large economic trends, and are thus more flexible.

Precious metals funds, often called **gold funds**, usually invest in stocks of gold-mining firms and other companies engaged in the business of precious metals. Some funds may actually purchase and store the metal itself. These funds tend to move in synchronization with precious metal prices. Historically, precious metals funds have been considered an inflation hedge, but lackluster performance in recent years has brought this into question.

Option funds. Stock options are so complex an investment that a well-managed fund is a very effective way of entering the market. Most option funds are conservative and income oriented. In a long-term bull market, option funds tend to perform poorly; they achieve their best payoff in a flat market.

Index funds own all the stocks in an index, the Standard & Poor's 500, for example. These "unmanaged" funds have attracted the attention of institutional investors who have had a very difficult time beating the market. By simply duplicating a broad section of the market, an institution can save substantial amounts on management and research and trading fees. Individual investors can do the same through an index fund.

MAJOR NO-LOAD MUTUAL FUND COMPANIES

This list can be used as a reference for information on investment companies offering no-load mutual funds. Some of the companies listed also offer load funds. The no-load funds do not charge sales commissions and can be purchased directly through the offering company without going through a broker. Call or write the specific company for information on their funds. Products and services vary from company to company.

Benham Management Corp.
755 Page Mill Road
Palo Alto, CA 94393
800-321-8321

Columbia Funds Management Co.
1301 SW Fifth
P.O. Box 1350
Portland, OR 97297
800-547-1037

Delaware Management Co.
Ten Penn Center Plaza
Philadelphia, PA 19103
215-988-1200

Dimensional Fund Advisors, Inc.
1299 Ocean Avenue, Suite 650
Santa Monica, CA 90401
213-395-8005

Dreyfus Corporation
666 Old Country Road
Garden City, NY 11530
800-645-6561

Federated Research Corp.
Federated Investors Tower
Pittsburgh, PA 15222-3779
800-245-0242

Fidelity Management & Research Corp.
82 Devonshire Street
Boston, MA 02109
800-544-6666

Financial Programs, Inc.
P.O. Box 2040
Denver, CO 80201
800-525-8085

Freedom Capital Management Corp.
One Beacon Street
Boston, MA 02108
800-225-6258

Heine Securities Corp.
(The Mutual Series Funds)

Heine Securities Corp.
(The Mutual Series Funds)
51 John F. Kennedy Parkway
Short Hills, NJ 07078
800-448-3863

Investors Research Corp.
(Twentieth Century Funds)
P.O. Box 200
Kansas City, MO 41920
800-345-2021

Keystone Custodian Funds, Inc.
99 High Street
Boston, MA 02104
800-343-2898

Loomis-Sayles & Co., Inc.
P.O. Box 449, Back Bay Annex
Boston, MA 02117
800-345-4048

Mutual Management Corp.
1235 Avenue of the Americas
22nd floor
New York, NY 10105
212-698-5349

Neuberger & Berman Management
342 Madison Avenue, Suite 1620
New York, NY 10173
800-877-9700

Nicholas Co., Inc.
700 Water Street, #1010
Milwaukee, WI 53202
414-272-6133

Price (T. Rowe) Associates
100 East Pratt Street
Baltimore, MD 21202
800-638-5660

Provident Institutional Management Corp.
Webster Bldg., Suite 204
3411 Silverside Road
Wilmington, DE 19810
800-221-8120

Reich & Tang LP
100 Park Avenue
New York, NY 10017
212-370-1110

Reserve Management Company
810 Seventh Avenue
New York, NY 10019
800-223-2213

Rodney Square Management Corp.
Rodney Square North
Wilmington, DE 19890
800-225-5084

Evergreen Asset Management Corp.
2500 Westchester Avenue
Purchase, New York 10577
800-235-0064

Scudder Stevens & Clark
160 Federal Street
Boston, MA 02110
800-225-2470

SEI Financial Management Corp.
53 State Street
Boston, MA 02109
800-345-1151

SteinRoe & Farham Inc.
P.O. Box 1143
Chicago, IL 60690
800-338-2550

Strong/Corneliuson Capital Management
100 Heritage Reserve
Menomonee Falls, WI 53051
800-368-3863

United States Trust Co. of NY
One Boston Place
Boston, MA 02108
800-233-1136

USAA Investment Management Co.
USAA Building
San Antonio, TX 78288
800-531-8000

Value Line Inc.
711 Third Avenue
New York, NY 10017
800-223-0818

Vanguard Group, Inc.
Vanguard Financial Center
Valley Forge, PA 19482
800-662-7447

Webster Management Co.
20 Exchange Place
New York, NY 10005
212-510-5041

TOP-PERFORMING MUTUAL FUNDS

Long-term performance is perhaps the most important criterion for selecting a mutual fund. On the other hand, short-term performance— that is 1 quarter or 1 year— is a very poor predictor of future performance. Table 5-2 is a list of top-performing mutual funds, by category, over the 5½- and 10½-year periods ending June 1990. The amounts represent the aggregate total return (interest and dividend income plus capital gains) over the periods indicated.

Table 5–2. Top-Performing Mutual Funds:
5½- and 10½-Year Periods Ending June 1990

	Total Return
Maximum Capital Gains Funds	5½ Years to 6/29/90
AIM Equity-Weingarten	221%
AIM Equity-Constellation	214
Fidelity Magellan Fund	209
Hartwell Emerging Growth Fund	201
Twentieth Century Growth	194
Pacific Horizon Aggr. Growth	192
SLH Aggressive Growth	189
Putnam Voyager Fund	183
New York Venture Fund	179
IDS Strategy-Aggressive	177
	10½ Years to 6/29/90
AIM Equity-Weingarten	633%
New York Venture Fund	557
WPG Tudor Fund	535
Sequoia Fund	532
American Cap Pace Fund	515
Alliance Quasar Fund	484
Twentieth Century Growth	481
Putnam Voyager Fund	448
Delaware GRP Trend Fund	448
Aim Equity-Constellation	447
Long-Term Growth Funds	5½ Years
Twentieth Century Giftrust	299%
Fidelity O-T-C Portfolio	214
IAI Regional Fund, Inc.	207
Hancock (John) Growth Trust	207
IDS New Dimensions Fund	195
Federated Growth Trust	191
New Perspective Fund	187
Fidelity Growth Company	186
Twentieth Century Vista Fund	183
Thomson McKinna Growth Fund	183

Table 5–2. (Cont.)

	Total Return
	10½ Years
CGM Capital Development	747%
New England Growth Fund	650
Janus Fund	612
IDS New Dimensions Fund	605
Lindner Fund	600
Twentieth Century Select Inv.	588
Steinroe Special Fund	576
Amev Growth Fund	569
United Vanguard Fund	560
Fidelity Destiny Port—Destiny I	553
Growth and Income Funds	**5½ Years**
Dodge & Cox Stock Fund	171%
Elfun Trusts	171
Nationwide Fund	162
Investment Co. of America	160
Fundamental Investors	156
Vanguard Index Trust-500	155
Oppenheimer Total Return	153
Amev Capital Fund	150
Founders Blue Chip Fund	150
Mass Investors Trust	149
	10½ Years
Amev Capital Fund	553%
Vanguard Index Trust-500	504
Dodge & Cox Stock Fund	471
Elfun Trusts	462
FPA Paramount Fund	449
Fundamental Investors	448
Investment Co. of America	445
Sentinel Common Stock Fund	435
American Mutual Fund	434
Merrill Lynch Capital Fund-A	431
Corporate Bond, Preferred Stock, and Convertible Funds	**5½ Years**
Dreyfus Convertible Securities	125%
Phoenix Convertible Fund	106
American Cap Harbor	97
Vanguard Preferred Stock Fund	95
Merrill Lynch Equi Bond Fund	93
JP Income Fund	86
Bond Fund of America	86

Table 5–2. (Cont.)

	Total Return
Corporate Bond, Preferred Stock, and Convertible Funds	5½ Years
IDS Selective Fund	84
Kemper High Yield Fund	83
United Bond Fund	83
	10½ Years
Phoenix Convertible Fund	416%
American Cap Harbor	334
Putnam Convertible Inc-Gro	328
GE S&S Long Term	271
Kemper High Yield Fund	258
Fidelity Intermediate Bond	248
Bond Fund of America	235
Vanguard Preferred Stock Fund	233
IDS Selective Fund	229
Fidelity High Income	226
Municipal Bond Funds	5½ Years
United Muni. Bond Fund	92%
Financial T/F Income Shares	90
Steinroe Managed Municipals	89
Putnam Tax Exempt Income Fund	89
Elfun Tax-Exempt Income Fund	88
Steinroe High Yield Munis	87
Safeco Municipal Bond	87
Delaware GRP T/F Fund-USA	86
Kemper California Tax-Free	86
Mutual of Omaha Tax-Free Inc.	86
	10½ Years
Elfun Tax-Exempt Income Fund	291%
MFS MGD Municipal Bond	210
Putnam T/F Income-High Yield	207
Merrill Lynch Muni Bond-Hy-A	179
Steinroe Managed Municipals	171
IDS High Yield Tax-Exempt Fund	160
Kemper Municipal Bond Fund	157
Oppenheimer Tax-Free Bond Fund	156
Tax-Exempt Bond Fund of America	154
Fidelity High Yield Municipals	148
Government Securities Funds	5½ Years
Kemper U.S. Gov't. Sec. Fund	80
Van Kampen Merritt U.S. Gov't.	79
Lord Abbett U.S. Gov't. Sec. (1984)	78

Table 5–2. (*Cont.*)

Government Securities Funds	Total Return 5½ Years
Vanguard Fixed Inc—GNMA	78
Federated GNMA Trust	77
Amev U.S. Gov't Securities (1985)	76
Merrill Lynch Federal Sec	75
Value Line U.S. Gov't. Sec	74
Smith, Barney Funds—U.S. Gov't.	73
Colonial Gov't Sec Plus Trust	72

Insufficient government securities funds in existence for 10½ years.

MUTUAL FUND PERFORMANCE SUMMARY

Table 5-3 summarizes annual total return performance of mutual funds, by category, for the years 1982 through 1989 and for the 6 months ended June 1990. When evaluating the performance of a mutual fund that you own, you should compare its return against the average return for the fund's category.

WIESENBERGER MUTUAL FUND PORTFOLIOS INDEX

While it is necessary to periodically review the performance of each mutual fund that you own, it is also critical to review how your total investment portfolio (mutual funds and directly owned invest-ments) has performed. One convenient basis of comparison is the Wiesenberger Mutual Fund Portfolios Index which consists of four balanced portfolios: aggressive, moderate, conservative, and income-oriented. After summarizing the performance of your investments, you can compare that performance against the Wiesenberger Index which is based upon average mutual fund performance. Another use of the index is to compare relative returns of various balanced portfolios. As Table 5-4 shows, aggressive portfolios, in spite of their higher risk, provided superior returns over the 5-year period surveyed. The compo-sition of each of the four portfolios follows the index.

Table 5-3. Annual Total Return Performance of Mutual Funds, by Category: 1982–1989 and the 6 months ending June 1990

Fund Category	Percent Increase or Decrease on Total Return Basis								
	6/90*	1989	1988	1987	1986	1985	1984	1983	1982
Max Capital Gains	5.2	26.9	14.6	0.1	12.0	27.3	−9.0	22.1	26.7
Long-Term Growth	4.2	25.2	14.1	1.6	13.1	28.0	−3.0	20.8	25.6
Growth & Income	1.9	23.5	15.3	1.2	15.8	28.2	4.0	20.4	24.2
Balanced	1.3	18.6	11.8	2.5	17.9	29	8.3	17.0	27.7
Income-Com Stk	−.04	19.5	15.6	−1.3	11.6	21.5	7.6	20.7	18.9
Income-Flexible	1.0	13.9	11.1	0.8	13.9	22.3	9.1	14.7	29.0
Corp. Bond	1.2	6.5	9.0	1.2	13.1	21.3	10.2	12.2	31.4
International	1.5	23.3	17.6	9.6	40.8	41.2	−12.7	16.0	21.8
Gold & Prec. Metal	−16.5	28.5	−16.8	36.8	38.9	−9.5	—	—	—
Sector	0.9	30.6	13.8	−0.6	14.6	31.6	3.8	17.8	17.1
Gov't Sec.	2.4	12.6	6.9	1.4	11.8	17.5	12.6	7.5	27.8
Tax-Exempt	2.3	9.3	10.6	−0.5	16.9	18.5	8.6	10.0	36.6
Specizd-Technology	19.1	17.6	6.9	−3.3	8.4	17.1	—	—	—
Dow Jones Industrial Average	6.6	32.2	16.1	5.5	27.1	33.5	1.2	25.9	25.8
Standard & Poor's 500-Stock Index	3.0	31.6	16.5	5.2	18.6	31.6	6.2	22.5	20.4

*Total return for the six months ended June 1990.

Source: Wiesenberger Investment Companies Service, *Investment Companies 1990* (New York, 1990).

Table 5–4. Wiesenberger Mutual Fund Portfolios Index

Performance Summary

Portfolio	Total Return First 6 Months 1990	1989 Total Return	1989 Yield	3-Year Total Return $10,000 Invested in July 1987 Would be Worth	5-Year Tota Return $10,000 Invested i July 1985 Would be Worth
Aggressive	2.7%	20.27%	3.88%	$12,428	$17,234
Moderate	2.3	17.13	5.43	12,482	16,073
Conservative	2.1	14.24	6.68	12,436	15,218
Income-Oriented	1.8	12.65	8.08	12,261	14,508

Allocation of Portfolio Assets

Fund Category	% of Assets in Portfolio			
	Aggressive	Moderate	Conservative	Income Oriente
Maximum Capital Gains	20%	10%	5%	—
Long-Term Growth/ Income Secondary	20	10	5	—
Growth and Current Income	10	20	15	20
International	20	10	5	—
Subtotal: Equity-Oriented	70	50	30	20
U.S. Government	10	20	30	45
Senior Securities	10	15	20	35
Tax-Exempt	10	15	20	—
Subtotal: Fixed-Income Oriented	30	50	70	80
	100%	100%	100%	100%

Total return for each portfolio is based upon the average performance of mutual funds o the periods indicated. The composition of each portfolio is: Aggressive: 70% equity funds, 30% fix income funds; Moderate: 50% equity funds, 50% fixed-income funds; Conservative: 30% equ funds, 70% fixed-income funds; Income-Oriented: 20% equity funds, 80% fixed-income funds. T index can be used to compare the performance of a managed portfolio against a diversified portfc of average performing mutual funds. The Wiesenberger Mutual Fund Portfolios Index is a service the Wiesenberger Investment Companies Service.

HOW TO INTERPRET A WIESENBERGER MUTUAL FUND DESCRIPTION

Figure 5-1 illustrates a typical Wiesenberger Mutual Fund report and provides explanations of the information contained therein. Most libraries subscribe to the Wiesenberger Investment Companies Service, which includes an annual reference book that provides descriptions of individual mutual funds.

Figure 5-1. Wiesenberger Mutual Fund Report

TWENTIETH CENTURY SELECT INVESTORS

The first two paragraphs provide an overview of the fund and its investment objectives and policies.

The largest of the twelve classes of shares of Twentieth Century Investors, Inc.. Select Investors was one of the two original classes offered in October 1958. Management adopted its present investment approach in 1971.

The primary objective of Select Investors is to seek capital growth through investment in securities which the management considers to have better than average prospects for appreciation in value, and which also pay dividends or interest.

At the October 31, 1989 fiscal year-end, the fund was 98.5% invested in common stocks, of which a substantial portion was in five industries: communications (15.1% of net assets); food & beverage (9.5%); financial services (7.5%); pharmaceuticals (7.4%), and retail (5.6%). The largest individual holdings were Federal National Mortgage Association (7% of assets); Philip Morris (4.1%); Pepsico and United Telecommunications (each 3.6%), and Procter & Gamble (3.1%). The rate of portfolio turnover during the latest fiscal year amounted to 93% of average assets. Unrealized appreciation in the portfolio at the calendar year-end totaled 23% of net assets.

The fund's investment position as of the latest calendar year-end is given, along with the rate of portfolio turnover and unrealized portfolio appreciation.

Special shareholder services, including automatic investment and withdrawal plans, retirement accounts, and investment minimums are described.

Statistical History

An eleven year statistical history lets you track asset growth, number of shareholder accounts, price and dividends, portfolio allocation, fund expenses, and yearly highs and lows.

	AT YEAR-ENDS				% of Assets in			ANNUAL DATA				
Year	Total Net Assets ($)	Number of Share-holders	Net Asset Value Per Share ($)	Yield (%)	Cash & Gov't	Bonds & Pre-ferreds	Com-mon Stocks	Income Div-idends ($)	Capital Gains Distribu-tion ($)	Expense Ratio (%)	Offering Price ($) High	Low
1989	2,858,684,199	333,785	36.51	3.1	1	—	99	1.116	—	1.00	38.32	26.77
1988	2,263,611,758	351,134	26.98	2.6	—	—	100	0.707	—	1.00	28.69	25.06
1987	2,393,303,005	372,145	26.22	2.6	1	—	99	0.861	6.367	1.00	44.60	25.93
1986	2,048,912,708	270,000	31.61	1.5	—	—	100	0.515	33.462	1.01	38.16	28.13
1985	1,335,523,625	182,719	29.56		1	—	99	0.465	—	1.01	29.85	22.02
1984	833,273,171	156,041	22.53	0.6	1	—	99	0.138	0.687*	1.02	25.74	19.79
1983	743,424,074	102,691	25.27	0.5	1	—	99	0.135	—	1.01	27.10	18.91
1982	130,347,036	22,829	19.57	0.6	1	1	98	0.12	0.31	1.08	20.28	12.06
1981	37,765,795	10,046	14.19	0.7	1	—	99	0.10	1.50*	1.09	16.31	12.38
1980	18,368,664	3,000	15.63	0.2	1	1	99	0.04	0.54	1.24	16.51	14.54
1979	6,276,022	1,350	15.63	0.8	1	—	99	0.10	1.35	1.56	11.17	9.95

* Includes $0.67 short-term capital gains in 1981; $0.128 in 1984.

Figure 5–1. Average Mutual Fund Portfolio Allocation (*Cont.*)

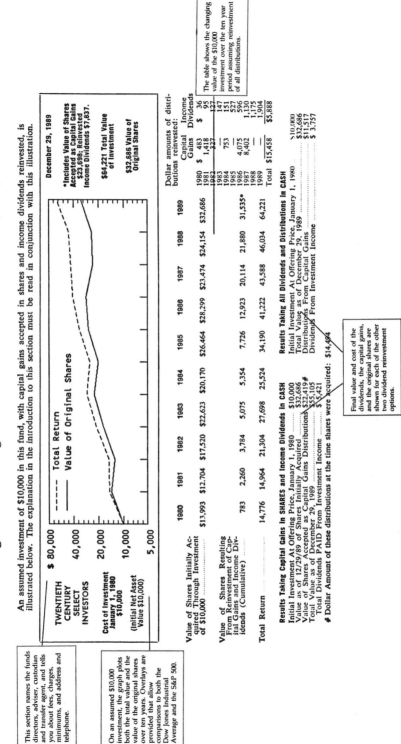

An assumed investment of $10,000 in this fund, with capital gains accepted in shares and income dividends reinvested, is illustrated below. The explanation in the introduction to this section must be read in conjunction with this illustration.

December 29, 1989

*Includes Value of Shares Accepted as Capital Gains $23,698; Reinvested Income Dividends $7,837.

$64,221 Total Value of Investment

$32,686 Value of Original Shares

$80,000
40,000
20,000
10,000
5,000

TWENTIETH CENTURY SELECT INVESTORS

Cost of Investment January 1, 1980 $10,000

(Initial Net Asset Value $10,000)

--- Total Return
— Value of Original Shares

Dollar amounts of distributions reinvested:

	Capital Gains	Income Dividends
1980	$ 483	$ 36
1981	1,418	95
1982	327	127
1983	—	147
1984	753	151
1985	—	527
1986	4,075	596
1987	8,402	1,130
1988	—	1,175
1989	—	1,904
Total	$15,458	$5,888

The table shows the changing value of the $10,000 investment over the ten year period assuming reinvestment of all distributions.

	1980	1981	1982	1983	1984	1985	1986	1987	1988	1989
Value of Shares Initially Acquired Through Investment of $10,000	$13,993	$12,704	$17,520	$22,623	$20,170	$26,464	$28,299	$23,474	$24,154	$32,686
Value of Shares Resulting From Reinvestment of Capital Gains and Income Dividends (Cumulative)	783	2,260	3,784	5,075	5,354	7,726	12,923	20,114	21,880	31,535*
Total Return	14,776	14,964	21,304	27,698	25,524	34,190	41,222	43,588	46,034	64,221

Results Taking Capital Gains in SHARES and Income Dividends in CASH

Initial Investment At Offering Price, January 1, 1980	$10,000
Value as of 12/29/89 of Shares Initially Acquired	$32,686
Value of Shares Accepted as Capital Gains Distributions	$22,419#
Total Value as of December 29, 1989	$55,105
Total Dividends PAID From Investment Income	$5,421

Dollar Amount of these distributions at the time shares were acquired: $14,494

Results Taking All Dividends and Distributions in CASH

Initial Investment At Offering Price, January 1, 1980	$10,000
Total Value as of December 29, 1989	$32,686
Distributions From Capital Gains	$11,517
Dividends From Investment Income	$ 3,757

Callout boxes:

This section names the funds directors, adviser, custodian and transfer agent, and tells you about fees, charges, minimums, and address and telephone.

On an assumed $10,000 investment, the graph plots both the total value and the value of the original shares over ten years. Overlays are provided that allow comparisons to both the Dow Jones Industrial Average and the S&P 500.

Final value and cost of the dividends, the capital gains, and the original shares are shown for each of the other two dividend reinvestment options.

NO-LOAD MUTUAL FUNDS WITH LOW MINIMUM
INITIAL PURCHASE REQUIREMENTS

Table 5-5 lists no-load mutual funds (excluding money market funds) that have minimum initial purchase requirements of $500 or less. New investors with limited resources will find this list quite useful. Mutual funds are particularly attractive to new investors in

Table 5–5. No-Load Mutual Funds with Minimum Initial Purchase
Requirements of $500 or Less

Name (Type of Fund)	Minimum Purchase Requireme
AARP Capital Growth Fund (CS)	$500
AARP General Bond Fund	500
AARP GNMA & U.S. Treasury Fund (GS)	500
AARP Growth & Income Fund (CS)	500
AARP Insured Tax-Free General Bond (Bond)	500
AARP Insured Tax-Free Short-Term (Bond)	500
Adtek Fund (CS)	250
Afuture Fund (CS)	500
Amana Mutual Fund Tr-Income (Flex)	100
American Capital Growth (CS)	25
American Pension Inv-Balanced (Bal)	100
American Pension Inv-Growth (Flex)	100
American Pension Inv-Income (Bond)	100
American Pension Inv-Precious Resources (Spec)	100
American Pension Inv-U.S. Gov't (GS)	100
Armstrong Associates (CS)	250
Babson Bond Fund-Portfolio L (Flex)	500
Babson Bond Fund-Portfolio S (Flex)	500
Babson Growth Fund (CS)	500
Caldwell Fund, Inc. (CS)	None
Century Shares Trust (Spec)	500
CGM Capital Development (CS)	250
CGM Mutual Fund (Bal)	250
Colonial VIP-Aggressive Growth (CS)	500
Colonial VIP-Diversified Return (Flex)	500
Colonial VIP-Federal Securities Fund (GS)	500
Colonial VIP-High Income (Bond)	500
Colonial VIP-High Yield Muni (Bond)	500
Colonial VIP-Inflation Hedge (CS)	500

Table 5–5. (Cont.)

Name (Type of Fund)	Minimum Purchase Requirement
Dividend Growth-Dividend Series (Flex)	300
Elfun Diversified Fund (Flex)	500
Elfun Global Fund (C&I)	500
Enterprise Group-Aggressive Growth (CS)	500
Enterprise Group-Gov't Secs (GS)	500
Enterprise Group-Growth Port (CS)	500
Enterprise Group-Growth & Income (CS)	500
Enterprise Group-High Yield Bond (Bond)	500
Enterprise Group-Int'l Growth (C&I)	500
Enterprise Group-Precious Metals (Spec)	500
Enterprise Group-T/E Income (Bond)	500
Fidelity Freedom Fund (CS)	500
Financial Bond-High Yield (Bond)	250
Financial Bond-Select Income (Bond)	250
Financial Bond-U.S. Gov't (Bond)	250
Financial Dynamics Fund (CS)	250
Financial Industrial Fund (CS)	250
Financial Industrial Income (Flex)	250
Financial Strategic-European (C&I)	250
Financial Strategic-Financial Services (Spec)	250
Financial Strategic-Gold (Spec)	250
Financial Strategic-Health (Spec)	250
Financial Strategic-Leisure (Spec)	250
Financial Strategic-Pacific (C&I)	250
Financial Strategic-Technology (Spec)	250
Financial Strategic-Utilities (Spec)	250
Financial T/F Income Shares (Bond)	250
Gateway Government Bond Fund (GS)	500
Gateway Growth Plus (CS)	500
Gateway Option Index Fund (CS)	500
General Securities (CS)	100
Home Investors Gov't Guar Inc (GS)	500
Insider Reports Fund (CS)	300
Investment Port-Diversified Income (CS)	250
Investment Port-Equity (CS)	250
Investment Port-Gov't Plus (GS)	250
Investment Port-High Yield (B&P)	250
Investment Port-Total Return (Flex)	250
Investment Series Tr-High Income (Bond)	500
Investment Series Tr-High Quality Stock (CS)	500
Investment Series Tr-Muni Secs Income (Bond)	500

Table 5–5. (*Cont.*)

Name (Type of Fund)	Minimum Purchase Requirement
Investment Series Tr-U.S. Gov't Bond (Bond)	500
Janus Flexible Income Fund (Flex)	None
Janus Fund (CS)	None
Janus Twenty Fund (CS)	None
Janus Venture Fund (CS)	None
Keystone B-1 (Inv. Bond) (Bond)	250
Keystone B-2 (Med. Grade Bd.) (Bond)	250
Keystone B-4 (Discount Bd.) (Bond)	250
Keystone International Fund (C&I)	250
Keystone K-1 (Income Fund) (Flex)	250
Keystone K-2 (Growth Fund) (CS)	250
Keystone S-1 (High Grade) (CS)	250
Keystone S-3 (Growth) (CS)	250
Keystone S-4 (Aggressive Gro.) (CS)	250
Lapercq-Istel Fund (CS)	500
MacKay-Shields Capital Appreciation (CS)	500
MacKay-Shields Convertible Fund (Bond)	500
MacKay-Shields Global Fund (Spec)	500
MacKay-Shields Gold & Precious Metals (Spec)	500
MacKay-Shileds Government Plus (GS)	500
MacKay-Shields High Yield Corp. Bond (Bond)	500
MacKay-Shields Total Return (CS)	500
MacKay-Shields T/F Bond Fund (Bond)	500
MacKay-Shileds Value Fund (CS)	500
Meeschaert Cap Accumulation (CS)	500
Meeschaert Int'l Bond Tr (C&I)	500
Merrill Lynch Euro Fund (B) (C&I)	500
Merrill Lynch Special Value (B) (CS)	250
Mutual of Omaha America Fund (GS)	250
One Hundred and One Fund (Flex)	250
One Hundred Fund (Flex)	250
Pax World Fund (Bal)	250
Prospector Fund (C&I)	100
Putnam Massachusetts T/E Income (Bond)	500
Putnam Michigan T/E Income (Bond)	500
Putnam Minnesota T/E Income (Bond)	500
Putnam Ohio T/E Income (Bond)	500
Putnam T/F Income-High Yield (Bond)	500
Putnam T/F Income-Insured (Bond)	500
Rainbow Fund (CS)	300
SEI Cash + Plus Tr-GNMA (GS)	None

Table 5–5. (*Cont.*)

Name (Type of Fund)	Minimum Purchase Requirement
SEI Cash + Plus Tr-Intermed Gov't (GS)	None
SEI Cash + Plus Tr-S/T Gov't (GS)	None
SEI Index Funds-Bond Index Port. (Bond)	None
SEI Index Funds-S&P 500 Index (CS)	None
SEI Inst'l Managed Tr-Bond Port (Bond)	None
SEI Inst'l Managed Tr-Cap Appr. (CS)	None
SEI Inst'l Managed Tr-Equity Inc. (CS)	None
SEI Inst'l Managed Tr-Ltd Volatility (Bond)	None
SEI Inst'l Managed Tr-Value Port (CS)	None
SFT Odd Lot Fund (CS)	500
SLH Basic Value Port (CS)	500
SLH European Portfolio (C&I)	500
SLH Global Bond Port (C&I)	500
SLH Global Equity Portfolio (C&I)	500
SLH Government Securities Port (GS)	500
SLH Growth Port (CS)	500
SLH Growth & Opportunity Port (CS)	500
SLH High Income Port (Bond)	500
SLH Intermediate Term Gov't (GS)	500
SLH International Port (C&I)	500
SLH Investment Grade (Bond)	500
SLH Mortgage Port (GS)	500
SLH Option Income Port (CS)	500
SLH Pacific Portfolio (C&I)	500
SLH Precious Metals Port (Spec)	500
SLH Sector Analysis Port (Spec)	500
SLH Special Equities Port (CS)	500
SLH Strategic Investors Port (B&P)	500
SLH Tax-Exempt Income (Bond)	500
SLH Utility Securities Port (Spec)	500
Special Portfolio, Inc-Cash (Bond)	500
Special Portfolio, Inc-Stock (CS)	500
State Farm Balanced Fund (Bal)	50
State Farm Growth Fund (CS)	50
State Farm Interim Fund (Flex)	50
Stralem Fund (CS)	100
Twentieth Century Balanced (Bal)	None
Twentieth Century Giftrust (CS)	100
Twentieth Century Growth (CS)	None
Twentieth Century Heritage (CS)	None
Twentieth Century Long-Term Bond (Bond)	None

Table 5–5. (*Cont.*)

Name (Type of Fund)	Minimum Purchase Requirement
Twentieth Century Select (CS)	None
Twentieth Century T/E-Intermediate (Bond)	None
Twentieth Century T/E-Long Term (Bond)	None
Twentieth Century Ultra (CS)	None
Twentieth Century U.S. Gov't (GS)	None
Twentieth Century Vista Fund (CS)	None
Unified Growth Fund (CS)	200
Unified Income Fund (Flex)	500
Unified Mutual Shares (Flex)	200
U.S. GNMA (GS)	100
U.S. Gold Shares (Spec)	100
U.S. Good & Bad Times (CS)	100
U.S. Growth Fund (CS)	100
U.S. Income Fund (CS)	100
U.S. LoCap (CS)	100
U.S. New Prospector (C&I)	100
U.S. Real Estate Fund (Spec)	100
U.S. Tax-Free Fund (Bond)	100
Vanguard Star Fund (Spec)	500
Variable Stock Fund (CS)	50
Volumetric Fund (CS)	500
Wade Fund (CS)	500

Type of Fund:

CS—Holdings are predominantly common stocks

Bal—Balanced; both bonds and common stocks are held at all times

B&P—Holdings are limited to bonds and preferred stocks

Bond—Investments concentrated in bonds

C&I—Holdings are predominantly in Canadian and/or international issues

Flex—Flexibly diversified; usually, but not necessarily, balanced

GS—Holdings in U.S. government securities

Spec—Specialized; holdings are concentrated in one or more specified industry group types of securities

that they can provide diversification and professional management at low cost with a small investment. Moreover, mutual funds can make a wonderful gift to children or grandchildren, at relatively low cost. Note, however, that many of these no-initial-load mutual funds do levy annual fees to compensate the selling broker and/or firm. Some also may impose substantial charges when the fund is sold.

6

Real Estate Investments

During much of the 1980s, real estate was widely considered a "can't lose" investment. Today, cooling markets in many areas of the country, combined with less attractive tax incentives, have made real estate investments somewhat less alluring, at least in the short term. Yet, real estate remains a worthwhile component in a well-balanced investment portfolio and, if chosen properly, can create opportunities for building up your investments, and, to a more limited extent, reducing income taxes.

The tax reform of the 1980s had a dramatic impact on the entire arena of real estate investment. Less generous depreciation schedules, as well as the inability to use real estate tax losses to offset other income, have severely curtailed investment in tax-loss-generating properties. Now, investors must look for real estate investments that can stand on economic merit alone—in other words, properties that generate a positive or close to positive cash flow. While weak real estate markets in many areas of the country may be viewed as an opportunity to make real estate investments, caution is advised in view of the possibility that the recession may further weaken these prices.

For those who have the resources and the inclination to purchase real estate on their own, two categories of investment are available: income-producing real estate and undeveloped land. Income-producing real estate can range from small apartment buildings to commercial and industrial properties. Undeveloped land is a more expensive way to invest in real estate because land with strong appreciation potential is very costly and difficult to finance. Direct ownership is the most desirable way to own real estate, although maintaining and managing a property can often require a more substantial time commitment than many people may be willing to make.

Other forms of real estate investment are available for investors who want to participate in the real estate market but who have neither the time nor the capital required for direct ownership. In real estate limited partnerships, many investors pool their money and invest in larger income producing properties including apartments, office buildings, and shopping centers. The liability for losses of the limited partners is usually limited to the amount of their investment. The general partner, who usually organizes the partnership, receives a share of the profits, plus fees and commissions. Usually, the partnership disbands after a period of time, ranging from a few years to over 10 years, and the partnership proceeds are distributed to the investors. Most of the limited partnerships on the market today stress income and capital gains because of decreased tax incentives. Investors should be very wary of limited partnerships in the current environment in which investors in older partnerships have suffered billions of dollars of losses. Some more recent deals have been attractive, but they are a distinct minority of what is being offered. Limited partnerships are generally not advisable for investors who may need access to their money in the near future, since selling the shares on the secondary market before the partnership is liquidated will usually result in substantial losses.

Real estate investment trusts, the second alternative to direct ownership of real estate, are the least expensive and most liquid way to invest in real estate. REITs are publicly traded stocks that invest in real estate projects and/or mortgages. Since they generally trade on the major stock exchanges, they are as easy to sell as any widely held stock.

Whatever form a real estate investment takes, its return will depend, to a large extent, on the overall health of the real estate market. Many regions of the country will continue to suffer from a severe downturn in this market; and while opportunities for direct investment in depressed real estate will present themselves, only investors with considerable resources and staying power should consider them. On a more positive note, because of lower prices, housing will finally become more affordable in many areas of the country, particularly for first-time homebuyers. And, offerings by real estate limited partnerships could eventually become more attractive as the industry begins to emerge from the ashes to attract justifiably wary investors. In short, real estate in the 1990s should become a more sensible, less frenzied area of investment than it was during the 1980s.

REAL ESTATE INVESTMENT ALTERNATIVES

This section describes of the characteristics of various real estate investment alternatives. Important characteristics of each category of real estate investment are highlighted to assist you either in evaluating a specific investment or in considering real estate investing in general. Investors generally have three different ways to invest in real estate: directly, indirectly via limited partnerships, and indirectly via shares of real estate investment trusts. Within each of those categories, of course, there are a range of alternative types of real estate that can be acquired.

Many investors overlook real estate as an investment candidate, yet real estate has proven to be an attractive wealth-creating component of many investment portfolios. On the other hand, real estate investments are difficult to evaluate and can prove to be financially penalizing. Moreover, direct investment in real estate, particularly income-producing real estate, can be very time-consuming. Yet the advantages of investing in real estate, either directly or indirectly, merits your attention.

Direct Real Estate Investment

Undeveloped Land.   Undeveloped land is the most speculative real estate investment. It has both the greatest potential for development and appreciation, and the greatest risk. An investor should try to purchase land that is currently of low value but that seems likely to increase in value. The four most important factors determining raw land value are: physical conditions, and governmental, economic, and sociological factors. A piece of land with poor drainage or water supply might be a problem, as could be undesirable subsoil foundations. A piece of land that is too small or irregularly shaped could also discourage development. Just as basic to the possibility of development as physical conditions are government rules and regulations; restrictive building codes and zoning could prohibit development and limit profit. Local tax laws and environmental regulations may also have significant implications for development.

Economic factors such as local employment rates, interest rates, and inflation are all important to consider. The more employment growth and diversification evident in a community, the more promising an adjacent raw land purchase might be. Growing populations with shrinking household sizes are favorable demographic trends, indicating a need for more residential housing. In order to understand the effect of all these various forces on a potential raw land purchase, an investor should consult a local broker, attorney, and perhaps an engineer or land surveyor.

The chief advantage of undeveloped land purchase is the potential for sizable appreciation. Disadvantages include a lack of any current income, and an accompanying reluctance on the part of bank lenders to finance raw land investment (because of the lack of income). Also, since few comparative appraisals are available for raw land, and industry standards are not well established, some land may be overpriced. Often, land with the lowest price is located in areas where values are unlikely to increase substantially or at all in the near future.

Residential Rental Property. Residential property's greatest benefit as an investment is that it produces income, which lessens out-of-pocket costs while the property increases in value. Location, structure type, and available utilities all may affect the property's value, as can local population movement and zoning changes. The primary categories of residential property are single-family homes, condominiums, multifamily houses, and apartment buildings.

Single-family Units. These investments may offer an advantage for a smaller investor in that they are affordable and provide rental income. A single-family unit does require active management, however. The most important factor in determining value is the property's neighborhood—availability of recreational facilities, transportation, and shopping are all important. One approach that has the potential to be very profitable is to purchase at low cost in an undesirable neighborhood that seems ready to improve. This technique is, of course, very speculative, and is not advisable for an unexperienced investor.

The potential for capital appreciation with single-family units is great. Such residences have been good insulators against inflation. In addition, small investments in cosmetic improvements can substantially improve the residence's selling price. On the other hand, single-family residences provide relatively low cash flow, and they tend not to be self-supporting; most predicted return will be realized through value appreciation. Probably the most important factor in single-family residential investment is location, as an area without rising property values will cause total stagnation. Also, prospective tenants must be carefully screened for their ability to pay rent reliably.

Condominiums and Cooperatives. Condominiums usually command lower prices than single-family homes, and often have collectively owned amenities, such as a swimming pool and parking facilities, that would otherwise be unavailable to a tenant. Cooperatives differ from condominiums primarily in the effects of an owner's default. Since a condominium's apartment units are individually financed, remaining tenants only need assume a defaulting owner's share of operating expenses. A cooperative, however, usually takes out a blanket mortgage on an entire building, so that if an owner defaults, remaining tenants must assume the extra share of carrying costs.

Condominiums and cooperatives are a viable investment in areas where rents can be significantly increased over time. In recent years, however, many areas of the country have been overbuilt with condos and co-ops, which subsequently caused declines in values.

Vacation Homes. A second home offers some of the tax benefits of a primary residence (although the IRS has restricted the tax shelter benefits of vacation homes used for rental purposes), as well as offering economic advantages through rental income. However, in most areas of the country prime rental season is limited to a few months of the year.

Time-sharing. Time-sharing, or interval ownership, is particularly suited to resort areas because owners can pay a smaller price for a piece of a more expensive property. Simple-fee ownership, in which an owner purchases a piece of the property and owns total rights to it, offers many of the same advantages as regular home equity. Right-to-use ownership grants a right to use a property for a specified period of time, after which point the possession of a property reverts to the "real" owner. Right-to-use owners are usually prohibited from transactions that simple-fee ownership allows.

Time-sharing property needs to be marketed very heavily, since developers need to find many owners for each unit. While many owners have been pleased with their investment, most of these projects are of dubious quality. The time-share resale market is almost nonexistent, and therefore, the vast majority of these projects should not be considered investment quality. However, as larger, well-established companies begin to enter this business, time-sharing may become a more viable investment.

Multifamily Units and Apartments. Multifamily units offer an investor greater opportunities for tax shelter and positive cash flow than single-family structures. Although large units require a greater initial investment, the cost per dwelling unit is lower. Multifamily units are relatively easy to finance for investors with sufficient resources, as lenders see the potential rental income as protection on their loans. A major problem with large apartment units is the presence of rent control restrictions (either present or potential). Other drawbacks include the possibility of overbuilding in a community and the illiquidity of the investment. As with any other real estate, the property's location can make or break the investment; a prospective buyer should avoid areas of depreciating property values. Proximity to main avenues of transportation, as well as to shopping, recreation, schools, and work, is particularly important to the apartment house dweller. If the physical condition of the property has been neglected, the costs of repair could erode profits. Unexpected expenses such as reroofing or replacing the electrical or heating systems may arise, so an investor who assumes an apartment building must have adequate reserves.

Commercial Property. Office buildings, shopping centers, other retail property, and industrial real estate all offer an investor with substantial resources an opportunity for significant appreciation. However, as potential rewards increase, buying and managing become more complicated, so the investor should be especially well-informed about the specifics of the purchase. With the exception of very small, well located, and fully occupied properties, commercial real estate is best left to the experts. If you want to participate, consider real estate limited partnerships or real estate investment trusts that invest in commercial properties.

Indirect Real Estate Investment

Limited Partnerships. In a real estate limited partnership, a group of individual investors pool their money to invest in either new construction or existing commercial or residential property. Shares in this partnership are offered to potential limited partners by a general partner in order to attract additional capital. Limited partners are generally liable only to the extent of the amount they invest. The general partner arranges the deal and is usually involved in the day-to-day management of the investment.

The various types of programs available allow an individual investor to shop for a real estate partnership that best suits his or her financial situation. A potential investor should carefully examine the offering memorandum or prospectus for information about risks and returns of the investment and about

the general partner's background and experience; the investor
should also look for independent sources of information about
similar limited partnerships.

Advantages to investment in real estate limited partnerships include:

Ease of buying in. While direct ownership requires a complex system of transfer, an investor in a limited partnership
needs only to complete some documentation and send a
check to the general partner. The partnership's prospectus
gives an investor access to information necessary to make a
reasonably quick decision.

Fixed cash requirements. After an investor makes the initial
payment, he or she will usually not be responsible for financing any further cost overruns.

No management responsibility. The general partner is responsible for construction, maintenance, bookkeeping, and
all other management duties.

Limited legal liability. An investor's other assets are not at
risk.

Smaller initial investment. A partner may need to invest as
little as $5000 to receive the benefits of a large real estate
project.

Lower overall risk. Diversification and professional management can make limited partnership investments less risky
than direct ownership.

Naturally, there are disadvantages which include:

No acquaintance with manager, and restricted knowledge of
the deal. You usually must base your knowledge of the
general partner on secondary sources; and an investor
might, despite the information available in the prospectus,
fail to identify hidden risks associated with the deal. The
limited partner's best interests will not always be served by
those of the general partner.

Less control. A limited partner has no say in the investment
policy.

Lower overall return. This is due to fees for participating in partnership.

Tax risks. Under the 1986 Tax Reform Act, tax shelter opportunities are either severely restricted or eliminated with limited partnerships.

Illiquidity. Because there is not a well-organized market for limited partnership investment units, they often are not able to be sold for a good price when desired.

The risk connected with real estate limited partnership deals is affected by three different factors: the amount of leverage used, the percentage specified, and the type of property and investment.

Leverage. Highly leveraged investments—those financed with a large amount of borrowed cash—require larger cash flows to make payments on the debt, and are thus riskier.

Percentage specified. A general partner may offer limited partners shares before selecting or specifying all specific properties. A deal with 0 percent specified—a "blind pool"—is the riskiest kind, since the investor cannot examine and evaluate the investment beforehand (although a general partner with a strong track record might not present too high a risk even with a blind pool). A further risk connected with blind pools is the possibility that, in a robust real estate market, the sponsor might be forced to lower his or her standards and make riskier investments in order to produce the promised results.

Type of property. Investments in existing property will have more information available, because of the property's operating history. Commercial property and established residential property will probably be more secure investments than hotels or undeveloped land.

The new tax laws are particularly stringent in tightening restrictions on the ability to use limited partnerships to reduce income taxes. Many limited partnerships now offer little more yield than a long-term bond, but with far less liquidity.

Real Estate Investment Trusts

REITs, like mutual funds, provide a way for an investor to acquire real estate with a small investment. Small investors pool their funds that are either invested in real estate ownership and/or loaned to real estate borrowers. Several REITs are traded on the stock market.

REITs can be excellent investment vehicles for small investors: All capital gains realized through the trust go directly to the shareholders, the diversified portfolio minimizes risks, and the ability to trade provides greater liquidity than other real estate investments. REITs, like mutual funds, bring the advantages of centralized, professional management to an investor; finally, REITs are subject to strict regulations and thus tend to be well managed.

You should realize, however, that REITs are very vulnerable to fluctuations in the real estate market, and at certain times in the recent past have performed very poorly. Today, many REITs are suffering from major cash flow problems as a result of overbuilding and recent low inflation. Under these circumstances, an investor may want to consider another, albeit indirect, means of real estate investment—investing in companies that have substantial undervalued real estate holdings on their balance sheets. Investment professionals often cite the large paper companies and some retailers as attractive "real estate rich" companies.

REAL ESTATE INVESTMENT EVALUATION FORMULAS

Experienced real estate investors are always on the lookout for reasonably priced properties. In order to do a quick initial evaluation of a property, investors typically use simple formulas which compare selling price to expected income from the property. If the price-income relationship seems reasonable, they will then conduct a more detailed analysis. A couple of commonly used real estate evaluation formulas are described below. They may be useful whether you are considering the purchase of a property yourself or through a limited partnership.

Rent Multiplier

The simplest formula involves comparing the total selling price with the current gross annual rental:

$$\text{Rent multiplier} = \frac{\text{Selling price}}{\text{Gross annual rental}}$$

For example, say a duplex selling for $180,000 generates $15,000 in annual rent. The rent multiplier is calculated as follows:

$$\text{Rent multiplier} = \frac{\text{Selling price}}{\text{Gross annual rental}} = \frac{\$180,000}{\$15,000} = 12$$

In other words, the property is selling for 12 times annual rental. A property that is selling for much more than 7 times the gross annual rental is likely to yield a negative cash flow. In the above example, until rents can be raised significantly, which may take years, you're probably going to be pouring more cash into the investment after you have bought it. If you put a sizable cash downpayment into the property to assure a positive cash flow, you're only fooling yourself because there's an opportunity cost associated with tying up a lot of cash that could otherwise be earning interest.

Similarly, if a general partnership pays more than 7 times the gross annual rental to buy a property, the partnership is probably paying too much, unless it can reasonably expect a dramatic increase in the value of the property (for example, immediate condo conversion). Of course, the salespeople always expect great things out of the deal, although a less optimistic prognosis would often be more accurate.

Capitalization Rate

A second real estate evaluation formula is the capitalization rate, usually referred to as the "cap rate." The formula is simple:

$$\text{Capitalization rate} = \frac{\text{Net operating income}}{\text{Total amount invested}}$$

For example, a limited partnership in an apartment building requiring a total investment of $3.5 million has an estimated net operating income of $300,000. The cap rate is calculated as follows:

$$\text{Capitalization rate} = \frac{\text{Net operating income}}{\text{Total amount invested}} = \frac{\$3,500,000}{\$300,000} = 8.6\%$$

A cap rate of 8 percent or greater is considered desirable. Whether you are investing in real estate yourself or through a limited partnership, make sure the amounts that go into the cap rate formula are realistic:

"Total amount invested" includes both the downpayment and the borrowed money necessary to buy the property.

"Net operating income" is the total rental income (allowing for vacancies) less all the expenses except debt service. A favorite trick of real estate agents and general partners is known as "bumping to market," which means raising rent projections from what they currently are to a supposed market level in order to make the deal look more attractive.

The above formulas are simply rules of thumb, and are just two of a multiplicity of relevant considerations that go into making real estate investments. In some instances, a promising location may outweigh a low cap rate, or tax advantages may compensate for a high rent multiplier. Those who are most successful in real estate investing, whether they do it themselves or through limited partnerships, share one characteristic—patience. When they find that real estate is overpriced, they are happy to wait until market conditions meet their criteria.

HOW TO EVALUATE REAL ESTATE LIMITED PARTNERSHIPS

This section outlines items that should be considered when evaluating a real estate limited partnership investment. The recent spate of failing real estate limited partnerships reinforces the need to evaluate thoroughly any potential partnership investment. In spite of their sullied reputation, many investors should still consider sound, thoroughly evaluated real estate limited partnerships as a component of their long-term investment portfolios.

Investor Suitability

1. Do you meet the investor suitability standards set forth in the offering memorandum?
2. Is your current and expected future tax bracket appropriate for this investment?
3. Do you have sufficient cash reserves to make the initial investment?
4. If the investment requires future payments, will you be able to afford making them out of cash reserves, or will funds have to be borrowed?
5. Can you afford to go without the money that is invested for a period at least as long as the estimated life of the partnership?
6. Can you afford to potentially lose your entire investment?
7. Is the investment appropriate in terms of your overall investment objectives?

Economic Risks

1. Do you understand the risks of the investment?
2. Are the business risks reasonable for the particular type of investment?
3. Are the risks appropriate when compared to the potential rewards?

Use of Proceeds

1. How much of the investor's dollar will go toward:
   A. Purchase of partnership assets?
   B. Fees to the general partner and affiliates?
   C. Sales, costs, and commissions?

D. Fees to other parties?

E. Rehabilitation of the project?

F. Covering projected negative cash flow from operations?

G. Being held for reserves?

2. Are the expenses associated with the investment reasonable, in light of this particular investment as well as in comparison to alternative investments?

Allocation of Benefits Between General Partner and Limited Partners

1. How are the following allocated between the general partner and the limited partners:

A. Tax benefits?

B. Cash flow from operations?

C. Sale or refinancing of partnership assets?

2. Are the limited partners entitled to the return of their capital contributions plus a return on the invested money, prior to the time the general partner receives any proceeds?

3. Do the allocation arrangements provide enough incentive to the general partner to maximize the performance of partnership assets during:

A. The operational phase?

B. The liquidation phase?

4. Are the overall allocation arrangements reasonable to all parties?

Partnership Assets

1. Does the real estate parcel have the potential to appreciate in value?

2. Are current economic conditions conducive to this type of real estate investment?

3. Are local real estate market conditions favorable to this kind of investment, considering current and projected competition in the area and vacancy rates?

4. Is the purchase price of the property reasonable in relation to appraisal value, current market data, and so on?

5. Will reasonable amounts of money be set aside to improve or rehabilitate the project?

6. Are the projections reasonable considering:

    A. Historical operating performance?

    B. Historical occupancy rates?

    C. Previous rate of increase in rent and expenses?

    D. Rents in the local market?

7. Are terms of the mortgage, if any, appropriate to the structure of the partnership?

8. If a negative cash flow is projected, are there enough reserves in the partnership to cover the cash shortfall?

9. Is the projected sales price of the asset at the time the partnership is expected to be liquidated reasonable?

General Partner Compensation

1. Is the compensation of the general partner adequately disclosed?

2. What percentage of the total equity to be raised from all limited partners are to be paid to the general partner and the salespeople? Are these fees reasonable?

3. Are the fees received by the general partner for performing services during the operational phase of the investment reasonable?

General Partner Track Record

1. How long has the general partner been in the real estate business?

2. How much experience does the general partner have in investing in and managing similar real estate projects?

3. Is the general partner's track record of all past projects satisfactory?

TAX BENEFITS OF HOME OWNERSHIP

After all the tax reform of the 1980s, home ownership is one of the few remaining tax shelters. Of course there are numerous benefits to owning your own home. Tax advantages, including deductions for mortgage interest and property taxes, are simply icing on the cake. The current tax rules relating to home ownership can be tricky in some areas. They are briefly in this section.

Mortgage Interest Deductibility

Home mortgage interest is generally fully deductible if paid on no more than two residences. On mortgages incurred before October 14, 1987, all interest on debt secured by a principal and second residence is deductible. After this date, interest deductions may be taken for debt of up to $1 million on two residences. The law distinguishes between:

1. debt to buy, construct, and improve a residence, and
2. home equity debt secured by a residence where the loan proceeds are used for nonresidential purposes.

In most cases, up to $1 million of acquisition debt and an additional $100,000 of home equity debt is deductible.

Acquisition debt is that which is secured by a principal or secondary residence and incurred in acquiring, constructing, or substantially improving that same residence. Home equity debt is any debt secured by a first or second residence that is not greater than the fair market value of the residence, less the amount of acquisition debt on the residence.

Interest on home construction loans for a first and second residence may be fully deductible, subject to the $1 million limit on acquisition debt, during a 24-month period of time beginning at the onset of construction.

Points, also called loan origination fees, are deductible if they are paid for your use of the mortgage proceeds and not for specific services performed by the lender. Points must be deducted over the period of the loan unless they are charged on a loan to buy or improve your principal residence and provided the payment meets certain other restrictions.

Deductions for Rental of a Home

Expenses which you allocate to the rented part of your home are deductible. If the expenses are greater than the rental income, the loss, up to a limit of $25,000, is deductible from any income (losses over the limit are only deductible from passive activity income). The $25,000 limitation is reduced for taxpayers with adjusted gross incomes in excess of $100,000 and is eliminated for adjusted gross incomes of $150,000 or greater. The following rules define the limitations on who may deduct rental losses:

1. If the house is rented for less than 15 days, expenses other than interest, real estate taxes, and casualty losses may not be deducted. If the home qualifies as a first or second home, interest is fully deductible.
2. If the number of days you use the house exceeds the greater of 14 days or 10 percent of the number of days the house is rented, then you are considered to have used the unit as a residence, and rental expenses are deductible only to the extent of gross rental income.
3. If the house is rented for 15 days or more, but your personal use does not meet the 14-day 15 percent minimum, then you are not considered to have made personal use of the residence, and expenses in excess of rental income may be deductible.
   When you personally use a home that is also used for rental, expenses must be allocated between personal and rental use.

Sale of Home

Although a gain on the sale or exchange of a principal residence is taxable, tax on the gain may be postponed if the cost of the new residence exceeds the adjusted sales price of the old one. In addition, the new residence must be purchased and moved into within the 4-year period starting 2 years *before* the day of the sale.

To determine the gain on the sale, the amount realized, adjusted sales price, and cost of the house must be calculated.

The amount realized is the selling price of the old residence, less expenses for all legal and title services involved with the sale. The selling price includes any mortgages on the property. The adjusted sales price is the amount realized less fix-up costs, such as painting and repair work, done within the 90-day period concluding on the day of the contract to sell, and paid for within 30 days after the sale. The cost of the new residence includes all cash payments and mortgages.

Once 2 years have passed since the sale date of the original home and you have not moved into the new home, the tax may not be postponed. (This rule is inflexible, even in a case of extraordinary circumstances preventing your move.) The only exceptions apply to certain members of the Armed Forces and individuals whose tax home is outside the United States.

If the 2-year rule is met, but the cost of the new residence is less than the adjusted sales price of your old residence, you may have to recognize gain to the extent that the adjusted sales price of the old residence exceeds the cost of the new residence.

If you are 55 or older, you are allowed a 1-time exclusion of a gain up to $125,000. To qualify, you must be 55 before the date of the sale and must have owned and occupied the residence for 3 out of the previous 5 years.

REAL ESTATE INVESTMENT TRUSTS

Real estate investment trusts are organizations, usually corporations, established for the accumulation of funds for investing in real estate holdings, or the extension of credit on real estate. Table 6-1 is a listing of some of the major publicly traded REITs, all of which trade on either the New York Stock Exchange or American Stock Exchange. There are three different REIT industry sectors: property owners, mortgage makers, and hybrids. Within each sector, you can select REITs that invest in or finance particular categories of real estate. For example, property-owner REITs may invest in such properties as shopping centers, office space, multifamily rental housing, distribution/service facilities, or, in the case of Santa Anita Realty, a racetrack. Therefore, the REIT selection process may not only focus on the value of the security per se, but also on the nature of the REIT's business.

Table 6–1. Major Publicly Traded Real Estate Investment Trusts

Name	Description
BRE Properties	Emphasis on income-producing real estate
Federal Realty	Emphasis on the ownership and renovation of shopping malls nationwide
First Union	Nationwide, emphasis on income-producing properties
HRE Properties	Invests in retail, office, and distribution-service facilities throughout the United States
L&N Housing	Invests in multifamily rental housing with a view toward conversion into condominiums; has diversified into apartment, retail, and office properties
L&N Mortgage	Emphasizes short-term mortgages on a nationwide basis
MGI Properties	Engages in geographically diverse real estate investments
New Plan Realty	Specializes in the ownership of income-producing shopping malls
Property Capital	Specializes in making equity participation loans on real estate properties
Santa Anita Realty	Owns Santa Anita racetrack and other real estate properties
Washington REIT	Emphasizes investing in and developing income-producing properties

Just like any real estate investment, REIT stocks should generally be considered longer-term investments.

BUYING A FIRST HOME

A family home is probably the single largest acquisition that most people make in their lifetimes. It usually requires a large cash outlay and the assumption of a major, long-term mortgage. Thus, the process of buying a home (or condominium, cooperative unit, duplex, triplex, or townhouse) should be initiated only after consideration and consultation with all family members. Nonetheless, home ownership has many advantages over renting or leasing, and if you can afford to buy a home, you probably should.

The Down Payment

Many people think the biggest stumbling block to home-ownership is qualifying for a mortgage, but undoubtedly the greatest difficulty most first-time homebuyers face is accumulating enough money for the down payment and closing costs, which will generally total between 5 and 20 percent of the home's value. Closing costs typically range up to several thousand dollars and include title insurance fees and sometimes loan origination fees (points) of 2 to 3 percent of the face amount of the mortgage.

Quite simply, the best way to save for a home is to live beneath your means by cutting, as much as possible, transportation costs, rental costs, discretionary expenses, and any corners you can find. Also, think about parents or other relatives as a source of loans or of some other arrangement to help cover the down payment.

The Mortgage

The cost of the house does not include only the down payment and monthly mortgage payments; there are additional costs that you must weigh in estimating the maximum amount of mortgage you will be able to carry. Total housing costs typically should not exceed 30 percent of your monthly net income (less if you carry other large debts). Housing costs may include maintenance or condominium fees, homeowner's insurance, property tax, and allowances for major repairs. If you have a variable rate mortgage, you will also have to consider whether or not expenses could continue to be met in the event that mortgage interest should increase.

Other Considerations

Buying a first home is not only a major financial undertaking, but it also involves some important emotional considerations. The emotional and financial factors are inextricably connected. For example, as a first-time home buyer, you may not be able to afford as large a home in as desirable a neighborhood as the one you grew up in. Nevertheless, don't postpone purchasing a home until you can afford your dream house. It makes more financial sense to buy now and trade up in the future.

Besides financial considerations, you should explore the following factors before buying your first home:

Location. Is the home convenient to work, shopping, school, and recreation? Is the general neighborhood declining or improving? How heavy are the property taxes?

Types of Houses. The traditional single-family home is facing stiff competition from newer types of housing such as condominiums and multifamily units. Even traditional housing offers a tremendous variety of choices, especially between older dwellings and newer ones.

Size of House. Is your family likely to grow in the future, or is it likely to shrink as children leave the nest? Will the size of the home facilitate resale?

Length of Stay. If you only expect to stay in a neighborhood 4 or 5 years, you may have different priorities than someone anticipating a permanent stay. If you may sell the house within a few years, make sure the size and location of the home fit the demands of the market.

Househunting. If possible, plan to devote several months to househunting. During that time, become familiar with various neighborhoods and the general price ranges of homes in these neighborhoods. Introduce yourself to several real estate brokers. You might also ask your bank to give you an idea of how much mortgage you will be able to qualify for. Learn as much as you can about the process of negotiating for a home purchase, including speaking with acquaintances who have bought several homes. Finally, never stop saving for the down payment.

7

Insurance

Having the appropriate insurance coverage can mean the difference between successfully coping with a financial emergency or being desperately ill-prepared for one. Yet few areas are as little understood, and inappropriately utilized, as insurance protection. You need to make sure that you have no gaps in insurance coverage.

Reduced to its simplest terms, insurance is a means of minimizing the losses of a few by spreading the cost among many. Insurance protection can be broadly divided into two categories: property and casualty, which insures your possessions such as a home, a car, and other personal property; and life and health, which covers loss of life, injury, or illness.

Beyond these basic definitions, however, lies a world of premiums, forms, deductibles, policy exceptions, and tax ramifications that are likely to be very confusing to most people. As a result, many people are underinsured, while others are over-insured or covered at much higher costs than necessary. Newer forms of tax-advantaged insurance products such as single premium, variable, and universal life insurance add to the confusion. Since policy features vary so widely, the task of selecting the right coverage has become very difficult.

Despite these roadblocks, you must periodically evaluate

your insurance needs; without proper insurance coverage, assets and future earnings could be severely jeopardized.

During your working years, you will need these basic forms of insurance:

Life Insurance. The main purpose of life insurance is to provide for dependents after your death, and ideally should replace most, if not all, of your wages for several years after your death.

Life insurance also helps provide liquidity for your estate. As the size of your estate grows, the need for life insurance to help pay estate taxes may increase.

Health Insurance. Although many employers provide health insurance, self-employed individuals and retirees who are no longer covered by a company plan must be particularly careful about selecting appropriate coverage.

As employers and health insurance companies search for ways to control health insurance costs, employees, too, will become increasingly diligent in seeking ways to monitor and reduce personal health care costs.

Disability Insurance. This crucial insurance replaces part or most of your wage income if a disability occurs. Disability is often the most overlooked area of insurance coverage, yet you are far more likely to become disabled than to die before you retire.

Homeowner's and Renter's Insurance. Theft, fire, or natural catastrophes are a fact of life for homeowners and apartment dwellers. Policy provisions should be carefully noted, since most policies cover only the depreciated cash value of an individual's possessions, and place severe limits on valuables.

Automobile Insurance. You should pay particular attention to the adequacy of bodily injury liability protection, since jury awards in some accident cases are very high.

Umbrella Liability Insurance. Umbrella insurance, also called extended personal liability insurance, takes over where your homeowners'-renters' and automobile insurance leaves off. It also covers you for potential personal (not job-related) liability not related to your home or the operation of your automobile. Having this coverage is a must.

Since few people are totally insured, one of the first steps to take when evaluating your insurance coverage is to look for any gaps. For example, you may be adequately covered if your home is burglarized, but inadequate life insurance could leave your family financially strapped in the event of your death.

On the other hand, it is also critical to guard against wasted premium dollars that are being spent on unnecessary coverage. You may be paying too much for the coverage that you do have. You should review the adequacy and appropriateness of your insurance coverage at least annually. A good insurance agent will offer to do this for you.

AVOIDING GAPS IN INSURANCE COVERAGE

A single gap in insurance coverage can wipe out years of hard-earned savings. Yet, most people lack complete insurance coverage. Often, they are overinsured in some areas and underinsured or uninsured in others, so they wouldn't have to spend much (if any) more money to obtain comprehensive coverage that is appropriate to their needs. Table 7-1 describes important areas of risk which you can protect against with appropriate insurance if the risks apply to you. Discuss your needs with an experienced insurance agent.

UNDERSTANDING LIFE INSURANCE

Life insurance has existed in America since the nineteenth century, but in recent years enough new varieties have been introduced to make the decision of which to buy a difficult and confusing one. The two basic types are term insurance, which provides insurance protection only, and cash-value insurance, which has a savings component. Within these two categories are many subspecies of insurance, as explained below. This section will help you make the right decisions to meet your life insurance needs.

Table 7–1. Risk Categories and Their
Appropriate Insurance Coverage

Risk Category	Appropriate Insurance Coverage
Loss of Income	
During your life	Disability insurance
After your death	Life insurance
Death of spouse	Life Insurance
Short-term disability	Short-term disability insurance
Long-Term disability	Long-term disability insurance
Permanent disability	Long-term disability insurance
Loss of Property	
Total loss	Homeowner's/renter's and automotive insurance
Loss of use	Homeowner's/renter's and automotive insurance
Repairs/Replacements	Homeowner's/renter's and automotive insurance
Loss of valuables	Floater policy on homeowner's/renter's and automotive insurance
Injury to Others	
Damage to property	Homeowner's/renter's, automotive, and umbrella liability insurance
Damage to person	Homeowner's/renter's, automotive, and umbrella liability insurance
Libel	Umbrella liability insurance
Illness/Injury	
Routine	Medical insurance
Catastrophic	Medical insurance
Old-age	Medicare gap and nursing home insurance
Occupational	
Professional liability	Professional liability insurance
Inflation	
Loss of income	Disability insurance with inflation provision
Loss of property	Homeowner's/renter's insurance with replacement cost provision
Estate Liquidity	
Final expenses	Life insurance
Estate taxes	Life insurance
Estate administration	Life insurance

Term Policies

Term life insurance is fairly straightforward. The policyholder pays an annual premium, and in exchange the insurance company pays a sum of money to the policyholder's beneficiaries if he or she dies within the time covered. Most term policies are renewable, meaning that when the policy expires (generally every 1 or 5 years) the policyholder may have the policy renewed, no matter what change in health he or she has undergone. The premium rises each term as the policyholder's age increases. The option to renew continues up to a specified age, usually 65 years or so. Renewability is a very important feature. Specific kinds of term insurance include:

Level Renewable Term Insurance. Maintains a fixed annual premium which increases each time the policy is renewed. A policyholder generally may reduce the amount of coverage when he or she renews, but may have to undergo a medical examination in order to increase coverage.

Level Nonrenewable Term Insurance. Maintains a fixed face amount and annual premium throughout the term of coverage—which might be 5, 10, or 20 years—and may not be renewed thereafter.

Decreasing or Declining Term Insurance. This policy's annual premium remains fixed, but its face amount gradually decreases. These policies, usually purchased for 10 to 25 or more years, are often used to provide for payment of an outstanding debt. Mortgage life insurance is a variety of decreasing term insurance that is specifically designed to pay off the balance of a mortgage upon the policyholder's death. Mortgage life insurance or credit life insurance (designed to pay off a loan) are both somewhat restrictive in that the policyholder's dependents will not have any option with the policy funds other than to pay the mortgage or loan. A term insurance policy that is large enough to cover a mortgage or debt has the advantages of greater flexibility and usually much lower cost than these targeted programs.

Group Term Insurance. Many Americans are covered by some form of group life insurance, through their employers, unions, professional and fraternal organizations, alumni associations, and so on. Group life insurance is generally less expensive than individual insurance and does not require a medical examination; eligibility for group coverage usually ends if the policyholder leaves the sponsoring group.

Cash Value Policies

These more complicated policies combine life insurance coverage with a savings plan. Like a savings account, a cash value insurance policy gradually builds up a cash value which the policyholder can borrow against or cash in. Cash value insurance thus enforces a regimented savings plan. It is much more expensive than term insurance, so that most people can't afford to obtain all of their life insurance needs with a cash value policy.

A cash value policy usually remains in effect for a holder's entire life, and a fixed annual premium is paid throughout. The policy's death benefit remains fixed even as the cash value rises with annual payments; when the policyholder dies, the beneficiary receives only the policy's face value. The savings component of a cash value policy is, thus, largely for the benefit of the policyholder, who may cash in the policy at any time, or may borrow against the cash value. Alternatively, the cash value can be used to pay premiums in later years of the policy's life or to purchase additional insurance.

A cash value policy may be participating or nonparticipating. With a "par" policy, a policyholder receives annual dividends representing whatever portion of his or her premium the insurance company did not use to pay death benefits and other expenses. Dividends may be received in cash, reinvested in insurance, or held by the company to reduce future premium payments.

Whole Life Insurance. As its name suggests, this policy covers a policyholder until death. The high annual premiums in a whole life policy will eventually begin to accumulate a substantial cash value, but only after several years, since in a policy's early years sales commissions and administrative costs absorb much of the premium payments. Only a total withdrawal of funds, canceling the policy, is permitted, but a holder may borrow against the cash value, generally at a low interest rate. Whole life policies, as well as other kinds of cash value insurance, have been treated as a tax-deferred investment up to the time of withdrawal (at which point part of the cash value is taxed).

Universal Life Insurance. While the company administering a whole life policy is not required to inform policyholders about the effective rate of interest that is being paid on a policy, universal life insurance allows a policyholder to see what percentage of premiums go respectively toward company expenses, protecting the client, and the savings component. The policyholder is also advised of the interest rate that the savings are earning. Universal life holders are permitted to withdraw a portion of the cash value account without terminating the policy. One form of universal life policy—which is for obvious reasons, more expensive—allows the policy's beneficiaries to receive the policy's accumulated cash value as well as its face value.

Many universal life insurance policies allow holders some flexibility in paying premiums; as long as they pay a minimum premium, they may pay more or less than usual, increasing or reducing the speed with which their cash value grows. Companies guarantee that they will credit a certain minimum interest rate to a policyholder's cash value, the rate sometimes increasing with higher cash values.

Variable Life Insurance. This kind of policy is similar to universal life insurance except that each policyholder is permitted to decide how his or her money is to be invested. He or she has a choice between various different investment vehicles—stocks, bonds, money market funds—from the company's portfolio, and can therefore tailor their own investment portfolio.

WAYS TO LOWER LIFE INSURANCE COSTS

Life insurance is so varied and complex that, all too often, people tend to give up and probably spend more on a life insurance policy than necessary. Some people are so life insurance poor that they can't afford to obtain sufficient coverage to provide adequately for their dependents. The following guidelines will help you shop around for the coverage you do need and avoid the added cost of coverage that you don't.

1. **Determine how much life insurance you need, if any.** Life insurance is designed primarily to provide for dependents in the event of the death of a breadwinner. If you have no dependents, your life insurance needs are probably nominal, if you need life insurance at all. People who fall into this category (who, for some reason, often buy a lot of life insurance anyway) include single individuals and "DINKS" (dual income couples with no kids), although DINKS may need some life insurance if a surviving spouse would suffer financial hardship upon the demise of his or her spouse.

    Don't rely too much on an insurance company's or agent's estimation of how much life insurance you need. Prepare your own independent estimate.

2. **Don't buy specific coverage.** You don't need air travel insurance because the risk of dying in a plane crash is so low, and you should already have enough life insurance to cover death from any cause. Mugging insurance is a waste of money, as is credit life insurance, which pays off a loan or mortgage if you die. In general, life insurance coverage for specific events or debts is wildly overpriced. Instead, buy more traditional, less expensive comprehensive life insurance that will cover you for a multitude of mishaps.

3. **Keep it simple.** With annual renewable term insurance, the simplest kind of life insurance, you pay a premium each year for coverage. Although the premium increases as you get older, most people's need for life insurance decreases as they age. Term insurance is often the best buy for many people, particularly those under age 50.

4. **Shop around for term insurance.** Premium rates for an otherwise identical term insurance policy can vary widely. Shop around for coverage. Many of the lowest price term insurance policies are available on a group basis. Check with your employer (you may be able to add to your company's group policy), professional or fraternal association, or any other group that you belong to or could join. Residents of Connecticut, Massachusetts, and New York should also investigate Savings Bank Life Insurance, which can be purchased through many savings institutions.

5. **Compare cash value policies.** Cash value (as opposed to term) life insurance can be a good investment for some people, especially when the tax advantages of these policies are considered. However, they remain an expensive way to obtain life insurance coverage since most of your premium goes into the investment component of the policy. Moreover, cash value policies can be difficult to understand and compare, and they're certainly not for everyone. As with any life insurance policy, be sure to understand the provisions, limitations, and fees associated with these policies before purchasing one. Also, shop around for the best overall deal.

6. **Stop smoking.** Smokers pay roughly 50 percent more for life insurance than healthy nonsmokers. Even if you don't need life insurance, that should tell you something about your odds when you light up.

DISABILITY INSURANCE POLICY PROVISIONS

Lack of adequate long-term disability insurance coverage is one of the two most common gaps in insurance coverage. (The other is lack of extended personal liability, or umbrella, insurance coverage.) Even if your employer provides long-term disability coverage, it may lack important policy features or provide insufficient benefits. Remember, you are far more likely to suffer a long-term disability before you retire than to die before retirement.

Disability insurance policies differ widely in features and benefits. For example, some policies terminate coverage when the disabled individual can perform any occupation, while others continue coverage until the disabled individual can perform his or her "usual and customary" occupation. Some policies offer the same benefits throughout the period of disability, while others adjust for inflation. Whether you need to check the adequacy of the disability insurance provided by your employer or you are evaluating privately purchased disability insurance, the following list of questions highlights various features and standards limitations of disability insurance policies. Don't expect your company plan to contain all of these features. Moreover, a very comprehensive individually purchased disability policy will be quite expensive.

1. What is the definition of total disability:
   • During initial period?
   • After initial period?
2. Is the contract noncancellable and guaranteed renewable to age 65 with guaranteed level premium?
3. Can total disability coverage be continued on a conditionally renewable basis to age 75 if the insured is employed full time?
4. Is a proportionate benefit for partial disability automatically included?
5. Is the contract participating?
6. Does the contract state that the number of days to satisfy the beginning date need not be continuous?
7. Does the contract have a presumptive total disability clause that starts on the day of a specified loss and provides for lifetime payments whether the insured is working or not?
8. What, if any, are the waiver of premium provisions?
9. What are the standard exclusions?
10. Is the policy incontestable after two years from date of issue?

11. Is a rehabilitation benefit automatically included?
12. Are lifetime benefits for total disability available?
13. Is a nonsmoker discount available?
14. Does the policy provide for inflation indexation of benefits?
15. Does the policy pay Social Security substitute benefits?
16. Does the policy offer additional regular disability coverage on an annually renewable, increasing premium basis?

HOMEOWNERS AND RENTERS INSURANCE POLICY COVERAGE OPTIONS

Obtaining comprehensive homeowners or renters insurance coverage is vitally important. Yet, many people are either underinsured or overinsured. For example, you may not realize the severe limits placed upon insurance coverage for valuable possessions located either in your home or in your safe deposit box. In order to be adequately insured for valuable possessions, you must obtain an endorsement on your policy.

Table 7-2 summarizes the risks covered under various homeowners and renters insurance plans. It shows the extent of coverage available under the various homeowners insurance plans and can be used to identify the appropriate level of coverage to meet your needs as well as to note risks that are not covered. Table 7-3 lists frequently used homeowners insurance policy endorsements, and can be used to identify risks and/or coverage modifications that can be added to a basic insurance plan to ensure that your coverage is comprehensive.

INSURANCE COMPANY RATING CATEGORIES

It is critical to do business with insurance companies that are financially strong. Recently, some insurers have experienced financial problems, although not yet serious enough to jeopardize their claims-paying obligations. A.M. Best Company provides a rating service of life and property-casualty insurance companies. These ratings are designed to reflect the companies' strengths and weaknesses in four areas: underwriting, expense control, reserve adequacy, and sound

Table 7-2. Comparison of Risks Covered Under Various Homeowners Insurance Plans

Risks	Basic HO-1	Broad HO-2	Special HO-3[1]	Renters HO-4	Unit Owners HO-6	Older Home HO-8
Fire or lightning	A,B	A,B	A,B	B	B	A,B
Windstorm or hail	A,B	A,B	A,B	B	B	A,B
Explosion	A,B	A,B	A,B	B	B	A,B
Riot or civil commotion	A,B	A,B	A,B	B	B	A,B
Damage from aircraft	A,B	A,B	A,B	B	B	A,B
Damage from vehicles	A,B	A,B	A,B	B	B	A,B
Damage from smoke	A,B	A,B	A,B	B	B	A,B
Vandalism and malicious mischief	A,B	A,B	A,B	B	B	A,B
Theft	A,B	A,B	A,B	B	B	A,B
Damage by glass or safety glazing material which is a part of a building	A,B	A,B	A,B	B	B	A,B
Volcanic eruption	A,B	A,B	A,B	B	B	A,B
Falling objects		A,B	A,B	B	B	
Weight of ice, snow, or sleet		A,B	A,B	B	B	
Accidental discharge or overflow of water or steam from within a plumbing, heating,		A,B	A,B	B	B	

Table 7-2. (*Continued*)

air-conditioning or automatic fire protective sprinkler system or from within a household appliance	A,B	A,B	B	B
Sudden and accidental tearing apart, cracking, burning, or bulging of a steam or hot water heating system, an air-conditioning, automatic fire protective sprinkler system or an appliance for hot water	A,B	A,B	B	B
Freezing of a plumbing, heating, air-conditioning or automatic fire protective sprinkler system or household appliance	A,B	A,B	B	
Sudden and accidental damage from artificially generated electrical current	A,B	A,B	B	
All perils except flood, earthquake, war, nuclear accident, and others specified in policy		A,B		

[1] Under new homeowners program, comprehensive coverage is available by endorsement to the HO-3 special policy, which otherwise covers only personal property.

A = Dwelling

B = Personal Property

Table 7–3. Frequently Used Homeowners Insurance Endorsements

Program	Endorsement
HO-40	Appurtenant Structures—Rented to Others
HO-41	Additional Insured—Designated Premises Only
HO-42	Office, Professional, Private School, or Studio Occupancy. Described Residence Premises Only
HO-43	Office, Professional, Private School, or Studio Occupancy. Additional Residence Premises (Section II only)
HO-45	Change Endorsement
HO-46	Theft Coverage Extension (Form HO-2, HO-3, or HO-4 only—Section I)
HO-47	Inflation Guard Endorsement
HO-48	Appurtenant Structures (Section I only)
HO-49	Secondary Residence Premises, Building Additions and Alterations. Increased Limit of Liability (Form HO-5 only—Section I)
HO-50	Additional Amount on Unscheduled Personal Property. In Secondary Residence (Form HO-5 only—Section I)
HO-53	Credit Card Forgery and Depositors Forgery Coverage Endorsement (Section I only)
HO-54, HO-54A, HO-54C	Earthquake Damage Assumption Endorsements (Form HO-1, HO-2, HO-3, or HO-4 only—Section I—variable in coverage for earthquake and/or volcanic eruption and deductibles)
HO-55, HO-55A, HO-55C	Earthquake Damage Assumption Endorsements (Form HO-5 only—Section I—variable in coverage for earthquake and/or volcanic eruption and deductibles)
HO-56	$100 Special Loss Deductible Clause (Form HO-1, HO-2, HO-3, or HO-4 only—Section I)
HO-57	$50 Loss Deductible Clause (Form HO-5 only—Section I)
HO-58	$250 Special Loss Deductible Clause (Section I only)
HO-59	$500 Special Loss Deductible Clause (Section I only)
HO-61	Scheduled Personal Property Endorsement
HO-65	Increased Limits on Money and Securities (Section I only)

Table 7–3. (*cont.*)

Program	Endorsement
HO-66	Additional Amount on Unscheduled Personal Property—Away From Premises (Form HO-1, HO-2, HO-3, or HO-4 only—Section I)
HO-67	Secondary Residence Premises Endorsement
HO-68	Scheduled Glass Endorsement (Section I only)
HO-69	Physicians, Surgeons, Dentists and Veterinarians—Away From Premises Endorsement (Form HO-2, HO-3, or HO-4 only—Section I)
HO-70	Additional Residence Premises—Rented to Others (1 or 2 families—Section II only)
HO-71	Business Pursuits Endorsement (Section II only)
HO-72	Farmers Comprehensive Personal Liability Endorsement
HO-75	Watercraft Endorsement (Section II only)
HO-114	$50 Loss Deductible Clause No. 1 and No. 2 (Form HO-5 only—Section I)
HO-122	Loss Deductible Clause No. 1—Windstorm or Hail (Form HO-1, HO-2, HO-3, or HO-4 only—Section I)
HO-148	$50 Modified Loss Deductible Clause No 2 (Form HO-2, HO-3, or HO-4 only—Section I)
HO-162	Credit for Existing Insurance Endorsement (for those states where permitted)
HO-164	Snowmobile Endorsement (Section II)
HO-171	Unscheduled Jewelry, Watches, and Furs Increased Limits of Liability (Form HO-1, HO-2, HO-3, or HO-4 only—Section I)
HO-172	Unscheduled Jewelry, Watches, and Furs Increased Limits of Liability (Form HO-5 only—Section I)
HO-174	$100 Loss Deductible Clause (Form HO-1, HO-2, HO-3, or HO-4 only—Section I)
HO-175	$100 Loss Deductible Clause No. 1—Windstorm or Hail (Form HO-1, HO-2, HO-3, or HO-4 only—Section I)
HO-192	Condominium Unit—Owner's Endorsement (Form HO-4 only—Section I)

Table 7–4. Explanations of A.M. Best's Insurance Ratings

Rating	Explanation
A+	**Superior.** Have demonstrated the strongest ability to meet policyholder and other contractual obligations.
A and A−	**Excellent.** Have demonstrated a strong ability to meet policyholder and other contractual obligations.
B+	**Very Good.** Have demonstrated a very good ability to meet policyholder and other contractual obligations.
B and B−	**Good.** Have demonstrated a good ability to meet policyholder and other contractual obligations.
C+	**Fairly Good.** Have demonstrated a fairly good ability to meet policyholder and other contractual obligations.
C and C−	**Fair.** Have demonstrated a fair ability to meet policyholder and other contractual obligations.
c	**Contingent Rating.** Temporarily assigned to a company when there has been a decline in performance of its profitability, leverage, and/or liquidity, but the decline has not been significant enough to warrant an actual reduction in the company's previously assigned rating.
w	**Watch list.** Indicates the company was placed on Best's Rating Watch List during the year because it experienced a downward trend in profitability, leverage and/or liquidity performance, but the decline was not significant enough to warrant an actual reduction in the assigned rating.

investments. While not infallible, Best's ratings are often used to gauge the ability of an insurance company to meet its obligations. Table 7-4 contains explanations of the Best's ratings. Note that many insurance companies are not eligible for a Best's rating, in which case these companies are placed in a "not assigned" classification (NA). When deciding upon a particular insurance policy, be sure to check the insurance company's Best's rating, and be wary of lower rated insurers.

8

Borrowing and Credit

Borrowing is a double-edged sword. On the one hand, it enables you to pursue wealth-building strategies such as investing in real estate, borrowing on margin, or starting and expanding a business. It permits you to pay gradually for goods and services. And equally important, it can, if necessary, allow you to deal promptly with financial emergencies without draining your savings and other personal resources.

On the other hand, its easy availability, along with the high interest rates on some forms of consumer credit, makes overextension a problem that is currently being seen with increasing frequency. In fact, the tightening of credit and the rise in mortgage delinquency rates in the early 1990s will, in all likelihood, result in tighter credit availability. The rising delinquency rate will also result in negative credit ratings or repossessions, and will severely restrict the use of credit by many individuals in the future.

You need to manage your credit much like a successful business manages its credit by borrowing only for worthwhile purposes and paying off loans over an appropriate period of time. Your first step should be to review your current loans, including home mortgages, home equity loans, installment loans, and credit card loans. Have these loans been taken out for a good reason? Is the interest charged on the loans reasonable, or can better interest rates be obtained elsewhere? If you are overextended, have you developed a plan to reduce your debt and get on sound financial footing?

In addition to your review of current indebtedness, you may also want to estimate your future borrowing requirements. This will enable the plan in advance to make the most of your credit. Sound use of credit involves knowing not only how much to borrow, but what type of loan to utilize and how to evaluate its terms. This is especially true today, since the consumer interest deduction, which is phased out as of January 1, 1991, will no longer partially subsidize what can sometimes be very costly credit mistakes.

As a result of this phase out, much attention is being focused on financing consumer purchases through home equity secured credit that is still deductible. Basically, this is a credit account, secured by a second mortgage, that operates like a checking account. Generally, the line of credit is 70 percent to 80 percent of the appraised value of the house, less what is already owed on it.

The popularity of home equity loans has increased enormously over the last several years. While home equity loans can be a cost-effective, tax-advantaged source of credit, you should guard against overusing them. If you fall behind on home equity loan payments, you put your home at risk. And the variable interest rates attached to many of these loans can lead to an unanticipated rise in payments. Finally, the application fees and other costs associated with such loans, combined with the lower tax rates, may make the resulting tax savings of marginal benefit anyway.

BUILDING A GOOD CREDIT RECORD

Good credit is difficult to achieve and easy to lose. This section will help you establish and maintain good credit as well as understand the mysteries behind the credit-granting process.

One of the best ways to establish credit is through judicious use of borrowing for sound purposes, particularly from banks. You may want to begin or continue a program of borrowing, even if there is no immediate need for borrowed funds. The borrowing relationship that you establish will be useful in the long run, and may even be crucial in case of a financial emergency. Consider the interest expense an investment in good credit.

Some people have a fear of borrowing and it can be stressful for them. The fear of rejection should never discourage you from attempting to borrow, however, since this rejection will not become part of your credit record. If rejected at one bank, you should try another.

Ideally, borrowing should be done on an unsecured basis. If this is not possible (as it may not be for young, first-time borrowers), you may have to pledge some assets to secure the loan.

As you begin to build up your credit, you may want to meet periodically with your banker to discuss your personal financial objectives and plans. Another way for you to maintain good banking relations is to send your personal financial statements to your banker regularly (at least once a year). Those who can demonstrate that they are in control of their financial situation have an advantage in securing ongoing bank credit.

The Three "Cs" of Credit

Lenders often summarize their credit rating system by referring to the "Three Cs." These are:

1. **Character.** Denotes a borrower's personal qualities; it is revealed through factual records that indicate to the lender how an individual is likely to perform as a borrower.
2. **Capacity.** The borrower's financial ability to repay the loan. It is judged on the basis of the job he or she holds, the amount of money earned, the length of time on the present or previous job, and future job prospects.
3. **Capital.** Includes all of the assets that can serve as collateral for the loan. The borrower's home, investments, bank accounts, and other tangible property are examples of such assets.

Although these three items form the foundation of a credit rating, the rating is far more complicated. More specifically, a rating as a credit risk is based upon the borrower's not meeting the lender's criteria in the following areas:

Employment record. The lender will want to know how long the borrower has worked with the same company and whether or not the borrower frequently moves or changes jobs. (If the borrower moves frequently because he or she is an upwardly mobile employee of a major corporation, however, this will not be taken as a negative.)

Previous loans. If the borrower has paid back a loan on time before, the bank is likely to anticipate that he or she will do so this time as well. If he or she has defaulted before, this will naturally be viewed as a negative.

Home ownership. It is generally a positive sign if the borrower owns a home (or has lived in the same apartment for several years); otherwise his or her condition might be judged as unstable.

Charge accounts. A record of paying charge accounts regularly indicates a sense of responsibility to pay.

Checking and savings accounts. Having a substantial amount in a bank account is a great help, especially if the account is at the bank at which one applies for the loan.

Once a satisfactory banking relationship has been established, you should usually endeavor to keep your business with that institution. Switching to another bank that is offering slightly better rates is sometimes short sighted, since good credit is usually built on long-term business dealings with one or a few financial institutions.

If You Have Bad Credit

If you have a bad credit rating, getting rid of it is often quite difficult. To even begin to do so, you must pay all of your bills. You will probably never be able to receive a loan if even one bill is left unpaid. Another positive step is to prove that you can pay off a secured installment loan—a car loan, for example. If the banks turn you down, you might try finance companies who charge higher rates but often take the customers the banks turn down. If you remain debt-free for about a year, you could probably get credit at a department store, however it will be contingent on your good bill-paying behavior. Even after taking these general steps toward a favorable credit rating, banks are still hard to convince. They will change their view eventually, after you have proven yourself in others' eyes.

How quickly you can restore a good credit rating ultimately depends on the reason it went bad originally. If there were outstanding circumstances, for example, illness, divorce, or unemployment, banks will usually find these excuses legitimate. On the other hand, lenders look very unfavorably and, in fact, resent the standard middle-class syndrome of running up huge bills and then taking months to pay them. These types tend to fall into a dangerous pattern and subsequently find it extremely difficult to establish a good credit rating or obtain any kind of loan. Also, the assumption that moving away immediately erases a bad credit rating is false. Computer-linked credit bureaus make it effortless for a loan officer to check your credit history.

Good credit, or restoring bad credit, is up to you. You must have the self-discipline to live beneath your means, even if it means taking the scissors to your credit cards.

PREPARING A PERSONAL BALANCE SHEET

If you apply for a loan, you will usually be asked to prepare a personal balance sheet, sometimes referred to as a net worth statement, which lists your assets and liabilities in dollar terms at a specific time. This section will help you prepare such a statement, which is seen in Figure 8-1.

Personal balance sheets are almost identical to business balance sheets. Balance sheets list assets which are things that you own and liabilities which are amounts that you owe to others. Net worth is found by subtracting your total liabilities from your total assets. Learning to fill out a reasonably accurate

Figure 8-1. Sample Personal Balance Sheet and Supplementary Financial Data Form

□ If you are applying for individual credit in your own name and are relying on your own income or assets and not the income or assets of another person as the basis for repayment of the credit requested, complete only Sections 1 and 3.

□ If you are applying for joint credit with another person, complete all Sections providing information in Section 2 about the joint applicant.

□ If you are applying for individual credit, but are relying on income from alimony, child support, or separate maintenance or on the income or assets of another person as a basis for repayment of the credit requested, complete all Sections, providing information in Section 2 about the person whose alimony, support, or maintenance payments or income or assets you are relying.

□ If this statement relates to your guaranty of the indebtedness of other person(s), firm(s) or corporation(s), complete Sections 1 and 3.

SECTION 1 - INDIVIDUAL INFORMATION (Type or Print)	SECTION 2 - OTHER PARTY INFORMATION (Type or Print)
Name	Name
Residence Address	Residence Address
City, State & Zip	City, State & Zip
Position or Occupation	Position or Occupation
Business Name	Business Name
Business Address	Business Address
City, State & Zip	City, State & Zip
Res. Phone Bus. Phone	Res. Phone Bus. Phone

SECTION 3 - STATEMENT OF FINANCIAL CONDITION AS OF _____ 19 __

ASSETS (Do not include Assets of doubtful value)	In Dollars (Omit Cents)	LIABILITIES	In Dollars (Omit cents)
Cash on hand and in banks		Notes payable to banks - secured	
U.S. Gov't. & Marketable Securities - see Schedule A		Notes payable to banks - unsecured	
Non-Marketable Securities - See Schedule B		Due to brokers	
Securities held by broker in margin accounts		Amounts payable to others - secured	
Restricted or control stocks		Amounts payable to others - unsecured	
Partial interest in Real Estate Equities - see Schedule C		Accounts and bills due	
		Unpaid income tax	
Real Estate Owned - see Schedule D		Other unpaid taxes and interest	
Loans Receivable		Real estate mortgages payable - see Schedule D	
Automobiles and other personal property			
Cash value-life insurance-see Schedule E		Other debts - itemize:	
Other assets - itemize:			
		TOTAL LIABILITIES	
		NET WORTH	
TOTAL ASSETS		TOTAL LIAB. AND NET WORTH	

SOURCES OF INCOME FOR YEAR ENDED _____ 19 _	PERSONAL INFORMATION
Salary, bonuses & commisions $	Do you have a will? _____ if so, name of executor.
Dividends	
Real estate income	Are you a partner or officer in any other venture? If so, describe.
Other income (Alimony, child support, or separate maintenance	
Income need not be revealed if you do not wish to have it	Are you obligated to pay alimony, child support or separate maintenance payments? If so, describe.
considered as a basis for repaying this obligation)	
	Are any assets pledged other than as described on schedules? If so, describe
TOTAL $	
CONTINGENT LIABILITIES	
Do you have any contingent liabilities? If so, describe.	Income tax settled through (date) _____
	Are you a defendant in any suits or legal actions?
As indorser, co maker or guarantor? $	Personal bank accounts carried at:
On leases or contracts? $	
Legal claims $	
Other special debt $	Have you ever been declared bankrupt? If so, describe.
Amount of contested income tax liens $	

P 1127

154

Figure 8-1. (Cont.)

SCHEDULE A - U.S. GOVERNMENTS & MARKETABLE SECURITIES

Number of Shares or Face Value (Bonds)	Description	In Name Of	Are These Pledged?	Market Value

SCHEDULE B - NON-MARKETABLE SECURITIES

Number of Shares	Description	In Name Of	Are These Pledged?	Source of Value	Value

SCHEDULE C - PARTIAL INTERESTS IN REAL ESTATE EQUITIES

Address & Type Of Property	Title In Name Of	% Of Ownership	Date Acquired	Cost	Market Value	Mortgage Maturity	Mortgage Amount

SCHEDULE D - REAL ESTATE OWNED

Address & Type Of Property	Title In Name Of	Date Acquired	Cost	Market Value	Mortgage Maturity	Mortgage Amount

SCHEDULE E - LIFE INSURANCE CARRIED, INCLUDING N.S.L.I. AND GROUP INSURANCE

Name Of Insurance Company	Owner Of Policy	Beneficiary	Face Amount	Policy Loans	Cash Surrender Value

SCHEDULE F - BANKS OR FINANCE COMPANIES WHERE CREDIT HAS BEEN OBTAINED

Name & Address Of Lender	Credit In The Name Of	Secured Or Unsecured?	Original Date	High Credit	Current Balance

The information contained in this statement is provided for the purpose of obtaining, or maintaining credit with you on behalf of the undersigned, or persons, firms or corporations in whose behalf the undersigned may either severally or jointly with others, execute a guaranty in your favor. Each undersigned understands that you are relying on the information provided herein (including the designation made as to ownership of property) in deciding to grant or continue credit. Each undersigned represents and warrants that the information provided is true and complete and that you may consider this statement as continuing to be true and correct until a written notice of a change is given to you by the undersigned. You are authorized to make all inquiries you deem necessary to verify the accuracy of the statements made herein, and to determine my/our creditworthiness. You are authorized to answer questions about your credit experience with me/us.

Signature (Individual) _____

S.S. No _____ Date of Birth _____

Signature (Other Party) _____

S S No _____ Date of Birth _____

personal balance sheet will not only be helpful when you apply for a loan, but will also assist you in monitoring your financial progress. By periodically preparing a personal balance sheet, say once per year, you will be able to gauge your progress by noting the increase in your net worth.

Be sure to refer to Figure 8-1, the sample personal balance sheet and supplementary financial data form that follows these explanations. This form is typical of those used by many lenders.

Assets should be realistically valued. Any overstatement of their actual market value will result in a corresponding overstatement of your net worth. The most difficult assets to value are real estate, including your home, automobiles, and other personal property. Many people tend to think their home is worth a lot more than it really is, so be careful. Also, remember that personal property such as furniture and clothing isn't worth very much if it has to be sold.

Liabilities include debt outstanding on your home mortgage, automobile, credit cards, and so on. Be sure to list all of your liabilities. Just like many people tend to overstate the value of their assets, others neglect to remember all of their liabilities.

Net worth is simply the difference between total assets and total liabilities. Some people, particularly those who are just starting out in their careers, have a negative net worth. In other words, their liabilities exceed their assets. Don't fret if you are in this boat—just make sure it is only a temporary condition. As you begin to save and pay off your debts, you will soon discover that you have a positive net worth—and it's all uphill from there!

THE INS AND OUTS OF CREDIT BUREAU REPORTS

Anyone who plans to take out a loan or mortgage or get a credit card needs to make sure that his or her credit rating is in good shape. A credit rating is a record of your historical performance in paying your bills, as well as a record of various factors such as your age and your type and duration of employment. (A professional or professor receives a boost to his or her rating, while a farmworker gets few "points" for his or her occupation.)

Potential creditors examine your rating in order to decide whether or not you pose a risk to them. Unfortunately, your credit rating—which you may never have seen—may for various reasons not fairly reflect the degree of conscientiousness with which you have conducted your financial affairs. Your always-prompt payment of rent, telephone and utility, medical and dental, and American Express bills will probably have no positive effect on your rating, while a mismanaged account with MasterCard or Visa or a national department store may damage your rating.

There's always a possibility that the credit bureau report on you may contain an error which will never be corrected unless you discover it. A bill on which you withheld payment because of a dispute over the services or goods purchased may be illegally included on your report. If you are a married woman, it is possible—despite the Equal Credit Opportunity Act— that your credit performance will be reported only under your husband's name, leaving you with no credit history.

How to Request a Report

All this proves how important it is that you periodically check your credit rating to make sure it contains no errors or distortions. Even if you have not yet had any difficulty in securing credit or a loan, you should obtain a copy of your report (for which a small fee is charged) in order to nip any problems in the bud. Your first step should be to ask your bank for the names of the major credit bureaus servicing your area or check the local Yellow Pages under "Credit Bureaus." Once you have located the bureau or bureaus that maintain a report on your credit, you should write them a letter requesting a copy, including your social security number, your addresses for the past 5 years, and a check for the fee.

How to Interpret a Report

A credit report, designed for computer processing rather than for reading by humans, is difficult to understand until you understand the codes and abbreviations it uses. A report includes a column called "Account Performance," containing the three categories "POS" (positive), "NEG" (negative), and "NON" (not evaluated). Every different account you now have or have had (with MasterCard or with a department store, for example) will be rated with one of these three codes. An account for which you have always paid your bills on time will, of course, be rated as "POS." If you have paid bills late or failed to pay any bills, the account may be labeled "NON" or "NEG." An occasional month-late payment will generally not affect an account's rating. The report will also include the date on which the account was opened; the type of charge account you have; the amount of charge authorized, and the current balance. If you have ever been late in paying an account, your report will include the amount you owed.

How to Correct Errors

If you find an error in your report, you must contact the creditor responsible for it, as the bureau will not correct it simply because you tell them it is inaccurate. Depending upon the type of error, your request to a company for correction of an error should say that you are writing under the provisions of the Fair Credit Reporting Act or the Fair Credit Billing Act.

Your Rights

Under the Fair Credit Reporting Act, a debtor has the following rights:

1. To learn the name and address of the consumer reporting agency whose report hurt him in connection with a credit or job application.
2. To discover upon request the nature and substance of all

information, except medical, that a credit agency has on file about him.

3. To know the sources of such information, except investigative sources.

4. To get the names of all people who have received reports on him within the previous 6 months, or within the previous year if the report was furnished for employment reasons.

5. To have all incomplete or incorrect information investigated, and if any information cannot be found or is found to be inaccurate, to have that information deleted from the file.

6. To have the credit bureau notify all agencies that the debtor names of the credit bureau's mistake, at no cost to himself.

7. To have the debtor's side of any controversy included in a creditor's report, if differences with that creditor cannot be resolved.

8. To have no information sent out that is more than 7 years old (10 years if the debtor has been bankrupt), with some exceptions if the individual is applying for an insurance policy or a job.

MORTGAGE LOAN ALTERNATIVES

Table 8-1 describes various types of mortgage loans, including advantages and drawbacks. If you are contemplating taking out or refinancing a mortgage, you should review the many alternatives so that you can choose the one that best meets your circumstances and needs.

Table 8-1. Various Types of Mortgage Loans

Technique	Description	Considerations
Fixed-rate mortgage	• Fixed Interest rate, usually long term. • Equal monthly payments of principal and interest until debt is paid in full.	• Offers stability and long-term tax advantages. • Limited availability. • Interest rates may be higher than other types of financing. • New fixed rates are rarely assumable.
Variable-rate mortgage	• Interest rate changes based on a financial index, resulting in possible changes in monthly payments, loan term, and/or principal. • May have rate or payment caps.	• Readily available. • Starting interest rate is slightly below market, but payments can increase sharply and frequently if index increases. • Payment caps prevent wide fluctuations in payments but may cause negative amortization. • Rate caps, while rare, limit amount total debt can expand.
Renegotiable rate mortgage (rollover)	• Interest rate and monthly payments are constant for several years; changes possible thereafter. • Long term.	• Less frequent changes in interest rate offer some stability.
Balloon mortgage	• Monthly payments based on fixed interest rate. • Usually short term.	• Offers low monthly payments but possibly no equity until loan is fully paid.

Table 8-1. Various Types of Mortgage Loans (*Cont.*)

Technique	Description	Considerations
Balloon mortgage	• Payments may cover interest only with principal due in full at term end.	• When due, loan must be paid off or refinanced. • Refinancing poses high risk if rates climb.
Graduated payment mortgage	• Lower monthly payments rise gradually (usually over 5 to 10 years), then level off for duration of term. • With variable interest rate, additional payment changes possible if index changes.	• Easier to qualify for. • Buyer's income must be able to keep pace with scheduled payment increases. • With a variable rate, payment increases beyond the graduated payments can result in additional negative amortization.
Shared-appreciation mortgage	• Below-market interest rate and lower monthly payments, in exchange for a share of profits when property is sold or on a specified date. • Many variations.	• If home appreciates greatly, total cost of loan jumps. • If home fails to appreciate, projected increase in value may still be due, requiring refinancing at possibly higher rates.
Assumable mortgage	• Buyer takes over seller's original, below-market rate mortgage.	• Lowers monthly payments. • May be prohibited if there is "due on sale" clause in original mortgage. • Not permitted on most new fixed-rate mortgages.

Table 8-1. Various Types of Mortgage Loans (*Cont.*)

Technique	Description	Considerations
Seller take-back	• Seller provides all or part of financing with a first or second mortgage.	• May offer below-market interest rate. • May have a balloon payment requiring full payment in a few years or refinancing at market rates, which could sharply increase debt.
Wrap-around mortgage	• Seller keeps original low-rate mortgage; buyer makes payments to seller, who forwards a portion to the lender holding original mortgage. • Offers lower effective interest rate on total transaction.	• Lender may call in old mortgage and require higher rate. • If buyer defaults, seller must take legal action to collect debt.
Growing equity mortgage (rapid payoff mortgage)	• Fixed interest rate but monthly payments may vary according to agreed-on schedule or index.	• Permits rapid payoff of debt because payment increases reduce principal. • Buyer's income must be able to keep up with payment increases.
Land contract	• Seller retains original mortgage. • No transfer of title until loan is fully paid. • Equal monthly payments based on below-market interest rate with unpaid principal due at loan end.	• May offer no equity until loan is fully paid. • Buyer has few protections if conflict arises during loan.
Buy-down	• Developer (or third party) provides an interest subsidy which lowers monthly payments during the first few years of the loan.	• Offers a break from higher payments during early years. • Enables buyer with lower income to qualify.

Table 8-1. Various Types of Mortgage Loans (*Cont.*)

Technique	Description	Considerations
Buy-down	• Can have fixed or variable interest rate.	• With variable-rate mortgage, payments may jump substantially at end of subsidy. • Developer may increase selling price.
Rent with option to buy	• Renter pays "option fee" for right to purchase property at specified time and agreed-on price. • Rent may or may not be applied to sales price.	• Enables renter to buy time to obtain down payment and decide whether to purchase. • Locks in price during inflationary times. • Failure to take option means loss of option fee and rental payments.
Reverse annuity mortgage (equity conversion)	• Borrower, who owns mortgage-free property and needs income, receives monthly payments from lender, using property as collateral.	• Can provide homeowners with needed cash. • At end of term, borrower must have money available to avoid selling property or refinancing.
Zero-rate and low-rate mortgage	• Appears to be completely or almost interest free. • Large down payment and one-time finance charge, then loan is repaid in fixed monthly payments over short term.	• Permits quick ownership. • May not lower total cost (because of possibly increased sales price). • Does not offer long-term tax deductions.

Source: Federal Trade Commission, *The Mortgage Money Guide.*

9

Education Planning

Meeting the cost of four years of college has always put some financial strain on the wallets of many middle- and even upper-income families. With college costs continuing to soar far in excess of the rate of inflation, paying for college is likely to become an even more difficult challenge in the years ahead.

The amount needed to pay educational costs indeed appears daunting. Universities estimate a 6.5 percent compound annual increase in tuition costs. This means that by the year 2000, the average public school's total cost will exceed $51,400. The cost of the average private school will top $92,000, with total costs of top-tier schools such as Harvard touching the $160,000 level.

Yet with careful planning, meeting a sizable portion of these expenses is possible for the average family. Indeed, widespread publicity about the rising cost of an education has resulted in an increased awareness among the general public of the need for a well-thought-out college savings plan.

The provisions of the 1986 Tax Reform Act will almost certainly influence decisions on how to invest college savings for many years to come. For children under age 14, unearned income under $500 is not taxed; unearned income between $500 and $1000 is taxed at the child's tax rate; and unearned income over $1000 is taxed at the parent's rate. If a child is age

14 or older, unearned income is taxed at the child's rate, regardless of the amount.

Many people are taking advantage of income-shifting devices such as trust accounts set up under the Uniform Gift to Minors Act (UGMA) or the Uniform Transfer to Minors Act (UTMA). These accounts are set up to allow a parent or other individual to give money to a child while keeping it in the hands of an adult custodian. The assets revert to the child when he or she reaches the age of majority. Other more individualized types of trusts are also available for wealthier investors. Before embarking upon any income-shifting programs, however, parents should weigh the tax-saving benefits against, in effect, giving the money to a child (who may opt not to go to college).

Certain parents whose income falls under specified, inflation-adjusted levels may also benefit from the tax-exempt status of interest on Series EE bonds if these bonds are used to pay for certain college expenses, such as tuition. This tax break is available for bonds purchased after December 31, 1989.

Of course, investment as well as tax considerations must be taken into account. If parents have a relatively long time to accumulate college savings, a portion of their portfolios should be earmarked for stock investments, which have historically performed better than other types of securities over the long term. On the other hand, as children approach college age, parents may want to consider moving a greater portion of their college funds into more liquid, less volatile investments.

Even the most diligent college savings plan, however, may need to be augmented by financial aid in the form of loans or scholarships, such as those detailed in this chapter. This aid is available from a number of sources, including the state or federal government, schools, or private foundations, and may be based on merit as well as financial need.

Because legislative initiatives as well as individual college aid programs change rapidly, it is important to keep abreast of them both before and during college. Although federal and state fiscal belt-tightening will almost certainly make obtaining financial aid more difficult except for the most needy of families, diligent parents and students will continue to benefit from uncovering the many sources of grants, scholarships, and loans that are available.

EDUCATION FUNDING ALTERNATIVES

A question facing many parents and students today is how to cope with the high cost of going to college. While colleges and most student aid sponsors expect parents or students to be the primary funding source, a host of financial aid alternatives, such as those summarized in this section, are also available. For more information on these alternatives, parents or students can contact their guidance counselor or the financial aid administrator of the school in which they are interested.

Grants and Scholarships

Grants are often awarded on the basis of need alone, while scholarships may be based on need as well as demonstrated athletic or academic achievement. Because federal funding has lagged the rise in college costs and the federal budget deficit has become increasingly burdensome, federal grants are becoming quite scarce and are usually available only to families of relatively limited resources. The largest federal need-based student aid program is the Pell Grant Program.

Scholarships from the National Honor Society and National Merit Scholarships are available to students with high grades who qualify. Foundations, religious organizations, and civic or trade groups may also offer sources of scholarship funding.

Individuals should keep in mind that scholarship awards will not necessarily lessen a family's financial burden. Because colleges and universities base their grant aid on financial need, the amount of such aid received may be reduced because of scholarship availability.

Some scholarships, most notably those offered by the Reserve Officers' Training Corps (ROTC) pay virtually all college costs. However, students must agree to serve in the military as commissioned officers after graduation.

Loans

As the cost of college rises, more students will find it necessary to turn to loans for financial assistance. Student loans, which usually bear low rates of interest compared to most other forms of commercial debt, are subsidized by the state or federal government, or by the colleges themselves. Common types of loans available from the federal government include PLUS loans for parents who want to borrow to help pay for a child's college education, and Supplemental Loans for Students (SLS) for student borrowers. Both carry variable interest rates which are lower than most commercial loans, but generally higher than some other types of student loans such as Stafford Student Loans.

Perkins Loans, available through college financial aid offices, have an interest rate of just 5 percent. In addition, some banks, credit unions, and other organizations have special loan programs that may carry more favorable rates than other consumer borrowing options.

If a student uses more than one student loan, he or she may be able to pay them all back using one repayment plan. A loan consolidation program, available from certain eligible lenders, is available to students who have loans totaling at least $5000. The repayment period is 10 to 25 years, depending on the amount to be repaid.

Both parents and students should review key loan provisions, including loan deferment, repayment terms, and refinancing and consolidation options. Of course, both students and their parents should be counseled on the responsible use of credit and how much they can realistically afford to borrow. Lenders should be kept informed of a change of address or any problems with loan repayment.

Also keep in mind that the interest on student loans will no longer be deductible beginning in 1991. For this reason, parents may want to consider using a home equity loan to help pay college costs, since interest on these loans generally remains fully deductible.

Work-Study Programs

Many students work part-time to help defray college expenses. The College Work-Study Program (CWS) provides jobs on and off campus for undergraduate and graduate students who need financial aid. Pay is at least minimum wage, but may be higher, depending on the type of work. Those whose jobs are on campus usually work for the school. Off-campus jobs generally involve work that is in the public interest, and the employer is usually a nonprofit organization or a local state or federal agency.

Many colleges have internship programs which offer part-time work for students, and at the same time, give them a chance to gain experience in their chosen fields. Others have instituted special programs which help match students with area employers.

Since a student's aid is determined largely by financial need, investment professionals should investigate ways in which an institution's estimate of the family's portion of the contribution may be reduced. First, it is important to avoid overstating the value of family assets, particularly the home. Second, if there is any possibility that a family might qualify for financial aid, parents should generally not transfer assets to their children because schools require a much higher percentage of assets in the student's name to be considered in meeting college expenses than they do assets in the parent's name. Finally, it is beneficial if a student can declare him- or herself financially independent, since the student's income and assets will generally be lower than that of his or her parents.

SUMMARY OF COLLEGE FINANCIAL AID PARAMETERS

To many parents, the college financial aid process is a big mystery. But, the more you know about it, the better chance you have for receiving assistance. Table 9-1 approximates the expected parents' annual contribution toward their children's education costs depending

Table 9–1. Expected Parents' Annual Contribution
Toward Children's Educational Costs

	Family size	Parents' pretax income					
		$30,000	$40,000	$50,000	$60,000	$70,000	$80,00
Assets							
	3	$ 2,768	$ 5,576	$ 8,444	$11,452	$14,460	$17,46
$40,000	4	2,119	4,487	7,474	10,482	13,490	16,49
	5	1,597	3,595	6,570	9,578	12,586	15,59
	6	1,056	2,767	5,534	8,542	11,550	14,55
	3	3,574	6,704	9,572	12,580	15,588	18,59
$60,000	4	2,792	5,615	8,602	11,610	14,618	17,62
	5	2,174	4,592	7,698	10,706	13,714	16,72
	6	1,584	3,573	6,662	9,670	12,678	15,68
	3	4,566	7,832	10,700	13,708	16,716	19,72
$80,000	4	3,607	6,743	9,730	12,738	15,746	18,75
	5	2,859	5,720	8,826	11,834	14,842	17,85
	6	2,160	4,565	7,790	10,798	13,806	16,81
	3	5,694	8,960	11,828	14,836	17,844	20,85
$100,000	4	4,605	7,871	10,858	13,866	16,874	19,88
	5	3,696	6,848	9,954	12,962	15,970	18,97
	6	2,840	5,693	8,918	11,926	14,934	17,94
	3	6,822	10,088	12,956	15,964	18,972	21,98
$120,000	4	5,733	8,999	11,986	14,994	18,002	21,01
	5	4,710	7,976	11,082	14,090	17,098	20,10
	6	3,673	6,821	10,046	13,054	16,062	19,07
	3	7,950	11,216	14,084	17,092	20,100	23,10
$140,000	4	6,861	10,127	13,114	16,122	19,130	22,13
	5	5,838	9,104	12,210	15,218	18,226	21,23
	6	4,683	7,949	11,174	14,182	17,190	20,19

Source: *Peterson's College Money Handbook 1990* and Peterson's College Database.

upon available assets (including equity in home) and pretax income. For example, the expected parents' annual contribution for a family of four with income of $50,000 and assets of $100,000 is $10,858. Increasingly limited resources for college grants and scholarships preclude many families from qualifying for any financial aid.

STRATEGIES FOR MEETING EDUCATION COSTS

The numerous details involved in planning for the financing of a child's education can be overwhelming. The multitude of financial sources available for college funding and the sophisticated financial aid analyses used by most educational institutions require thorough research by both parents and student. The strategies outlined below can assist you in organizing a precise and comprehensive approach to financing college costs.

Step 1: Begin a savings program for the long term.

Ideally, parents should begin planning and saving for their child's education as soon as the child is born. Depending upon the parents' current and expected financial circumstances, a variety of investment vehicles may be appropriate. For children under age 14, any funds in the child's name should usually be invested so as to avoid or minimize the Kiddie Tax. Moreover, the form in which the college-earmarked savings are held, for example, custodianship accounts or in trust, should be carefully evaluated.

Parents should also keep abreast of innovative programs designed to facilitate college savings. For example, one commercial college tuition plan offers a unique savings opportunity. The program, Collegeaire, is sponsored by the Student Financial Services in Atlanta. Collegeaire allows a family to begin saving several years prior to a student's matriculation for his future college cash need. The savings account, established at a bank designated by Student Financial Services, then becomes the down payment for a line of credit worth up to 2.5 times the value of the savings. Once the line of credit has been opened, the family has approximately 6 to 7 years to repay the debt, at which point the original savings plus interest is returned.

Step 2: Organize financing for the short term.

Often, parents delay planning for a child's college education and are left with little time to organize financing. Sometimes, however, even after maintaining a responsible and farsighted savings program, parents still find that the cost of college far exceeds the amount saved. Both situations necessitate a methodical examination of financing alternatives, including the steps outlined below.

Assess all family resources available for funding college costs. Resources may include the equity that has accumulated in the family home, gifts from grandparents, and inheritances.

Exhaustively review all possible sources of scholarships. A multitude of scholarship opportunities exist. Scholarships for academic, athletic, and leadership achievement are very common. Parents and students should also consider any military, company, union, trade, civic, religious, or ethnic affiliations they have that could lead to other sources of funds.

Parents and students must realize that scholarship awards do not necessarily lessen the family's financial burden. More often than not, outside awards ease the institution's burden by reducing the family's projected need and, therefore, the amount of grant aid the college or university must supply. On the other hand, some scholarships, such as ROTC scholarships, alleviate a family's burden by paying all of the educational expenses of a qualified candidate.

Investigate available loan and grant opportunities. Not all loans are created equal. Students displaying appropriate financial need may qualify for other federally sponsored low-interest loans aside from Stafford Student Loans (formerly GSLs). Programs such as the Pell Grant, College Work Study, and the Perkins Loan (formerly the NDSL) provide funds for the neediest candidates in the form of outright grants or very-low-interest loans. In addition, many states offer their own educational assistance programs aside from the GSL and PLUS programs. Finally, institutions themselves offer loans on favorable terms, although resources are usually limited. Candidates should apply for such loans as early as possible in order to be considered while funds last.

The PLUS Loan Program can provide another source of funds. These loans are incurred by the parents of a student. While their interest rates are relatively low compared to those of commercial loans, they usually run about 4 percent above those of GSLs. Also, repayment of the loan begins 2 months after it has been granted. Therefore, parents should assume a PLUS loan only if they do not qualify for a GSL.

Step 3: Reduce college costs.

The Family Contribution. Since a student's need, and therefore eligibility for aid, is directly determined by the family's expected ability to pay (family contribution), the client and planner should investigate ways in which an institution's estimates of this figure can be reduced.

First, in completing the section of a financial aid application concerning the family's asset evaluation, the client should try to avoid overstating the value of family assets, particularly the home.

Secondly, if there is any possibility that a family might qualify for financial aid, parents should generally not transfer assets to their children. Such a transfer might result in lower taxes, since the parents are usually in a higher tax bracket. However, the transfer could backfire because colleges and universities require a much higher percentage of assets in the student's name to be used to meet college expenses than they do assets in the parent's name.

Finally, if a student can declare him- or herself financially independent, he or she should do so. The federal government, state governments, and educational institutions cannot consider the parents' income and assets if a student is independent. The income and assets of the student are normally more limited if he is independent, and this usually results in a larger aid package. However, tests to establish independence vary from state to state and from institution to institution, and federal criteria for establishing independence may be more or less strict than those of the student's state and college. One must consider all criteria when using this approach.

The Aid Package. Students should attempt to obtain packages that consist of few loans and many grants and work-study awards. Since much student aid is distributed on a first-come, first-served basis, students must be prompt in applying to college and financial aid programs. Obtaining outside sources of funding through scholarships is also an ideal way to reduce a student's loan obligation.

Miscellaneous Costs. The student should never sacrifice quality of education for a few dollars' savings that can be repaid in the future when a fine education is in hand. However, frugal living while in school is one way that a student may significantly reduce the amount of money, and therefore the amount of aid, needed. A few ways of minimizing expenditures are listed below.

Books. Although it is easier to go to the campus bookstore and purchase new texts, shopping for used books can result in substantial savings.

Room and board. Many colleges provide a choice between on- or off-campus housing. Although it is often more convenient to live on-campus, a student may find room and board to be cheaper off-campus. Students and parents should investigate this possibility.

Insurance. Often, the parents' medical insurance policies will cover a child through college until graduation. The client should avoid enrolling his child in a college-sponsored program when, in fact, the student is already insured.

INVENTORY OF COLLEGE FUNDING SOURCES

Most families end up funding college education costs from a variety of sources, including grants, scholarships, fellowships, education loans, personal loans, and personal resources. The list below illustrates common sources of money used to pay for higher education.

Grants, scholarships, and fellowships:
Pell Grant
Supplemental Education Opportunity Grant
State financial assistance
School financial assistance
School scholarship/fellowship
Private aid programs
Military benefits or officer-training program
Social security benefits
Education loans:
Perkins Loan (formerly National Direct Student Loan)
Stafford Student Loan (formerly Guaranteed Student Loan)
Parent Loans for Undergraduate Students
School loan programs
State loan programs
Private education loan programs
Personal loans:
Home equity loan
Other secured financing
Unsecured loans
Personal resources allocable to funding education costs:
Income of parents
Income of student—school jobs
Income of student—summer jobs
Parents' savings/investments
Student's savings/investments
Gifts from relatives

10

Tax Planning

The Revenue Reconciliation Act of 1990 added even more complexity to the tax legislation that had been enacted almost every year during the 1980s. Middle- and lower-income tax payers will probably see no change in their income tax bill as a result of the 1990 legislation. High-income taxpayers, however, may see somewhat higher taxes beginning in 1991. For tax years beginning after 1990, income will be taxed at three rates: 15 percent, 28 percent, and 31 percent. The previous top rate was 33 percent. The maximum tax rate imposed on capital gains is 28 percent beginning in 1991. Previously, some taxpayers faced a 33 percent capital gains rate. Many experts expect that even more tax legislation will be enacted so as to address fiscal woes. States are facing financial difficulty as well and are increasingly turning to taxpayers to help overcome financial difficulties. These developments make it more crucial than ever for you to keep attuned to new developments and legislation, and to adjust your tax planning and investment strategies in order to minimize the potentially onerous effect of taxes.

The Tax Reform Act of 1986, considered by many to be the most significant tax reform measure in over 30 years, is already playing a significant role in virtually all areas of financial planning, and will no doubt continue to do so in the 1990s. This section outlines some steps that you may be able to take now to help minimize the impact of recent tax changes on the individual in the coming decade

Review Children's Investments. Unearned income of a child under age 14 which exceeds $1000 is subject to tax at the parents' marginal rate—the Kiddie Tax. The first $500 of the child's income is fully offset by standard or itemized deductions, while the second $500 is taxable at the child's rate. This provision may make it advisable for some parents to utilize investments that can help avoid the kiddie tax, such as U.S. savings bonds, municipal securities, or growth stocks which produce little or no dividend income.

Pare Down Personal Debt. After 1990, the deduction for interest on car loans, credit cards, and other forms of personal interest will be completely eliminated. This will give added incentive for many individuals to trim their debt burden.

Adjust Investments to Lower Tax Rates. Unless Congress passes legislation to change the tax rates, the two basic rates are 15 percent and 28 percent. For higher-income individuals, a 33 percent rate may apply to a portion of taxable income. If you are in the 33 percent bracket, you may be able to lower your taxes somewhat by judicious timing of the receipt of income and payment of tax-deductible expenses. While tax-exempt investments such as municipal bonds may still be attractive for some individuals, it will become increasingly important to compare taxable and tax-exempt yields to determine which will offer the better return after taxes. Also review possible ways to minimize state and local taxes, which are becoming a significant burden in a number of states.

Review Child Care Credit Provisions. The credit for child care expenses may only be claimed for children under age 13 (previously 15). Individuals must now list the provider's name, address, and social security number on the return in order to claim the credit. In addition, the dollar amount of expenses eligible for the credit must be reduced by any amounts that have been excluded from income under a salary reduction program or similar arrangement.

Check Your Exposure to the Alternative Minimum Tax (AMT). Many people who were not concerned with the AMT in previous years should review their exposure to it now. A combination of factors including the increase in the AMT rate from 21 percent to 24 percent effective 1991, the higher number of so-called preference items, and the phase-out of the exemption for high-income taxpayers, will make an increasing number of individuals subject to the tax. If you find that you may be subject to the AMT, you may be able to take some action to minimize its impact.

Maximize Your Investment in Retirement Savings Plans. Although the deduction for IRA contributions has been reduced or eliminated for many individuals, you should still save regularly for retirement through tax-deferred plans, since earnings can continue to accrue on a tax-deferred basis.

Future developments on the tax front are likely to add even more confusion to your tax planning. The federal government may reintroduce tax-advantaged savings incentives, reflecting an increasing concern about individual savings for the average American, particularly in the area of retirement. While upper-income taxpayers could eventually benefit from continued pressure for a reduction in the capital gains tax rate, they may also face higher taxes in other areas in order to help foot the bill for these savings programs. Also be on the lookout for new and potentially more attractive means of achieving tax deferral through products that are likely to be developed by the beleaguered financial services industry.

INCOME TAX DUE DATE CALENDAR

Table 10-1 lists the 1991 due dates for commonly used tax returns.

LISTING OF TAX-DEDUCTIBLE ITEMS

Figure 10-1 is an alphabetical list of commonly used tax-deductible items for individual taxpayers. Of course, more detailed explanations should be sought in considering any single item as a tax

Table 10–1. Calendar for 1991 Tax Returns

Date	
Jan. 15	Final installment of 1990 estimated tax by individuals due, unless income tax return is filed with final payment by January 31, 1991 (Form 1040-ES). Farmers and fishermen must pay estimated tax in full unless income tax return filed with payment by March 1, 1991 (Form 1040-ES).
Jan. 31	Individuals (other than farmers or fishermen) who owed, but did not pay, estimated tax on January 15 must pay tax in full to avoid penalty (Form 1040).
Mar. 1	Last day for farmers and fishermen who owed, but did not pay, estimated tax on January 15 to file 1990 calendar-year income tax return to avoid late payment penalty.
Apr. 15	Last date for filing income tax and self-employment tax returns of individuals for the calendar year 1990 and income tax returns of calendar-year decedents who died in 1990 (Form 1040, 1040A, or 1040EZ). Last day for calendar-year individuals to file application for automatic 4-month extension to file 1990 income tax return (Form 4868). Payment of first installment of 1991 estimated income taxes by calendar-year individuals (other than farmers and fishermen) (Form 1040ES).
June 17	Last day for nonresident alien individuals not subject to withholding, as well as U.S. citizens and resident aliens who were abroad on April 15, to file income tax return for calendar year 1990. Payment of second installment of 1991 estimated tax by individuals other than farmers and fishermen. Nonresident aliens who have no wages subject to U.S. withholding must make first payment.

Table 10–1. Calendar for 1991 Tax Returns (*Continued*)

Date	
July 31	Last day for pension, profit-sharing, stock-bonus or other employee benefit plans that use a calendar year to file for calendar year 1990 (Form 5500, Form 5500EZ, Form 5500-C or Form 5500-R).
Aug. 15	Last day for filing 1990 income tax return by calendar-year individuals who obtained an automatic 4-month filing extension.
Sept. 16	Payment of third installment of 1991 estimated tax by individuals other than farmers and fishermen.

Figure 10–1. Commonly Used Tax-Deductible Items

Accelerated cost recovery on business equipment
Accounting and auditing expenses paid for keeping your business books and accounts and preparation of tax returns
Alimony, if it meets certain tax tests
Alterations and repairs on business or income-producing property
Amortization of bond premiums, with some exceptions
Appraisal costs for tax and business purposes
Attorney fees related to:
  Your job or business
  Estate planning
  Libel suits, business reputation
  Obtaining taxable alimony
  Tax advice
Automobile expenses incurred during business trips, job-related moving, trips for charitable organizations, and trips for medical care

Back pay, expenses to collect
Bad debts
Bank deposit loss by failure of bank
Burglary losses
Business expense and losses

Capital asset loss
Capital loss carryover
Casualty losses

Figure 10–1. Commonly Used Tax-Deductible Items (*Continued*)

Charitable contributions paid to religious, charitable, scientific, literary, educational, and other organizations (including family foundations) which qualify under tax law

Christmas presents and other holiday gifts paid to employees, customers or prospects up to $25 per person

Clothing—uniforms, costumes, and working clothes—cost, laundering, and cleaning if required by job and not adaptable to regular wear

Collection of income and business debts, expenses connected with

Commissions paid to agents (press agents, literary agents, booking agents, etc.)

Commissions paid in connection with rented property

Condominium owners' interest and realty taxes

Contributions to IRAs, subject to limits and restrictions

Contributions to disability insurance funds in certain states

Convention expenses

Custodian fees paid to banks or investment counsel, fees incurred in the management of your investments where they produce taxable income

Damage to property held for personal use, as a result of a casualty such as a fire and storm

Debts, uncollectible

Depreciation on business or income-producing property

Directors' expenses

Disability insurance deductions in certain states

Disaster losses

Donations to qualified charities

Drugs and medicines, subject to limitations

Dues to:

Clubs and associations which employer requires you to belong to in order to hold your job

Membership in organized labor unions

Professional societies

Trade associations

Education—tuition fees, books, traveling expenses, etc.—if required to keep your employment or professional standards; carrying charges on installment payments of tuition

Employment agency fees

Entertainment of customers

Estate tax paid on income reported by heirs

Figure 10–1. Commonly Used Tax-Deductible Items (*Continued*)

Expenses paid for the production and collection of income, and expenses to maintain, manage, and conserve property held for investment

Farm expenses, if operated for profit
Fees paid:
  To bank acting as dividend agent in automatic dividend reinvestment plan
  To secure employment, within limits of
  To secure readmission to organized labor union
  For passports on a business trip
Finance charges
Fire insurance premiums (on business or income-producing property)
Flood losses
Food and drinks (for business entertainment)
Forced sales, losses
Foreign taxes paid

Gambling losses (only to extent of gambling gains)
Gifts for business purposes up to certain limits

Home office expenses, subject to limitations
Household or personal assets stolen or destroyed by fire or other casualty
Housing costs while working abroad if self-employed or costs not employer-financed
Hurricane losses

Income tax return, fees for preparation
Income tax, state or city
Individual retirement account (IRA) contributions, subject to limits
Information, cost of obtaining, including cost of standard services for business, tax, or investment use
Injury benefits to employees (not compensated by insurance)
Interest paid or imputed (subject to limits)
Interest, prepaid, must be allocated over life of loan
Interest, although not stated, on tuition installment plans or personal property purchases
Interest paid in form of dividends from stock pledged for your loan
Investment counsel fees
Involuntary conversion, loss

Figure 10–1. Commonly Used Tax-Deductible Items (*Continued*)

Job expenses
Joint venture losses

Keogh plan contributions

Labor union dues
Library expenses used only for business or profession
License and regulatory fees for business
Loans, uncollectible
Lodging on trips to obtain medical care
Losses (except to the extent covered by insurance) arising from:
    Abandoned property
    Abandonment of worthless business machinery
    Bad debts
    Bonds sold or exchanged
    Bonds, worthless
    Business operations
    Capital assets, sale of
    Casualties such as fire, theft, storm, shipwreck
    Deposits in closed banks
    Endorser or guarantor compelled to pay for principal when transaction was entered into for profit
    Forced sales
    Foreclosures
    Forfeitures
    Futures account closed by broker
    Gambling to the extent of gains
    Goodwill, sale or abandonment
    Investments, worthless
    Joint ventures, syndicates, pools, etc., participation in
    Loans not repaid
    Mortgaged property sold (business or investment)
    Net operating loss carried over and back
    Obsolescence of business asset
    Partnership operations
    Profit-seeking transactions
    Sale of capital assets
    Sale of inherited residence
    Sales and exchanges of property
    Securities, sale or exchange
    Securities, worthless
    Seizures by the government
    Short sales

Figure 10–1. Commonly Used Tax-Deductible Items (*Continued*)

Losses (*Cont.*)
   Stocks, worthless
   Transactions entered into for profit, even though not connected
     with a business
   Worthless securities

Magazines, technical or in waiting room of professional
Malpractice, expenses of professional in defense of suit for
Materials and supplies used in your business
Meals and lodging
Medical expenses, subject to limitations
Membership dues
Mortgage foreclosure losses
Moving expense of business property

National Defense Education Act grants under Title IV to graduate
   students preparing for college teaching careers

Ordinary and necessary business expenses

Penalty paid for prepaying mortgage payments
Periodicals used in your business or profession
Plane fare for business trips
Points paid for loan under certain circumstances
Preparation of tax returns, cost of
Professional dues
Professional's expenses, including books and equipment of short life
Property damage
Property taxes

Real estate, expenses of rental or investment property
Real estate sales losses
Real estate taxes
Religious organizations, contributions to
Rents, including payments for the use of safe deposit box used for
   business or investment purposes
Repairs of business or income-producing property
Repairs to a residence or property which you can rent to others

Safe deposit box costs for records used in your business or for
   income-producing or investment property
Salespersons' expenses
Securities as charitable contributions
Security transactions, cost of

Figure 10–1. Commonly Used Tax-Deductible Items (*Continued*)

Short sales losses

Short selling costs

Simplified employee pension plan contributions

State income and other taxes

Storm damage

Subscriptions to professional or trade journals

Supplies used in profession or business

Support of a student, unrelated to you, in your home, up to $50 per
month

Tax preparation fees

Taxes paid (property, state income)

Teachers' expenses of attending summer school

Technical magazines used in your business

Tenants—payment of real estate taxes, interest or other items for your
landlord (if property is leased for income-producing purposes)

Theft losses

Trade associations' dues

Traveling and entertaining expenses

Traveling between two jobs

Traveling to professional convention, subject to limits

Traveling to get medical care

Traveling to look after income-producing property

Trustees' expenses, certain commissions

Uncollectible debts

Uniforms, required for your job and not generally adaptable for
ordinary wear

Union assessments

Union dues

Unreimbursed volunteer expenses for charity

Unstated interest

Upkeep, care and maintenance of real estate held for investment or
rented to others

Worthless bonds or stocks

Note: The above deductions are subject to the 2% limit even if they are
passed through to the taxpayer from certain entities (for example, partnerships, S corporations, and certain mutual funds).

deduction. Note that many of the items listed are deductible only under certain circumstances. This information, as well as more detailed checklists, are available in many of the popular tax preparation guides as well as in IRS publications. Figure 10-2 is a compilation of miscellaneous deductions subject to the 2 percent of adjusted gross income limit, and Figure 10-3 lists nondeductible expenses.

Figure 10–2. Miscellaneous Deductions Subject to the 2%
of Adjusted Gross Income Limit

Certain appraisal fees
Certain legal fees
Clerical help and office rent in caring for investments
Custodial fees in connection with property held for producing income
Dues to professional societies
Employment-related education
Fees to collect interest and dividends
Hobby expenses, but generally not more than hobby income
Investment counsel fees
Laboratory breakage fees
Liquidated damages paid to former employer for breach of employment contract
Looking for a new job
Malpractice insurance premiums
Medical examinations required by employer
Occupational taxes paid by an employee
Part of home used regularly and exclusively in work
Research expenses of a college professor
Safe deposit box rental
Small tools and supplies used in taxpayer's work
Subscriptions to professional journals and trade magazines related to taxpayer's work
Tax preparation fees
Union dues and expenses
Work clothes and uniforms

Note: The above deductions are subject to the 2% limit even if they are passed through to the taxpayer from certain entities (for example, partnerships, S corporations, and certain mutual funds).

Figure 10–2. Miscellaneous Deductions Subject to the 2%
of Adjusted Gross Income Limit (*Continued*)

Gambling losses to the extent of gambling winnings
Federal estate tax on income in respect of a decedent
Amortizable bond premium on bonds purchased before October 23, 1986
Deduction for repayment of substantial amounts under a claim of right
Unrecovered investment in pension
Impairment-related work expenses of a handicapped individual

Figure 10–3. Nondeductible Expenses

Adoption expenses for children with special needs
Burial or funeral expenses
Campaign expenses
Capital expenses
Certain fees and licenses
Commuting expenses
Fines and penalties, such as parking tickets
Gifts to influence legislation
Health spa expenses
Hobby losses
Home repairs, insurance, and rent
Illegal bribes and kickbacks
Life insurance
Losses from the sale of taxpayer's home, furniture, personal car, etc.
Lost or misplaced cash or property
Lunches and meals while working late
Personal legal expenses
Personal, living, or family expenses
Political contributions
Professional accreditation fees
Relief fund contributions for fellow employee
Self-improvement expenses
Stockholders' meeting, expenses of attending
Tax-exempt income expenses
Voluntary unemployment benefit fund contributions

FEDERAL INCOME TAX RATES

Table 10-2 presents federal income tax rates for taxable years beginning 1990. Note that the income tax brackets are adjusted for inflation each year.

DIRECTORY OF FEDERAL INCOME TAX PUBLICATIONS

Table 10-3 lists many publications, available at no cost from the Internal Revenue Service, that can be very helpful in your tax planning and tax return preparation. They may be ordered by calling the IRS. Check your local phone listings.

FEDERAL TAX RETURN FORMS

Table 10-4 is a listing of the more commonly used federal income tax forms. They may be obtained by calling the Internal Revenue Service. Check your local phone listings.

Table 10–2. Federal Income Tax Rates for Taxable Year Beginning in 1990

Single Individuals (Other Than Surviving Spouses and Heads of Households)

	Taxable income	Tax on lower amount	Rate on excess
Not over	$ 19,450	15%	—
	19,450	$ 2,917.50	28%
	47,050	10,645.50	33%
	97,620	27,333.60	See below

For taxable income over $97,620, the tax is $27,333.60 plus 28% of the amount over $97,620 plus an adjustment (for phaseout of personal exemptions) computed as follows:
1. Subtract $97,620 from taxable income.
2. Multiply $11,480 by the number of personal exemptions.
3. Multiply the lesser of (1) or (2) by 5%.

Table 10–2. Federal Income Tax Rates for Taxable Year
Beginning in 1990 (*Continued*)

Married Individuals Filing Separate Returns:

	Taxable income	Tax on lower amount	Rate on excess
Not over	$ 16,225	15%	—
	16,225	$ 2,433.75	28%
	39,200	8,866.75	33%
	123,570	36,708.85	See below

For table income over $123,570, the tax is $36,708.85 plus 28% of the amount over $123,570 plus an adjustment (for phaseout of personal exemptions) computed as follows:
1. Subtract $123,570 from taxable income.
2. Multiply $11,480 by the number of personal exemptions.
3. Multiply the lesser of (1) or (2) by 5%.

Married Individuals Filing Joint Returns and Surviving Spouses:

	Taxable income	Tax on lower amount	Rate on excess
Not over	$ 32,450	15%	—
	32,450	$ 4,867.50	28%
	78,400	17,733.50	33%
	162,770	45,575.60	See below

For taxable income over $162,770, the tax is $45,575.60 plus 28% of the amount over $162,770 plus an adjustment (for phaseout of personal exemptions) computed as follows:
1. Subtract $162,770 from taxable income.
2. Multiply $11,480 by the number of personal exemptions.
3. Multiply the lesser of (1) or (2) by 5%.

Heads of Households

	Taxable income	Tax on lower amount	Rate on excess
Not over	$ 26,050	15%	—
	26,050	$ 3,907.50	28%
	67,200	15,429.50	33%
	134,930	37,780.40	See below

For taxable income over $134,930, the tax is $37,780.40 plus 28% of the amount over $134,930 plus an adjustment (for phaseout of personal exemptions) computed as follows:
1. Subtract $134,930 from taxable income.
2. Multiply $11,480 by the number of personal exemptions.
3. Multiply the lesser of (1) or (2) by 5%.

Table 10–3. Internal Revenue Service Publications

Publication Number	Title
1	Your Rights as a Taxpayer
15	Circular E, Employer's Tax Guide
17	Your Federal Income Tax
51	Circular A, Agricultural Employer's Tax Guide
54	Tax Guide for U.S. Citizens and Resident Aliens Abroad
80	Circular SS, Federal Tax Guide for Employers in the Virgin Islands, Guam, and American Samoa
179	Federal Tax Guide for Employers in Puerto Rico (in Spanish)
225	Farmer's Tax Guide
334	Tax Guide for Small Businesses
349	Federal Highway Use Tax on Heavy Vehicles
378	Fuel Tax Credits and Refunds
448	Federal Estate and Gift Taxes
463	Travel, Entertainment, and Gift Expenses
501	Exemptions, Standard Deduction, and Filing Information
502	Medical and Dental Expenses
503	Child and Dependent Care Credit
504	Tax Information for Divorced or Separated Individuals
505	Tax Withholding and Estimated Tax
508	Educational Expenses
509	Tax Calendars
510	Excise Taxes
513	Tax Information for Visitors to the United States
514	Foreign Tax Credit for Individuals
515	Withholding of Tax on Nonresident Aliens and Foreign Corporations
516	Tax Information for U.S. Government Civilian Employees Stationed Abroad
517	Social Security for Members of the Clergy and Religious Workers
519	U.S. Tax Guide for Aliens
520	Scholarships and Fellowships
521	Moving Expenses
523	Tax Information on Selling Your Home
524	Credit for the Elderly or the Disabled
525	Taxable and Nontaxable Income
526	Charitable Contributions
527	Residential Rental Property
529	Miscellaneous Deductions
530	Tax Information for Homeowners (Including Owners of Condominiums and Cooperative Apartments)
531	Reporting Income From Tips

Table 10–3. Internal Revenue Service Publications (*Continued*)

Publication Number	Title
533	Self-Employment Tax
534	Depreciation
535	Business Expenses
536	Net Operating Losses
537	Installment Sales
538	Accounting Periods and Methods
539	Employment Taxes
541	Tax Information on Partnerships
542	Tax Information on Corporations
544	Sales and Other Dispositions of Assets
545	Interest Expense
547	Nonbusiness Disasters, Casualties, and Thefts
548	Deduction for Bad Debts
549	Condemnations and Business Casualties and Thefts
550	Investment Income and Expenses
551	Basis of Assets
552	Recordkeeping for Individuals and a List of Tax Publications
554	Tax Information for Older Americans
555	Community Property and the Federal Income Tax
556	Examination of Returns, Appeal Rights, and Claims for Refund (also available in Spanish; Publication 556S)
557	Tax-Exempt Status for Your Organization
559	Tax Information for Survivors, Executors, and Administrators
560	Self-Employed Retirement Plans
561	Determining the Value of Donated Property
564	Mutual Fund Distributions
570	Tax Guide for Individuals in U.S. Possessions
571	Tax-Sheltered Annuity Programs for Employees of Public Schools and Certain Tax-Exempt Organizations
572	General Business Credit
575	Pension and Annuity Income
579S	How to Prepare the Federal Income Tax Return (in Spanish)
583	Information for Business Taxpayers
584	Nonbusiness Disaster, Casualty, and Theft Loss Workbook
586A	The Collection Process (Income Tax Accounts) (also available in Spanish; Publication 586S)
587	Business Use of Your Home
588	Tax Information for Homeowners Associations
589	Tax Information on S Corporations

Table 10–3. Internal Revenue Service Publications (*Continued*)

Publication Number	Title
590	Individual Retirement Arrangements (IRAs)
593	Tax Highlights for U.S. Citizens and Residents Going Abroad
594	The Collection Process (Employment Tax Accounts)
595	Tax Guide for Commercial Fishermen
596	Earned Income Credit
597	Information on the United States-Canada Income Tax Treaty
598	Tax on Unrelated Business Income of Exempt Organizations
686	Certification for Reduced Tax Rates in Tax Treaty Countries
721	Comprehensive Tax Guide to U.S. Civil Service Retirement Benefits
794	Favorable Determination Letter
850	English-Speaking Glossary of Words and Phrases Used in Publications Issued by the Internal Revenue Service
901	U.S. Tax Treaties
904	Interrelated Computations for Estate and Gift Taxes
907	Tax Information for Handicapped and Disabled Individuals
908	Bankruptcy and Other Debt Cancellation
909	Alternative Minimum Tax for Individuals
910	Guide to Free Tax Services
911	Tax Information for Direct Sellers
915	Social Security Benefits and Equivalent Railroad Retirement Benefits
916	Information Returns
918	Business Use of a Car
919	Is My Withholding Correct?
924	Reporting of Real Estate Transactions to IRS
925	Passive Activity and At-Risk Rules
926	Employment Taxes for Household Employers
927	Tax Obligations of Legalized Aliens
929	Tax Rules for Children and Dependents
934	Supplemental Medicare Premium
936	Limits on Home Mortgage Interest Deduction
1004	Identification Numbers Under ERISA
1045	Information for Tax Practitioners
1048	Filing Requirements for Employee Benefit Plans
1212	List of Original Issue Discount Instruments
1244	Employee's Daily Record of Tips (Form 4070A) and Employee's Report of Tips to Employer (Form 4070)

Table 10–4. Common Federal Income Tax Forms

706	United States Estate Tax Return
709	United States Gift Tax Return
709A	U.S. Short Form Gift Tax Return
1040	U.S. Individual Income Tax Return
	☐ Schedule A—Itemized Deductions
	☐ Schedule B—Interest and Dividend Income
	☐ Schedule C—Profit (Loss) From Business or Profession (Sole Proprietorship)
	☐ Schedule D—Capital Gains and Losses
	☐ Schedule E—Supplemental Income Schedule
	☐ Schedule F—Farm Income and Expenses
	☐ Schedule R—Credit for the Elderly and the Permanently and Totally Disabled
	☐ Schedule SE—Computation of Social Security Self-Employment Tax
1040A	U.S. Individual Income Tax Return (Short Form)
1040ES	Payment-Voucher for Estimated Tax by Individuals
1040EZ	U.S. Income Tax Return (Short Form for Single Filers With No Dependents)
1040X	Amended U.S. Individual Income Tax Return
1041	U.S. Fiduciary Income Tax Return
	☐ Schedule D—Capital Gains and Losses
	☐ Schedule J—Trust Allocation of an Accumulation Distribution
	☐ Schedule K-1—Beneficiary's Shares of Income, Deductions, Credits, etc.
1065	U.S. Partnership Return of Income
	☐ Schedule D—Capital Gains and Losses
	☐ Schedule K—Partner's Share of Income, Credits, Deductions, etc. [*required only when there are more than 10 schedules*]
	☐ Schedule K-1—Partners' Shares of Income, Credits, Deductions, etc. [*filed with Form 1065*]
1096	Annual Summary and Transmittal of Certain Information Returns
1098	Mortgage Interest Statement
1099-B	Statement for Recipients of Proceeds From Broker and Barter Exchange Transactions
1099-DIV	Statement for Recipients of Dividends and Distributions
1099-G	Statement for Recipients of Certain Government Payments
1099INT	Statement for Recipients of Interest Income
1099MISC	Statement for Recipients of Miscellaneous Income
1099OID	Statement for Recipients of Original Issue Discount

Table 10–4. Common Federal Income Tax Forms (*Continued*)

1099R	Statement for Recipients of Total Distributions From Profit-Sharing, Retirement Plans, Individual Retirement Arrangements, Insurance Contracts, etc.
1099S	Statement for Recipients of Proceeds From Real Estate Transactions
1116	Computation of Foreign Tax Credit ☐ Schedule A—Schedule of Foreign Taxable Income and Foreign Taxes Paid or Accrued
1120S	Income Tax Return, S Corporation ☐ Schedule D—Capital Gains and Losses ☐ Schedule K-1—Shareholder's Share of Undistributed Taxable Income, etc.
1310	Statement of Person Claiming Refund Due to a Deceased Taxpayer
2106	Employee Business Expenses
2119	Sale or Exchange of Personal Residence
2120	Multiple Support Declaration
2210	Underpayment of Estimated Tax by Individuals
2439	Notice to Shareholder of Undistributed Long-Term Capital Gains
2440	Disability Income Exclusion
2441	Credit for Child Care and Dependent Care Expenses
2688	Application for Extension of Time to File
2848	Power of Attorney and Declaration of Representative
3468	Computation of Investment Credit
3559	Alimony or Separate Maintenance Statement
3903	Moving Expenses Adjustment
4136	Computation of Credit for Federal Tax on Gasoline, Special Fuels, and Lubricating Oils
4137	Computation of Social Security Tax on Unreported Tax Income
4469	Computation of Excess Medicare Tax Credit
4562	Depreciation
4684	Casualties and Thefts
4768	Application for Extension of Time to File U.S. Estate Tax Return and/or Pay Estate Tax
4782	Employee Moving Expense Information
4797	Supplemental Schedule of Gains and Losses
4835	Farm Rental Income and Expenses
4868	Automatic Extension to File
4952	Investment Interest Expense Deduction
4970	Tax on Accumulation Distribution of Trusts
4972	Special Ten-Year Averaging Method

Table 10–4. Common Federal Income Tax Forms (*Continued*)

5329	Return for Individual Retirement Arrangement Taxes
5498	Individual Retirement Arrangement Information
5544	Multiple Recipient Special Ten-Year Averaging
5695	Residential Energy Credits
5884	Job Credit (and WIN Credit Carry-over)
6251	Alternative Minimum Tax Computation
6252	Computations of Installment Sale Income
6781	Gains and Losses From Regulated Futures Contracts and Straddles
8027	Employer's Annual Information Return of Tip Income and Allocated Tips
8283	Noncash Charitable Contributions
8332	Release of Claim to Exemption for Child of Divorced or Separated Parents
8582	Passive Activity Loss Limitations
8598	Home Mortgage Interest
8606	Nondeductible IRA Contributions, IRA Basis, and Nontaxable IRA Distributions
8615	Computation of Tax for Children Under Age 14 Who Have Investment Income of More than $1,000
8801	Credit for Prior Year Minimum Tax
SSA-1099	Social Security Benefit Statement
W-2	Wage and Tax Statement
W-2c	Statement of Corrected Income and Tax Amounts
W-2P	Statement for Recipients of Annuities, Pensions, Retired Pay, or IRA Payments
W-3	Transmittal of Income and Tax Amounts
W-4	Employee's Withholding Allowance Certificate
W-4P	Withholding Certificate for Pension or Annuity Payments
W-4S	Request for Federal Income Tax Withholding From Sick Pay
W-5	Earned Income Credit Advance Payment Certificate
W-9	Payer's Request for Taxpayer Identification Number

WHERE TO FILE FEDERAL INCOME TAX RETURNS

Table 10-5 indicates the mailing addresses for filing income tax returns. The IRS requests that, if an addressed envelope came with the return, the taxpayer should use it. A fiduciary of an estate or trust should generally file form 1041 with the Internal Revenue Service Center for the state in which the fiduciary resides or has his or her

Table 10–5. Mailing Addresses for Filing Income Tax Returns

If you are located in:	Use this address:
Florida, Georgia, South Carolina	Atlanta, GA 39901
New Jersey, New York (New York City and counties of Nassau, Rockland, Suffolk, and Westchester)	Holtsville, NY 00501
Connecticut, Maine, Massachusetts, New Hampshire, New York (all other counties), Rhode Island, Vermont	Andover, MA 05501
Illinois, Iowa, Minnesota, Missouri, Wisconsin	Kansas City, MO 64999
Delaware, District of Columbia, Maryland, Pennsylvania, Virginia	Philadelphia, PA 19255
Indiana, Kentucky, Michigan, Ohio, West Virginia	Cincinnati, OH 45999
Kansas, New Mexico, Oklahoma, Texas	Austin, TX 73301
Alaska, Arizona, California (counties of Alpine, Amador, Butte, Calaveras, Colusa, Contra Costa, Del Norte, El Dorado, Glenn, Humboldt, Lake, Lassen, Marin, Mendocino, Modoc, Napa, Nevada, Placer Plumas, Sacramento, San Joaquin, Shasta, Sierra, Siskiyou, Solano, Sonoma, Sutter, Tehama, Trinity, Yolo and Yuba), Colorado, Idaho, Montana, Nebraska, Nevada, North Dakota, Oregon, South Dakota, Utah, Washington, Wyoming	Ogden, UT 84201
California (all other counties), Hawaii	Fresno, CA 93888
Alabama, Arkansas, Louisiana, Mississippi, North Carolina, Tennessee	Memphis, TN 37501
American Samoa	Philadelphia, PA 19255

Table 10–5. Mailing Addresses for Filing Income Tax Returns
(*Continued*)

Guam	Commissioner of Taxes Agana, GU 96910

Puerto Rico (or if excluding
  income under section 933)
Virgin Islands:
  Nonpermanent residents
	Philadelphia, PA 19255

Virgin Islands Permanent residents	V.I. Bureau of Internal Revenue Lockharts Garden No. 1A Charlotte Amalie, St. Thomas, VI 00802

Foreign country:
  U.S. citizens and those filing
  form 2555 or Form 4563, even
  if you have an A.P.O. or
  F.P.O. address
	Philadelphia, PA 19255

A.P.O. or F.P.O. address of:	Miami—Atlanta, GA 39901 New York—Holtsville, NY 00501 San Francisco—Fresno, CA 93888 Seattle—Ogden, UT 84201

*principal place of business. If you moved during the year, the return
should be mailed to the Internal Revenue Service Center for the place
where you live. No street address is needed.*

HOW TO DETERMINE TAX BASIS OF SECURITIES

*One of the most vexing problems that investors must confront
when filling out their tax returns is determining the tax basis of
investments that they have sold. Good record keeping can avoid many
of these problems. This section will help you sort out the confusion
surrounding tax basis.*

The cost basis of stocks or bonds is the purchase price plus
the various costs of purchase, such as commissions and transfer fees. If you bought your stocks or bonds in another way, the
basis is determined by the fair market value or the donor's

adjusted basis. After you make the purchase, the basis may be adjusted for certain situations; for example, if you receive additional shares from nontaxable dividends or stock splits, you have to reduce the basis of the original stock. You must also reduce your basis when you receive nontaxable distributions, because these are a return of capital. There are varying ways of determining the bases of your stocks and bonds, depending on how you acquired them. Automatic investment programs, dividend reinvestment plans, and stock rights are different ways to acquire stocks and bonds, each of which requires special record keeping.

Stock Splits

Say that in 1988 you purchased 100 shares of a stock called XYZ at $10 dollars per share, thus paying a total amount of $1000 dollars. Then, the following year, you purchased 100 more shares of the same stock at a price of $16 a share, paying $1600 dollars in total. In 1990, a 2 for 1 stock split is declared. You now own 200 shares of XYZ with a basis of $5 dollars per share and 200 shares with a basis of $8 dollars per share.

Selecting Securities to be Sold

If your stock portfolio contains various lots of the same stock acquired at different times and at different costs, you must exercise caution when you consider selling a portion of these shares. For example, assume you own five different lots of stock XXX that you acquired at different times which range in cost from $50 to $100 dollars per share. If the stock is currently selling for $70 dollars per share and you sell a lot with a basis of $50 dollars per share, you recognize a gain. But, if you sell a lot with a basis of $100 dollars per share, you sustain a loss. This situation could end up being more complicated if the the company has paid stock dividends or if it has split its stock one or more times. The best way to simplify this situation is to take the shares you receive as a result of a stock dividend or a stock split and combine them with those they originated from. In other words, have your broker make all related stock certificates into one certificate. Thus, each block of stock with a distinguishable cost basis is separately maintained. This simplifies your record keeping and keeps your portfolio more organized as well.

It is considered an adequate identification if you deliver certificates for securities that you purchased on a certain date or for a specific price to your broker or agent. If you left the certificates with your broker or agent, or if you have one certificate for securities which you bought in different lots at different times, then you have made an adequate identification if you inform the broker of the security to be sold or transferred.

FIFO Basis

It may be difficult for you to identify the securities that you sell if you buy and sell varying quantities at different times. If you cannot identify the basis of a particular block of securities that you sold, the basis is figured by the first-in/first-out (FIFO) method. This means that the first securities that you acquired are the first sold.

Incentive Stock Options

If you acquired the shares you are selling through an Incentive Stock Option (ISO), with previously owned employer shares, special rules will apply in determining the basis of those shares. For instance, what is known as a disqualifying disposition is the sale or transfer of stock acquired through the exercise of an Incentive Stock Option within one year of the option's exercise date. If your sale constitutes a disqualifying disposition of the ISO shares, the lowest basis shares are considered to be sold first, regardless of your effort to identify and sell specific shares.

Charitable Contributions of Appreciated Securities

Charitable contributions of blocks of appreciated stocks with the lowest tax basis are generally to your advantage if you are not subject to the alternative minimum tax in the year you make the contribution. At the time you make the contribution, be sure to be clear in designating which shares are to be contributed, and tell your broker or agent the date you purchased the shares you are now donating.

Current tax rules treat the untaxed appreciation deducted as a charitable contribution as a preference item for the purpose of calculating the alternative minimum tax. Depending upon your tax situation, the effect of this may be to limit your deduction to your tax basis. Thus, prior to your decision of whether or not to donate appreciated property, you should carefully consider the effect of a donation on your regular tax and the AMT.

Other Matters Pertaining to Tax Basis

When you purchase a taxable bond at a premium and choose to amortize the premium paid, you must reduce the basis of the bond by the amount of the amortized premium (despite the fact that you cannot take a deduction for the premium on tax-exempt bonds).

In an original issue discount (OID) bond instrument, you must increase your basis by the amount of OID that you included in income for that instrument. OID on tax-exempt bonds is not taxable. However, there are special rules for determining basis on tax-exempt original issue discount bonds issued after September 3rd, 1982 and acquired after March 1, 1984.

SURVIVING A TAX AUDIT

Maybe you've filled out your tax return strictly by the book. Maybe not. Whatever the reason, you've received that dreaded notice in the mail that your tax return has been selected by the IRS for further examination.

Don't panic. Most IRS examinations are routine, and in many cases you will not have to pay additional tax—provided you know a little about the audit game and how it is played.

The audit process begins when you send your tax return to 1 of 10 IRS Service Centers, where it is reviewed for routine mistakes or omissions. The income you've reported is also matched against the information sent to the IRS by employers, banks, companies who have contracted your services, and so on. Computerization has made the matching process much more efficient than it was in the past, so be sure to tally your income carefully so you won't be snared for a mismatch.

Next stop is West Virginia, where the information on your return is fed into a master computer. Based on previous IRS audits, this mechanized watchdog weeds out returns that are likely to produce additional tax assessments. Although the formula used to segregate audit targets is more closely guarded than the recipe for Coca-Cola, it is possible to reduce your odds of becoming acquainted with your local IRS agent.

A couple of red flags that examiners look for are suspiciously rounded figures; if you have to make an educated guess, do so in odd numbers. Also, identical numbers that appear on a return for two different items, such as a $2000 deduction for an IRA and a $2000 credit for estimated tax, may seem suspicious. Unusually large deductions are another audit magnet. If you do have such a deduction, it's a good idea to attach supporting documentation to substantiate it.

Although it may not seem important, the way you fill out your occupation will also be scrutinized by an examining officer. Salaried occupations will arouse less suspicion than occupations involving self-employment, because there is less opportunity to hide income or exaggerate deductions. Thus, someone who is a music teacher should write "teacher" rather than "musician." Obviously, the word "consultant" should be avoided, too. Finally, be sure the information on your state tax return jibes with your federal return. In many states, entries on federal and state tax returns are checked against each other for consistency.

Even a squeaky clean return may be selected for an audit, since the IRS plucks a certain number of returns at random. If you're tapped for a correspondence audit, the IRS will simply write a letter asking for further information. With an office audit, you will be required to bring documentation to your local IRS office. Or, you may be subject to a field audit in which the IRS agent comes to your home or office.

The letter informing you of an office audit will list the time and place. You have the right to rearrange both, and this is often a good idea. The best time to schedule an audit is just before lunch or at the end of the day, when the auditor is more likely to have his or her eye on the door than on your documentation. The end of the month is a good time, too, since auditors may be anxious to close their cases.

You can request that the audit be moved to a different location if you have a good reason, such as working in another area or moving to a different district. If you're lucky, there will be substantial delays in transferring your case and it will go to the bottom of the stack when it's assigned to a new agent. By that time, the statute of limitations for auditing your return could expire.

The notification letter from the IRS will contain a checklist of items being questioned. Bring only the documentation necessary to substantiate this list. If additional questions crop up during the audit, the auditor will probably be deterred from pursuing them by the fact that you don't have the necessary documents, and may need to schedule another appointment to bring them.

11

Retirement Planning

To a large extent, everything you do during your working years, from saving regularly to maintaining adequate insurance coverage, is directed toward one overriding financial planning objective—to be able to retire comfortably. During the 1990s, retirement planning is likely to become an even more important issue, as the postwar baby boom generation enters their fifties and begins to ponder the prospect of achieving financial security in their "golden years."

Increasingly, both employers and the federal government expect that individuals can and should be prepared to fund a substantial portion of retirement income from personal savings. On the employer's side, pension plans are already under pressure because of the increasing costs associated with funding those plans. Many companies, in fact, are replacing traditional pension plans, which provide a guaranteed income at retirement, with plans that base corporate contributions on annual profits. In addition, many pensions do not provide postretirement cost-of-living increases; and those that do have generally not kept pace with inflation in recent years.

Many experts feel that Social Security benefits—once considered a legislative sacred cow—will eventually be subject to a means-based test. Should this occur, relatively affluent workers may find that their Social Security benefits will be less than they had planned on.

On the other hand, the federal government has introduced a number of tax-advantaged retirement savings programs to help boost a sagging personal savings rate. Employers, too, now offer tax-advantaged savings plans, like 401(k) plans, that often have incentives such as matching contributions. Financial institutions also feature numerous products and services to take advantage of the growing retirement market. So, while it is becoming increasingly important to save for your own retirement, there are an attractive array of investment and savings alternatives to help you do so. It is largely up to you, however, to acquaint yourself with these varied opportunities.

Ideally, retirement planning should be a process that starts when individuals are in their twenties or thirties. While it is difficult to predict retirement income or expenses at this point, younger individuals can begin saving for retirement by taking advantage of an Individual Retirement Account (IRA) or other tax-advantaged savings plan, determining an appropriate investment strategy, and making regular plan contributions.

Chances are that you haven't yet accumulated a substantial nest egg for retirement. If you are like most people, you have experienced more pressing and immediate concerns, such as buying a home and raising and educating children. Whatever your circumstances, however, you should regularly direct some attention to planning for your retirement.

The first step in retirement planning is determining how much income will be needed and what its sources will be. Retirement is often compared to a three-legged stool, consisting of Social Security, pension plans, and personal savings. These resources should be examined carefully to determine if they can adequately meet your postretirement lifestyle expectations. If you don't want to change your lifestyle very much when you retire, you will probably need to accumulate considerable resources during your working years.

After this initial step, you should make an estimate of anticipated expenses at retirement. Since most people enjoy a long retirement, it is important to factor inflation into the picture as well. Fortunately, for many retirees, the cost of living falls for several reasons. Senior citizens pay less in taxes than they did during their working years. For example, there is no longer any Social Security withholding when you stop working. Also, saving for retirement is no longer an expense, since that money is being consumed rather than subtracted from family income. Work-related expenses are eliminated, and retirees have at their disposal numerous discounts on everyday goods and services, such as entertainment and transportation.

Medical expenses and insurance costs, however, are often higher for retirees than other segments of the population. Individuals who retire before age 65, and thus not yet eligible for Medicare, may be particularly vulnerable to unexpected medical expenses and high insurance costs. Therefore, if you are considering early retirement, you should inquire about your company's policy on providing health insurance for early retirees. Those age 65 or over should examine the features of health insurance policies that supplement Medicare.

As you periodically review your retirement planning, be sure to consider income tax and estate planning opportunities that may help you maximize your retirement investments and ensure smooth transfer of your estate. In addition, appropriate saving and investment techniques should be explored to assure that you accumulate sufficient retirement funds without taking too much risk.

TAX-FAVORED RETIREMENT PLANS

The best way for people to prepare for retirement is to make regular contributions to one or more tax-favored retirement plans, such as an IRA, a 401(k) plan, or a Keogh plan. Whether they are offered by your employer or if you set one up yourself, these plans offer the powerful advantage of tax deferral of investment earnings until the funds are withdrawn (usually during retirement). In addition, contributions to some of these plans are also tax-deductible. This section will help you evaluate the various types of commonly used tax-deferred retirement savings plans and determine if your are eligible to use them.

Company Qualified Plans

General Considerations. A company-qualified pension or profit-sharing plan offers several benefits. First, if your employer makes contributions to the plan on your behalf, they are not included in your current income for tax purposes. Second, income earned on the funds compounds tax-free. Finally, your employer may allow you to make voluntary contributions. Although you can't deduct these contributions, income earned on voluntary contributions is not taxed until withdrawn.

Tax Treatment of Distributions. If you receive a lump sum when you retire, taxes on the distribution may be reduced by special averaging rules. Alternatively, the lump-sum payment could be rolled over to an IRA account in order to further postpone taxation. Distributions from qualified plans before age 59½ are generally subject to penalties, but there are exceptions. IRA rollovers of lump-sum payments may also be elected to defer taxes on the distribution. Finally, a penalty may apply to distributions from a pension plan that exceed specified ceilings.

Keogh Plans

General Considerations. If you earn income from self-employment, you may be able to set up a Keogh even if you already participate in a pension plan through your employer. You may deduct contributions up to a specified limit, and income earned on Keogh investments is not taxed until withdrawn. The plan must be set up by the end of tax year, although contributions may be made up to the date of filing your tax return (including extensions). If you have employees, they must be included under specified rules.

Tax Treatment of Distributions. Self-employed persons may not generally withdraw Keogh plan funds until age 50½ unless they are disabled. Premature withdrawals are subject to penalty. Lump-sum distributions to self-employed persons after age 59½ or beneficiaries at death of the self-employed person may qualify for favored lump-sum distribution treatment under specified rules.

Deferred Compensation [401(k)] Plans

General Considerations. 401(k) plans generally involve joint contributions by you and your employer. Your contributions are, in effect, deducted from your salary and, therefore, you don't pay taxes on them until they are withdrawn during retirement. Income earned on the funds accumulates tax-free until it is withdrawn. Many of these plans offer some choice among a number of investment possibilities. If you work for a charitable or educational organization, your employer may offer similar deferred compensation arrangements known as tax-sheltered annuities or 403(b) plans. Participation in 401(k) or 403(b) plans is usually too good to pass up.

Tax Treatment of Distributions. Withdrawals are penalized if received before age 59½ with some exceptions, although you may be able to borrow from your account. At the time of withdrawal, the tax on proceeds may be computed under specified rules.

Simplified Employee Pension (SEP) Plans

General Considerations. A SEP plan may be set up by your employer (or you alone if you are a sole proprietor). The company makes contributions on behalf of the employees up to specified limits which are deposited in each employee's IRA account. There is less red tape with SEPs than there is with Keogh plans. Some employers may qualify for SEP plans that allow employees to contribute to the SEP through salary reduction.

Tax Treatment of Distributions. Withdrawals are taxable under the rules which follow for IRAs.

Individual Retirement Accounts (IRAs)

General Considerations. Anyone who has earned income may contribute to an IRA, but the contribution is fully or partially deductible only if certain requirements are met. Your level of income and whether or not you participate in a company pension plan are the determining factors. Whether your IRA contribution is deductible or not, income earned on IRA accounts is not taxed until the funds are withdrawn. IRAs continue to be an excellent way to build up money for retirement, even if you can't deduct the contribution.

Tax Treatment of Distributions. You may not withdraw funds without penalty until you are 59½, disabled, or receive IRA distributions in the form of a lifetime annuity. Premature withdrawals are subject to penalty. Participants who can afford to delay withdrawing from their IRA (so that it can continue to increase tax-free) must begin to take money out at age 70½ according to specified rules.

CONSIDERING A NONDEDUCTIBLE IRA INVESTMENT

Table 11-1 compares the result over two time periods—10 years and 20 years—of hypothetical investments made inside and outside a nondeductible IRA. Earnings of an investment outside an IRA are taxed each year, thus reducing the true yield. The taxes on earnings of an investment inside an IRA are deferred until the investor withdraws funds from the IRA.

The table assumes reinvestment of all earnings. For investment inside the nondeductible IRA, the part of this sum that represents earnings on investment is subject to taxation on withdrawal. The remaining portion, the sum of the annual investments, represents after-tax dollars and is not subject to taxation on withdrawal.

The after-tax value is based on 15 percent and 28 percent tax rates. The 15 percent rate might apply to withdrawals made in installments; the 28 percent rate might apply to lump-sum withdrawals and to periodic withdrawals made in years with substantial other income.

Table 11-1. Investments Made Inside and Outside a Nondeductible IRA

	Annual investment	Assumed annual yield	10 Years			20 Years		
			Accumulation	After-tax value at 15% rate	After-tax value at 28% rate	Accumulation	After-tax value at 15% rate	After-tax value at 28% rate
Inside	$2000	12%	$39,909	$36,413	$33,902	$161,397	$143,187	$127,406
Outside	2000	8.6% net	32,449	32,449	32,449	106,769	106,769	106,769
Inside	2000	10%	35,062	32,803	30,845	126,005	113,104	101,924
Outside	2000	7.2% net	29,904	29,904	29,904	89,838	89,838	89,838
Inside	2000	8%	31,291	29,597	28,130	98,846	90,019	82,369
Outside	2000	5.8% net	27,568	27,568	27,568	75,831	75,831	75,831
Inside	2000	6%	27,943	26,752	25,719	77,985	72,287	67,349
Outside	2000	4.3% net	25,424	25,242	25,424	64,233	64,233	64,233
Inside	2000	4%	24,973	24,227	23,581	61,938	58,647	55,795
Outside	2000	2.9% net	23,485	23,458	23,458	54,619	54,619	54,619

This table does not include the effect of any state and local income taxes that may be due on withdrawal.

Contrary to popular belief, you are almost always better off making nondeductible IRA investments for retirement-earmarked savings than you would be if you invested these monies outside of an IRA.

ESTIMATING SOCIAL SECURITY BENEFITS

The computation of Social Security benefits is quite complicated. Fortunately, the Social Security Administration will provide you with an accounting of your yearly salary history, a total of how much you've paid in Social Security taxes to date, estimates of your retirement benefits at ages 65, 70 and an age that you designate on the form, and estimates of survivors' and disability benefits. You can obtain Form SSA-7004 (Request for Earnings and Benefit Estimate Statement) from your Social Security office or by calling 800/937-2000. You must provide your name, Social Security number, current earnings, and an estimate of average future earnings. You should receive an answer within three to six weeks.

While you should request an estimate of your Social Security benefits directly from the Social Security Administration, you may want to make a rough estimate of your benefits now. Tables 11-2 and 11-3 show the approximate monthly retirement and survivors benefits, respectively, based upon your current age and income. Remember that the amounts indicated are expressed in current dollars which, of course, will have much less purchasing power when you retire than they would have today.

HOW EARLY OR LATE RETIREMENT AFFECTS SOCIAL SECURITY BENEFITS

Tables 11-4 and 11-5 show the percentage amounts that Social Security benefits are reduced in the event you begin collecting them before age 65 or increased if collection of benefits is postponed until after age 65. Deciding upon when to begin receiving benefits is no easy chore, particularly for early retirees. The prospect of beginning to collect Social Security at age 62 may seem enticing. On one hand, by receiving benefits 3 years early, you would need to collect benefits at

Table 11-2. Approximate Monthly Retirement Benefits if the Worker Retires at Normal Retirement Age and Had Steady Lifetime Earnings

Worker's Age in 1988	Worker's Family	Retired Worker's Earnings in 1987						
		$10,000	$15,000	$20,000	$25,000	$30,000	$35,000	$43,800 or more
25	Retired worker only	$ 618	$ 801	$ 983	$ 1,129	$ 1,214	$ 1,300	$ 1,471
	Worker and spouse[1]	927	1,201	1,474	1,693	1,821	1,950	2,206
35	Retired worker only	572	740	908	1,045	1,123	1,203	1,358
	Worker and spouse[1]	858	1,110	1,362	1,567	1,684	1,804	2,037
45	Retired worker only	523	677	831	958	1,030	1,092	1,201
	Worker and spouse[1]	784	1,015	1,246	1,437	1,545	1,638	1,801
55	Retired worker only	475	614	754	862	910	946	1,003
	Worker and spouse[1]	712	921	1,131	1,293	1,365	1,419	1,504
65	Retired worker only	425	550	675	768	797	816	838
	Worker and spouse[1]	637	825	1,012	1,152	1,195	1,224	1,257

[1]Spouse is assumed to be the same age as the worker. Spouse may qualify for a higher retirement benefit based on his or her work record.

Note: The accuracy of these estimates depends on the pattern of the worker's actual past earnings and his or her earnings in the future.

Source: Social Security Administration Publication No. 05-10035.

Table 11-3. Approximate Monthly Survivors Benefits if the Worker Dies in 1988 and Had Steady Earnings

Worker's Age in 1988	Worker's Family	Deceased Worker's Earnings in 1987						
		$10,000	$15,000	$20,000	$25,000	$30,000	$35,000	$43,800 or more
25	Spouse and 1 child[1]	$ 668	$ 864	$ 1,060	$ 1,226	$ 1,318	$ 1,410	$ 1,572
	Spouse and 2 children[2]	717	1,073	1,263	1,432	1,539	1,646	1,834
	1 child only	334	432	530	613	659	705	786
	Spouse at age 60[3]	318	412	505	584	628	672	749
35	Spouse and 1 child[1]	662	856	1,048	1,220	1,310	1,400	1,516
	Spouse and 2 children[2]	706	1,056	1,252	1,424	1,529	1,635	1,769
	1 child only	331	428	524	610	655	700	758
	Spouse at age 60[3]	316	408	500	581	624	667	722
45	Spouse and 1 child[1]	662	854	1,046	1,216	1,286	1,332	1,384
	Spouse and 2 children[2]	705	1,054	1,251	1,420	1,502	1,555	1,616
	1 child only	331	427	523	608	643	666	692
	Spouse at age 60[3]	315	407	499	579	613	635	660
55	Spouse and 1 child[1]	660	866	1,046	1,194	1,242	1,272	1,306
	Spouse and 2 children[2]	703	1,067	1,250	1,395	1,451	1,485	1,524
	1 child only	330	433	523	597	621	636	653
	Spouse at age 60[3]	315	412	498	569	592	606	622
65	Spouse and 1 child[1]	638	824	1,012	1,152	1,194	1,224	1,256
	Spouse and 2 children[2]	682	1,021	1,206	1,345	1,395	1,429	1,468
	1 child only	319	412	506	576	597	612	628
	Spouse at age 60[3]	304	393	482	549	570	583	599

[1]Spouse who has substantial earnings and care for two children also receives this benefit.

[2]Equals the maximum family benefit.

[3]Amounts payable in 1988. Spouse turning 60 in the future would receive higher benefits.

Source: Social Security Administration Publication No. 05-10084.

Table 11–4. Social Security Benefit Reductions for Early Retirees

Multiply your estimated benefits at age 65 as provided by the Social Security Administration by the appropriate reduction factor.

Months before Age 65	Reduction Factor
1	.994
2	.988
3	.983
4	.977
5	.972
6	.966
7	.961
8	.955
9	.950
10	.944
11	.938
12	.933
13	.927
14	.922
15	.916
16	.911
17	.905
18	.900
19	.894
20	.888
21	.883
22	.877
23	.872
24	.866
25	.861
26	.855
27	.850
28	.844
29	.838
30	.833
31	.827
32	.822
33	.816
34	.811
35	.805
36	.800

Retiree benefits cannot commence before age 62. Dependent spouses who retire early have a somewhat greater reduction factor; a dependent spouse who retires 36 months before age 65 has a reduction factor of .750 (versus .800 for the early retiree).

Table 11–5. Social Security Benefit Increases for Late Retirees

Increase your estimated benefits at age 65 as provided by the Social Security Administration by the appropriate percentage factor. For example, assuming that you become age 65 in 1992, and you expect to begin collecting Social Security at age 67, your initial Social Security benefits will be 8 percent higher (yearly percentage of 4 percent times 2 years) than they would have been had you begun collecting benefits at age 65.

Year Age 65 Attained	Monthly Percentage (of 1 percent)	Yearly Percentage
1990–91	7/24%	3.5%
1992–93	1/3	4
1994–95	3/8	4.5
1996–97	5/12	5
1998–99	11/24	5.5
2000–2001	1/2	6
2002–2003	13/24	6.5
2004–2005	7/12	7
2006–2007	5/8	7.5
2008 or later	2/3	8

the full rate for 12 years to make up the difference in total income. On the other hand, once you begin receiving Social Security benefits at a reduced rate, you will always receive benefits at a reduced rate.

ANNUITY PAYMENT CONTRACT OPTIONS

Table 11-6 shows the various payment options that are commonly available for annuitants. Some are designed to provide income for one recipient only, while other options arrange for coverage of both the annuitant and a spouse or other dependent. You should review these options carefully and consider factors such as age, health, other sources of income, and income tax ramifications before making the important and usually irreversible decision regarding the form of annuity payment to take. Also, if you have the option of selecting an annuity from any insurance company, be sure to shop around. Benefit levels vary considerably among insurance companies on an otherwise identical policy.

Table 11–6. Payment Options Available for Annuitants

Annuity	Description
One annuitant annuity	The annuitant receives payments for the rest of his or her life.
Temporary annuity	The annuitant receives payment until death or until the end of a specified limited period, whichever occurs earlier.
Uniform joint and survivor annuity	The annuitant receives payments for the rest of his or her life, and after death, the same amount is paid to another annuitant. The expected return is based on the combined life expectancies of both annuitants.
One annuitant stepped-up annuity	The annuitant receives smaller payments at first, and after reaching a certain age, usually upon retirement, receives larger payments.
One annuitant stepped-down annuity	The annuitant receives larger payments at first, and then, when he or she reaches a certain age, smaller payments commence.
Variable payment joint and survivor annuity with lesser annuity to survivor	The annuitant and spouse receive payments while both are alive, and, on the death of one, a lesser amount is paid to the survivor—regardless of who dies first.
Variable payment joint and survivor annuity with first and second annuitants specified	The annuitant receives payments of a certain amount, and on his or her death another annuitant gets a lesser amount. The exclusion ratio remains the same for both annuitants.

RETIREMENT FUND WITHDRAWAL CHART

Retirees and people who are planning for retirement must be particularly careful to avoid withdrawing (or planning to withdraw) too much of their personal investments each year. Stories abound of retired people who, either through overspending or failing to anticipate

Table 11–7. Number of Years Retirement Funds Can Last

Annual Withdrawal Rate	Return on Retirement Funds:				
	5%	6%	7%	8%	9%
10%	14	15	17	20	26
9%	16	18	22	28	
8%	20	23	30		
7%	25	33			
6%	36				

a long life, have run out of money. Table 11-7 shows the number of years that retirement savings will last, assuming a given annual withdrawal rate and rate of return. For example, if you withdraw 8 percent of your retirement funds each year and you earn 7 percent on them, your funds will be depleted in 30 years.

IRA MINIMUM WITHDRAWAL TABLES

Tables 11-8 and 11-9 are the Internal Revenue Service tables used to determine the annual minimum withdrawals from an IRA at various ages for single life and joint and last survivor life expectancies. Retirees who can afford to go without the money can allow their IRA funds to continue to accumulate tax-free well into old age by postponing withdrawal of these funds until age 70½ when they have to commence making annual withdrawals, and thereafter taking out only the minimum amounts required by the IRS.

For example, the minimum annual withdrawal for a single person, age 79, is ¹/₁₀ of the amount contained in his or her IRA account (See Table 11-8). The minimum annual withdrawal for a couple who are both age 77 is ¹/₁₅ of the amount contained in their IRA accounts (See Table 11-9).

SUMMARY OF HEALTH CARE ALTERNATIVES FOR RETIRED PERSONS

Most older Americans and their families are justifiably worried about meeting the health care costs of the elderly. All elderly persons as

Table 11–8. Single Life Expectancies

Age	Multiple	Age	Multiple
5	76.6	61	23.3
6	75.6	62	22.5
7	74.7	63	21.6
8	73.7	64	20.8
9	72.7	65	20.0
10	71.7	66	19.2
11	70.7	67	18.4
12	69.7	68	17.6
13	68.8	69	16.8
14	67.8	70	16.0
15	66.8	71	15.3
16	65.8	72	14.6
17	64.8	73	13.9
18	63.9	74	13.2
19	62.9	75	12.5
20	61.9	76	11.9
21	60.9	77	11.2
22	59.9	78	10.6
23	59.9	79	10.0
24	58.9	80	9.5
25	57.9	81	8.9
26	56.0	82	8.4
27	55.1	83	7.9
28	54.1	84	7.4
29	53.1	85	6.9
30	52.2	86	6.5
31	51.2	87	6.1
32	50.2	88	5.7
33	49.3	89	5.3
34	48.3	90	5.0
35	47.3	91	4.7
36	46.4	92	4.4
37	45.4	93	4.1
38	44.4	94	3.9
39	43.5	95	3.7
40	42.5	96	3.4
41	41.5	97	3.2
42	40.6	98	3.0
43	39.6	99	2.8
44	38.7	100	2.7
45	37.7	101	2.5
46	36.8	102	2.3
47	35.9	103	2.1
48	34.9	104	1.9
49	34.0	105	1.8
50	33.1	106	1.6
51	32.2	107	1.4
52	31.3	108	1.3
53	30.4	109	1.1
54	29.5	110	1.0
55	28.6	111	.9
56	27.7	112	.8
57	26.8	113	.7
58	25.9	114	.6
59	25.0	115	.5
60	24.2		

well as their children should be aware of the different options that are available. These may include:

1. Medicare

2. Retiree medical benefits

3. Medicare supplemental health insurance

4. Health maintenance organizations

Table 11–9. Joint and Last Survivor Life Expectancies

Ages	45	46	47	48	49	50	51	52	53	54
45	44.1	43.6	43.2	42.7	42.3	42.0	41.6	41.3	41.0	40.7
46	43.6	43.1	42.6	42.2	41.8	41.4	41.0	40.6	40.3	40.0
47	43.2	42.6	42.1	41.7	41.2	40.8	40.4	40.0	39.7	39.3
48	42.7	42.2	41.7	41.2	40.7	40.2	39.8	39.4	39.0	38.7
49	42.3	41.8	41.2	40.7	40.2	39.7	39.3	38.8	38.4	38.1
50	42.0	41.4	40.8	40.2	39.7	39.2	38.7	38.3	37.9	37.5
51	41.6	41.0	40.4	39.8	39.3	38.7	38.2	37.8	37.3	36.9
52	41.3	40.6	40.0	39.4	38.8	38.3	37.8	37.3	36.8	36.4
53	41.0	40.3	39.7	39.0	38.4	37.9	37.3	36.8	36.3	35.8
54	40.7	40.0	39.3	38.7	38.1	37.5	36.9	36.4	35.8	35.3
55	40.4	39.7	39.0	38.4	37.7	37.1	36.5	35.9	35.4	34.9
56	40.2	39.5	38.7	38.1	37.4	36.8	36.1	35.6	35.0	34.4
57	40.0	39.2	38.5	37.8	37.1	36.4	35.8	35.2	34.6	34.0
58	39.7	39.0	38.2	37.5	36.8	36.1	35.5	34.8	34.2	33.6
59	39.6	38.8	38.0	37.3	36.6	35.9	35.2	34.5	33.9	33.3
60	39.4	38.6	37.8	37.1	36.3	35.6	34.9	34.2	33.6	32.9
61	39.2	38.4	37.6	36.9	36.1	35.4	34.6	33.9	33.3	32.6
62	39.1	38.3	37.5	36.7	35.9	35.1	34.4	33.7	33.0	32.3
63	38.9	38.1	37.3	36.5	35.7	34.9	34.2	33.5	32.7	32.0
64	38.8	38.0	37.2	36.3	35.5	34.8	34.0	33.2	32.5	31.8
65	38.7	37.9	37.0	36.2	35.4	34.6	33.8	33.0	32.3	31.6
66	38.6	37.8	36.9	36.1	35.2	34.4	33.6	32.9	32.1	31.4
67	38.5	37.7	36.8	36.0	35.1	34.3	33.5	32.7	31.9	31.2
68	38.4	37.6	36.7	35.8	35.0	34.2	33.4	32.5	31.8	31.0
69	38.4	37.5	36.6	35.7	34.9	34.1	33.2	32.4	31.6	30.8
70	38.3	37.4	36.5	35.7	34.8	34.0	33.1	32.3	31.5	30.7
71	38.2	37.3	36.5	35.6	34.7	33.9	33.0	32.2	31.4	30.5
72	38.2	37.3	36.4	35.5	34.6	33.8	32.9	32.1	31.2	30.4
73	38.1	37.2	36.3	35.4	34.6	33.7	32.8	32.0	31.1	30.3
74	38.1	37.2	36.3	35.4	34.5	33.6	32.8	31.9	31.1	30.2
75	38.1	37.1	36.2	35.3	34.5	33.6	32.7	31.8	31.0	30.1
76	38.0	37.1	36.2	35.3	34.4	33.5	32.6	31.8	30.9	30.1
77	38.0	37.1	36.2	35.3	34.4	33.5	32.6	31.7	30.8	30.0
78	38.0	37.0	36.1	35.2	34.3	33.4	32.5	31.7	30.8	29.9
79	37.9	37.0	36.1	35.2	34.3	33.4	32.5	31.6	30.7	29.9
80	37.9	37.0	36.1	35.2	34.2	33.4	32.5	31.6	30.7	29.8
81	37.9	37.0	36.0	35.1	34.2	33.3	32.4	31.5	30.7	29.8
82	37.9	36.9	36.0	35.1	34.2	33.3	32.4	31.5	30.6	29.7
83	37.9	36.9	36.0	35.1	34.2	33.3	32.4	31.5	30.6	29.7
84	37.8	36.9	36.0	35.0	34.2	33.2	32.3	31.4	30.6	29.7
85	37.8	36.9	36.0	35.0	34.1	33.2	32.3	31.4	30.5	29.6
86	37.8	36.9	36.0	35.0	34.1	33.2	32.3	31.4	30.5	29.6
87	37.8	36.9	35.9	35.0	34.1	33.2	32.3	31.4	30.5	29.6
88	37.8	36.9	35.9	35.0	34.1	33.2	32.3	31.4	30.5	29.6
89	37.8	36.9	35.9	35.0	34.1	33.2	32.3	31.4	30.5	29.6
90	37.8	36.9	35.9	35.0	34.1	33.2	32.3	31.3	30.5	29.6
91	37.8	36.8	35.9	35.0	34.1	33.2	32.2	31.3	30.4	29.5
92	37.8	36.8	35.9	35.0	34.1	33.2	32.2	31.3	30.4	29.5
93	37.8	36.8	35.9	35.0	34.1	33.1	32.2	31.3	30.4	29.5
94	37.8	36.8	35.9	35.0	34.1	33.1	32.2	31.3	30.4	29.5
95	37.8	36.8	35.9	35.0	34.0	33.1	32.2	31.3	30.4	29.5
96	37.8	36.8	35.9	35.0	34.0	33.1	32.2	31.3	30.4	29.5
97	37.8	36.8	35.9	35.0	34.0	33.1	32.2	31.3	30.4	29.5
98	37.8	36.8	35.9	35.0	34.0	33.1	32.2	31.3	30.4	29.5
99	37.8	36.8	35.9	35.0	34.0	33.1	32.2	31.3	30.4	29.5
101	37.8	36.8	35.9	35.0	34.0	33.1	32.2	31.3	30.4	29.5
102	37.8	36.8	35.9	35.0	34.0	33.1	32.2	31.3	30.4	29.5
103	37.7	36.8	35.9	34.9	34.0	33.1	32.2	31.3	30.4	29.5
104	37.7	36.8	35.9	34.9	34.0	33.1	32.2	31.3	30.4	29.5
105	37.7	36.8	35.9	34.9	34.0	33.1	32.2	31.3	30.4	29.5
106	37.7	36.8	35.9	34.9	34.0	33.1	32.2	31.3	30.4	29.5
107	37.7	36.8	35.9	34.9	34.0	33.1	32.2	31.3	30.4	29.5
108	37.7	36.8	35.9	34.9	34.0	33.1	32.2	31.3	30.4	29.5
109	37.7	36.8	35.9	34.9	34.0	33.1	32.2	31.3	30.4	29.5
110	37.7	36.8	35.9	34.9	34.0	33.1	32.2	31.3	30.4	29.5
111	37.7	36.8	35.9	34.9	34.0	33.1	32.2	31.3	30.4	29.5
112	37.7	36.8	35.9	34.9	34.0	33.1	32.2	31.3	30.4	29.5
113	37.7	36.8	35.9	34.9	34.0	33.1	32.2	31.3	30.4	29.5
114	37.7	36.8	35.9	34.9	34.0	33.1	32.2	31.3	30.4	29.5
115	37.7	36.8	35.9	34.9	34.0	33.1	32.2	31.3	30.4	29.5

5. Medicaid

6. Long-term care insurance

7. Continuous care communities

These health care programs are discussed at length in this section.

Table 11–9. Joint and Last Survivor Life Expectancies (*Continued*)

Ages	55	56	57	58	59	60	61	62	63	64
55	34.4	33.9	33.5	33.1	32.7	32.3	32.0	31.7	31.4	31.1
56	33.9	33.4	33.0	32.5	32.1	31.7	31.4	31.0	30.7	30.4
57	33.5	33.0	32.5	32.0	31.6	31.2	30.8	30.4	30.1	29.8
58	33.1	32.5	32.0	31.5	31.1	30.6	30.2	29.9	29.5	29.2
59	32.7	32.1	31.6	31.1	30.6	30.1	29.7	29.3	28.9	28.6
60	32.3	31.7	31.2	30.6	30.1	29.7	29.2	28.8	28.4	28.0
61	32.0	31.4	30.8	30.2	29.7	29.2	28.7	28.3	27.8	27.4
62	31.7	31.0	30.4	29.9	29.3	28.8	28.3	27.6	27.3	26.9
63	31.4	30.7	30.1	29.5	28.9	28.4	27.6	27.3	26.9	26.4
64	31.1	30.4	29.8	29.2	28.6	28.0	27.4	26.9	26.4	25.9
65	30.9	30.2	29.5	28.9	28.2	27.6	27.1	26.5	26.0	25.5
66	30.6	29.9	29.2	28.6	27.9	27.3	26.7	26.1	25.6	25.1
67	30.4	29.7	29.0	28.3	27.6	27.0	26.4	25.8	25.2	24.7
68	30.2	29.5	28.8	28.1	27.4	26.7	26.1	25.5	24.9	24.3
69	30.1	29.3	28.6	27.8	27.1	26.5	25.8	25.2	24.6	24.0
70	29.9	29.1	28.4	27.6	26.9	26.2	25.6	24.9	24.3	23.7
71	29.7	29.0	28.2	27.5	26.7	26.0	25.3	24.7	24.0	23.4
72	29.6	28.8	28.1	27.3	26.5	25.8	25.1	24.4	23.8	23.1
73	29.5	28.7	27.9	27.1	26.4	25.6	24.9	24.2	23.5	22.9
74	29.4	28.6	27.8	27.0	26.2	25.5	24.7	24.0	23.3	22.7
75	29.3	28.5	27.7	26.9	26.1	25.3	24.6	23.8	23.1	22.4
76	29.2	28.4	27.6	26.8	26.0	25.2	24.4	23.7	23.0	22.3
77	29.1	28.3	27.5	26.7	25.9	25.1	24.3	23.6	22.8	22.1
78	29.1	28.2	27.4	26.6	25.8	25.0	24.2	23.4	22.7	21.9
79	29.0	28.2	27.3	26.5	25.7	24.9	24.1	23.3	22.6	21.8
80	29.0	28.1	27.3	26.4	25.6	24.8	24.0	23.2	22.4	21.7
81	28.9	28.1	27.2	26.4	25.5	24.7	23.9	23.1	22.3	21.6
82	28.9	28.0	27.2	26.3	25.5	24.6	23.8	23.0	22.3	21.5
83	28.8	28.0	27.1	26.3	25.4	24.6	23.8	23.0	22.2	21.4
84	28.8	27.9	27.1	26.2	25.4	24.5	23.7	22.9	22.1	21.3
85	28.8	27.9	27.0	26.2	25.3	24.5	23.7	22.8	22.0	21.3
86	28.7	27.9	27.0	26.1	25.3	24.5	23.6	22.8	22.0	21.2
87	28.7	27.8	27.0	26.1	25.3	24.4	23.6	22.8	21.9	21.1
88	28.7	27.8	27.0	26.1	25.2	24.4	23.5	22.7	21.9	21.1
89	28.7	27.8	26.9	26.1	25.2	24.4	23.5	22.7	21.9	21.1
90	28.7	27.8	26.9	26.1	25.2	24.3	23.5	22.7	21.8	21.0
91	28.7	27.8	26.9	26.0	25.2	24.3	23.5	22.6	21.8	21.0
92	28.6	27.8	26.9	26.0	25.2	24.3	23.5	22.6	21.8	21.0
93	28.6	27.8	26.9	26.0	25.1	24.3	23.4	22.6	21.8	20.9
94	28.6	27.7	26.9	26.0	25.1	24.3	23.4	22.6	21.7	20.9
95	28.6	27.7	26.9	26.0	25.1	24.3	23.4	22.6	21.7	20.9
96	28.6	27.7	26.9	26.0	25.1	24.2	23.4	22.6	21.7	20.9
97	28.6	27.7	26.8	26.0	25.1	24.2	23.4	22.5	21.7	20.9
98	28.6	27.7	26.8	26.0	25.1	24.2	23.4	22.5	21.7	20.9
99	28.6	27.7	26.8	26.0	25.1	24.2	23.4	22.5	21.7	20.9
100	28.6	27.7	26.8	26.0	25.1	24.2	23.4	22.5	21.7	20.8
101	28.6	27.7	26.8	25.9	25.1	24.2	23.4	22.5	21.7	20.8
102	28.6	27.7	26.8	25.9	25.1	24.2	23.3	22.5	21.7	20.8
103	28.6	27.7	26.8	25.9	25.1	24.2	23.3	22.5	21.7	20.8
104	28.6	27.7	26.8	25.9	25.1	24.2	23.3	22.5	21.6	20.8
105	28.6	27.7	26.8	25.9	25.1	24.2	23.3	22.5	21.6	20.8
106	28.6	27.7	26.8	25.9	25.1	24.2	23.3	22.5	21.6	20.8
107	28.6	27.7	26.8	25.9	25.1	24.2	23.3	22.5	21.6	20.8
108	28.6	27.7	26.8	25.9	25.1	24.2	23.3	22.5	21.6	20.8
109	28.6	27.7	26.8	25.9	25.1	24.2	23.3	22.5	21.6	20.8
110	28.6	27.7	26.8	25.9	25.1	24.2	23.3	22.5	21.6	20.8
111	28.6	27.7	26.8	25.9	25.0	24.2	23.3	22.5	21.6	20.8
112	28.6	27.7	26.8	25.9	25.0	24.2	23.3	22.5	21.6	20.8
113	28.6	27.7	26.8	25.9	25.0	24.2	23.3	22.5	21.6	20.8
114	28.6	27.7	26.8	25.9	25.0	24.2	23.3	22.5	21.6	20.8
115	28.6	27.7	26.8	25.9	25.0	24.2	23.3	22.5	21.6	20.8

Medicare

Medicare, a health insurance program administered by the federal government, provides hospital and medical insurance for people 65 years of age or older, as well as to disabled people. It consists of:

Part A, or Hospital Insurance, which helps pay for certain hospital, hospice, skilled nursing facility care, and home health care; and

Table 11–9. Joint and Last Survivor Life Expectancies (*Continued*)

Ages	65	66	67	68	69	70	71	72	73	74
65	25.0	24.6	24.2	23.8	23.4	23.1	22.8	22.5	22.2	22.0
66	24.6	24.1	23.7	23.3	22.9	22.5	22.2	21.9	21.6	21.4
67	24.2	23.7	23.2	22.8	22.4	22.0	21.7	21.3	21.0	20.8
68	23.8	23.3	22.8	22.3	21.9	21.5	21.2	20.8	20.5	20.2
69	23.4	22.9	22.4	21.9	21.5	21.1	20.7	20.3	20.0	19.6
70	23.1	22.5	22.0	21.5	21.1	20.6	20.2	19.8	19.4	19.1
71	22.8	22.2	21.7	21.2	20.7	20.2	19.8	19.4	19.0	18.6
72	22.5	21.9	21.3	20.8	20.3	19.8	19.4	18.9	18.5	18.2
73	22.2	21.6	21.0	20.5	20.0	19.4	19.0	18.5	18.1	17.7
74	22.0	21.4	20.8	20.2	19.6	19.1	18.6	18.2	17.7	17.3
75	21.8	21.1	20.5	19.9	19.3	18.8	18.3	17.8	17.3	16.9
76	21.6	20.9	20.3	19.7	19.1	18.5	18.0	17.5	17.0	16.5
77	21.4	20.7	20.1	19.4	18.8	18.3	17.7	17.2	16.7	16.2
78	21.2	20.5	19.9	19.2	18.6	18.0	17.5	16.9	16.4	15.9
79	21.1	20.4	19.7	19.0	18.4	17.8	17.2	16.7	16.1	15.6
80	21.0	20.2	19.5	18.9	18.2	17.6	17.0	16.4	15.9	15.4
81	20.8	20.1	19.4	18.7	18.1	17.4	16.8	16.2	15.7	15.1
82	20.7	20.0	19.3	18.6	17.9	17.3	16.6	16.0	15.5	14.9
83	20.6	19.9	19.2	18.5	17.8	17.1	16.5	15.9	15.3	14.7
84	20.5	19.8	19.1	18.4	17.7	17.0	16.3	15.7	15.1	14.5
85	20.5	19.7	19.0	18.3	17.6	16.9	16.2	15.6	15.0	14.4
86	20.4	19.6	18.9	18.2	17.5	16.8	16.1	15.5	14.8	14.2
87	20.4	19.6	18.8	18.1	17.4	16.7	16.0	15.4	14.7	14.1
88	20.3	19.5	18.8	18.0	17.3	16.6	15.9	15.3	14.6	14.0
89	20.3	19.5	18.7	18.0	17.2	16.5	15.8	15.2	14.5	13.9
90	20.2	19.4	18.7	17.9	17.2	16.5	15.8	15.1	14.5	13.8
91	20.2	19.4	18.6	17.9	17.1	16.4	15.7	15.0	14.4	13.7
92	20.2	19.4	18.6	17.8	17.1	16.4	15.7	15.0	14.3	13.7
93	20.1	19.3	18.6	17.8	17.1	16.3	15.6	14.9	14.3	13.6
94	20.1	19.3	18.5	17.8	17.0	16.3	15.6	14.9	14.2	13.6
95	20.1	19.3	18.5	17.8	17.0	16.3	15.6	14.9	14.2	13.5
96	20.1	19.3	18.5	17.7	17.0	16.2	15.5	14.8	14.2	13.5
97	20.1	19.3	18.5	17.7	17.0	16.2	15.5	14.8	14.1	13.5
98	20.1	19.3	18.5	17.7	16.9	16.2	15.5	14.8	14.1	13.4
99	20.0	19.2	18.5	17.7	16.9	16.2	15.5	14.7	14.1	13.4
100	20.0	19.2	18.4	17.7	16.9	16.2	15.4	14.7	14.0	13.4
101	20.0	19.2	18.4	17.7	16.9	16.1	15.4	14.7	14.0	13.3
102	20.0	19.2	18.4	17.6	16.9	16.1	15.4	14.7	14.0	13.3
103	20.0	19.2	18.4	17.6	16.9	16.1	15.4	14.7	14.0	13.3
104	20.0	19.2	18.4	17.6	16.9	16.1	15.4	14.7	14.0	13.3
105	20.0	19.2	18.4	17.6	16.8	16.1	15.4	14.6	13.9	13.3
106	20.0	19.2	18.4	17.6	16.8	16.1	15.3	14.6	13.9	13.3
107	20.0	19.2	18.4	17.6	16.8	16.1	15.3	14.6	13.9	13.2
108	20.0	19.2	18.4	17.6	16.8	16.1	15.3	14.6	13.9	13.2
109	20.0	19.2	18.4	17.6	16.8	16.1	15.3	14.6	13.9	13.2
110	20.0	19.2	18.4	17.6	16.8	16.1	15.3	14.6	13.9	13.2
111	20.0	19.2	18.4	17.6	16.8	16.0	15.3	14.6	13.9	13.2
112	20.0	19.2	18.4	17.6	16.8	16.0	15.3	14.6	13.9	13.2
113	20.0	19.2	18.4	17.6	16.8	16.0	15.3	14.6	13.9	13.2
114	20.0	19.2	18.4	17.6	16.8	16.0	15.3	14.6	13.9	13.2
115	20.0	19.2	18.4	17.6	16.8	16.0	15.3	14.6	13.9	13.2

Part B, or Medical Insurance, which covers certain types of outpatient care, such as visits to a physician, laboratory fees, and certain outpatient prescription drugs.

Most people over age 65 have Medicare coverage and anyone who has worked long enough to receive Social Security is automatically eligible for Part A Hospital Insurance. Spouses and certain dependents of eligible workers are also eligible, as are certain divorced persons and widows and widowers. Eligible people are covered by Part A without payment, but others who are not eligible may purchase Part A. Almost anyone over age 65 may enroll for Medicare Part B, which requires a

Table 11–9. Joint and Last Survivor Life Expectancies (*Continued*)

Ages	75	76	77	78	79	80	81	82	83	84
75	16.5	16.1	15.8	15.4	15.1	14.9	14.6	14.4	14.2	14.0
76	16.1	15.7	15.4	15.0	14.7	14.4	14.1	13.9	13.7	13.5
77	15.8	15.4	15.0	14.6	14.3	14.0	13.7	13.4	13.2	13.0
78	15.4	15.0	14.6	14.2	13.9	13.5	13.2	13.0	12.7	12.5
79	15.1	14.7	14.3	13.9	13.5	13.2	12.8	12.5	12.3	12.0
80	14.9	14.4	14.0	13.5	13.2	12.8	12.5	12.2	11.9	11.6
81	14.6	14.1	13.7	13.2	12.8	12.5	12.1	11.8	11.5	11.2
82	14.4	13.9	13.4	13.0	12.5	12.2	11.8	11.5	11.1	10.9
83	14.2	13.7	13.2	12.7	12.3	11.9	11.5	11.1	10.8	10.5
84	14.0	13.5	13.0	12.5	12.0	11.6	11.2	10.9	10.5	10.2
85	13.8	13.3	12.8	12.3	11.8	11.4	11.0	10.6	10.2	9.9
86	13.7	13.1	12.6	12.1	11.6	11.2	10.8	10.4	10.0	9.7
87	13.5	13.0	12.4	11.9	11.4	11.0	10.6	10.1	9.8	9.4
88	13.4	12.8	12.3	11.8	11.3	10.8	10.4	10.0	9.6	9.2
89	13.3	12.7	12.2	11.6	11.1	10.7	10.2	9.8	9.4	9.0
90	13.2	12.6	12.1	11.5	11.0	10.5	10.1	9.6	9.2	8.8
91	13.1	12.5	12.0	11.4	10.9	10.4	9.9	9.5	9.1	8.7
92	13.1	12.5	11.9	11.3	10.8	10.3	9.8	9.4	8.9	8.5
93	13.0	12.4	11.8	11.3	10.7	10.2	9.7	9.3	8.8	8.4
94	12.9	12.3	11.7	11.2	10.6	10.1	9.6	9.2	8.7	8.3
95	12.9	12.3	11.7	11.1	10.6	10.1	9.6	9.1	8.6	8.2
96	12.9	12.2	11.6	11.1	10.5	10.0	9.5	9.0	8.5	8.1
97	12.8	12.2	11.6	11.0	10.5	9.9	9.4	8.9	8.5	8.0
98	12.8	12.2	11.5	11.0	10.4	9.9	9.4	8.9	8.4	8.0
99	12.7	12.1	11.5	10.9	10.4	9.8	9.3	8.8	8.3	7.9
100	12.7	12.1	11.5	10.9	10.3	9.8	9.2	8.7	8.3	7.8
101	12.7	12.1	11.4	10.8	10.3	9.7	9.2	8.7	8.2	7.8
102	12.7	12.0	11.4	10.8	10.2	9.7	9.2	8.7	8.2	7.7
103	12.6	12.0	11.4	10.8	10.2	9.7	9.1	8.6	8.1	7.7
104	12.6	12.0	11.4	10.8	10.2	9.6	9.1	8.6	8.1	7.6
105	12.6	12.0	11.3	10.7	10.2	9.6	9.1	8.5	8.0	7.6
106	12.6	11.9	11.3	10.7	10.1	9.6	9.0	8.5	8.0	7.5
107	12.6	11.9	11.3	10.7	10.1	9.6	9.0	8.5	8.0	7.5
108	12.6	11.9	11.3	10.7	10.1	9.5	9.0	8.5	8.0	7.5
109	12.6	11.9	11.3	10.7	10.1	9.5	9.0	8.4	7.9	7.5
110	12.6	11.9	11.3	10.7	10.1	9.5	9.0	8.4	7.9	7.4
111	12.5	11.9	11.3	10.7	10.1	9.5	8.9	8.4	7.9	7.4
112	12.5	11.9	11.3	10.6	10.1	9.5	8.9	8.4	7.9	7.4
113	12.5	11.9	11.2	10.6	10.0	9.5	8.9	8.4	7.9	7.4
114	12.5	11.9	11.2	10.6	10.0	9.5	8.9	8.4	7.9	7.4
115	12.5	11.9	11.2	10.6	10.0	9.5	8.9	8.4	7.9	7.4

Ages	85	86	87	88	89	90	91	92	93	94
85	9.6	9.3	9.1	8.9	8.7	8.5	8.3	8.2	8.0	7.9
86	9.3	9.1	8.8	8.6	8.3	8.2	8.0	7.8	7.7	7.6
87	9.1	8.8	8.5	8.3	8.1	7.9	7.7	7.5	7.4	7.2
88	8.9	8.6	8.3	8.0	7.8	7.6	7.4	7.2	7.1	6.9
89	8.7	8.3	8.1	7.8	7.5	7.3	7.1	6.9	6.8	6.6
90	8.5	8.2	7.9	7.6	7.3	7.1	6.9	6.7	6.5	6.4
91	8.3	8.0	7.7	7.4	7.1	6.9	6.7	6.5	6.3	6.2
92	8.2	7.8	7.5	7.2	6.9	6.7	6.5	6.3	6.1	5.9
93	8.0	7.7	7.4	7.1	6.8	6.5	6.3	6.1	5.9	5.8
94	7.9	7.6	7.2	6.9	6.6	6.4	6.2	5.9	5.8	5.6
95	7.8	7.5	7.1	6.8	6.5	6.3	6.0	5.8	5.6	5.4
96	7.7	7.3	7.0	6.7	6.4	6.1	5.9	5.7	5.5	5.3
97	7.6	7.3	6.9	6.6	6.3	6.0	5.8	5.5	5.3	5.1
98	7.6	7.2	6.8	6.5	6.2	5.9	5.6	5.4	5.2	5.0
99	7.5	7.1	6.7	6.4	6.1	5.8	5.5	5.3	5.1	4.9
100	7.4	7.0	6.6	6.3	6.0	5.7	5.4	5.2	5.0	4.8
101	7.3	6.9	6.6	6.2	5.9	5.6	5.3	5.1	4.9	4.7
102	7.3	6.9	6.5	6.2	5.8	5.5	5.3	5.0	4.8	4.6
103	7.2	6.8	6.4	6.1	5.8	5.5	5.2	4.9	4.7	4.5
104	7.2	6.8	6.4	6.0	5.7	5.4	5.1	4.8	4.6	4.4
105	7.1	6.7	6.3	6.0	5.6	5.3	5.0	4.8	4.5	4.3
106	7.1	6.7	6.3	5.9	5.6	5.3	5.0	4.7	4.5	4.2
107	7.1	6.6	6.2	5.9	5.5	5.2	4.9	4.6	4.4	4.2
108	7.0	6.6	6.2	5.8	5.5	5.2	4.9	4.6	4.3	4.1
109	7.0	6.6	6.2	5.8	5.5	5.1	4.8	4.5	4.3	4.1
110	7.0	6.6	6.2	5.8	5.4	5.1	4.8	4.5	4.3	4.0
111	7.0	6.5	6.1	5.7	5.4	5.1	4.8	4.5	4.2	4.0
112	7.0	6.5	6.1	5.7	5.4	5.0	4.7	4.4	4.2	3.9
113	6.9	6.5	6.1	5.7	5.4	5.0	4.7	4.4	4.2	3.9
114	6.9	6.5	6.1	5.7	5.3	5.0	4.7	4.4	4.1	3.9
115	6.9	6.5	6.1	5.7	5.3	5.0	4.7	4.4	4.1	3.9

monthly premium that is automatically deducted from the Social Security check.

Insurance protection starts automatically for some, while others need to apply for Parts A and B about 3 months before turning 65. A current copy of a handbook explaining Medicare coverage in detail may be obtained at your local Social Security office. Anyone expecting to need Medicare coverage should read this handbook carefully, because Medicare, contrary to common belief, does not provide complete health care coverage. Its gaps include deductibles, copayments, limits or reimbursement for certain services, as well as a lack of coverage for some services, notably long-term nursing home confinements.

Medicare Part A pays for unlimited number of days of hospitalization, but a Medicare beneficiary who is hospitalized must pay an annual hospital deductible, set once a year at the average national cost for a day of hospitalization. Once the deductible is met, Medicare pays for all medically necessary inpatient hospital care for the remainder of the year regardless of the cost or frequency of this care.

Part A also covers up to 150 days of skilled nursing facility care each year, with a copayment for each of the first 8 days of care. A skilled nursing facility is a specialized facility; most nursing homes in the United States are not skilled nursing facilities, and many skilled nursing facilities are not certified by Medicare. In addition, Medicare will not pay for a stay even in a certified skilled nursing facility if the services received are mainly personal or custodial services.

Part A pays for the intermittent services of a skilled nurse for a homebound beneficiary, and physical and speech therapist services furnished by a certified home health agency. However, Part A does not cover full-time nursing care, drugs, meals delivered to a home, or homemaker services. Services such as routine medical examinations and most dental services and hearing and vision testing are also excluded from coverage.

Medicare beneficiaries who are certified as terminally ill may elect to receive hospice care for an unlimited duration in lieu of other benefits. Part A will pay the full cost necessary for the symptom management and pain relief of a terminally ill beneficiary. There are no deductibles or copayments aside from limited cost sharing for outpatient drugs and inpatient respite care.

Anyone enrolled in Medicare Part A is automatically enrolled in Part B unless he or she states the desire not to be enrolled. There is a deductible for outpatient care covered by Part B, after which Medicare pays 80 percent of the amount that Medicare approves for covered services. Medicare sets a rate for doctors' fees based upon the average fee for a geographical area, and then reimburses the doctor or patient 80 percent of that amount. If a doctor charges more than the Medicare assignment, then the patient may have to pay the difference. For example, if a doctor charges $100, but Medicare's approved charge is $80, then Medicare will pay $64 (80 percent of $80). Supplemental insurance would probably cover the remaining 20 percent of the $80 ($16), but would likely not cover the difference between the actual charge and the Medicare assignment amount. In some states, doctors are prohibited from charging more than the Medicare approved charge. Patients should, in any case, check whether or not their doctor accepts Medicare assignment.

Services covered by Part B include:

Physicians' and surgeons' services, whether received at home or at a facility of any kind. Routine physical exams are excluded.

Home health visits. For a patient who does not have Part A, Part B pays the full cost of medically necessary home health visits for patients requiring skilled care. The only copayment is 20 percent of the cost of durable medical equipment.

Physical therapy and speech pathology services.

Certain other services and supplies, such as outpatient hospital services, X-rays and laboratory tests, certain ambulance services, and purchase or rental of durable medical equipment (such as wheelchairs).

Medicare coverage of outpatient prescription drugs is presently being phased in.

Expenses not covered by Medicare include:

Private duty nursing

Skilled nursing home care costs beyond 150 days a year

Custodial care in a nursing home or at home

Intermediate nursing home care

Physician charges above Medicare's approved amount

Most kinds of outpatient drugs

Care received outside the United States, except under certain circumstances in Mexico and Canada;

Dental care or dentures, checkups, most routine immunizations, cosmetic surgery, routine foot care, examinations for and the cost of eyeglasses or hearing aids.

Starting in 1990, the upper limit on a Medicare beneficiary's out-of-pocket expenses for Part B benefits will be set at $1370, due to rise with inflation. Once this limit has been reached, Medicare will pay 100 percent of all reasonable charges, instead of 80 percent.

Hospitals and other institutions file Medicare claims directly, and the patient receives notice of such charges and payments. Medicare frequently takes a long time to process these claims. Patients do need to file claims for Part B insurance services. If a doctor accepts Medicare assignments, he or she will file the claim and bill the patient the remaining 20 percent, but if a doctor does not accept the assignment, the patient will be billed directly and will be responsible for submitting a request for payment from Medicare.

If a patient believes Medicare's coverage of a claim is inappropriate, he or she may appeal the decision. Depending on whether the decision is part of Part A or Part B coverage, and on how large an amount the claim is for, this appeal should be addressed to different authorities.

Medicare has introduced the Prospective Payment System for Hospital Reimbursement, limiting payments to hospitals to a fixed amount per illness. Some patients have complained that this system has forced them to be discharged before they feel they are ready to be released. In order to prevent problems, a patient (or his or her family caretaker) should get in touch with the doctor and the hospital's discharge planner at the beginning of a hospital stay. A hospital social worker can make arrangements for services to assist the patient when he or she returns home. The more information the social worker is provided with and the more time he or she has to work on a discharge plan, the more smooth the departure is likely to be.

Retiree Medical Benefits

These benefits are provided by some companies to their former employees; they fill in some of the gaps in Medicare's coverage, meaning that the retiree may not need to purchase Medicare Supplemental Health Coverage.

Medicare Supplemental Health Coverage

This coverage, also known as "Medigap" insurance, can help pay for Medicare deductibles, the remaining 20 percent of a medical bill, or specific items not covered by Medicare. Supplemental insurance rarely covers a service that Medicare determines to be medically unnecessary. Before purchasing a supplemental health plan, the following policy features should be considered:

Deductibles. Many supplemental health plans, while paying for Medicare deductibles, also have their own deductibles.

Exclusions. Possible exclusions include routine physical or eye examinations, podiatric and dental care.

Preexisting illness. Some policies require a waiting period before they will provide coverage for a preexisting illness.

Renewability. Some policies can be cancelled on the basis of too many claims.

Maximum coverage limits. A health insurance plan may, for example, limit its coverage to $500 a year for prescription drugs.

State regulations. Insurance regulated by a policyholder's own state may provide more consumer protection.

Health Maintenance Organizations

HMOs emphasize a preventive approach to health care, and many cover the cost of a routine physical examination. With some HMOs, all out-of-pocket expenses not covered by Medicare are eliminated and replaced by a single monthly premium paid to the HMO. Advantages of an HMO may include:

A doctor assigned to coordinate all the patient's health care, eliminating fragmentary care

No deductibles

Coverage for preventive care

Convenient 24-hour daily access to health care

No paperwork

Many health care services available in one location

Fully covered office visits (with a small copayment, often $5 or so)

Possible disadvantages are:

Patient can only use physicians associated with the HMO, and may have fewer choices in selecting specialists

Members must use the hospitals and facilities with which the HMO is affiliated

If an older person using an HMO decides to change health care coverage, the following should be done before making the change:

Check to make sure the health plan is accepting new members

Make sure new coverage is in effect before cancelling old coverage

Let the HMO know that coverage is being terminated

Medicaid

Medicaid is funded by the state and federal governments. Unlike Medicare, Medicaid will pay for extended nursing home care for eligible individuals. All older persons receiving Supplemental Security Income (SSI) are eligible. In some states, individuals whose incomes are too high to qualify normally for Medicaid may qualify if their medical expenses are so large that their net income is reduced to a level within state requirements. This process whereby individuals become eligible for Medicaid is called spending down. Formulas and criteria for spending down vary from state to state. Elderly persons and their children should be cautioned about certain techniques that are sometimes used to qualify an elderly person or couple for Medicaid, such as giving all of their assets to their children or placing their assets in an irrevocable trust.

Long-Term Care Insurance

This is a relatively new type of insurance policy designed to fill the large gaps left by Medicare with respect to nursing home and home health care. The amount of coverage, deductibles, exclusions, and other factors all vary depending on the policy. Comprehensive coverage can be very expensive, particularly if the person who obtains the coverage is already quite old. A thorough evaluation of several competing policies is recommended for those who want to purchase this coverage.

Continuous Care Communities

A recent innovation in care for senior citizens is the continuous care community. The individual or couple typically pays a substantial admission fee in addition to monthly payments in return for lifetime residential accommodations and nursing home care when needed. These communities offer the elderly

Table 11–10. Life Expectancy Tables

Age in 1986 (years)	Expectation of Life in Years					Expected Deaths per 1,000 Alive at Specified Age[1]				
		White		Black			White		Black	
	Total	Male	Female	Male	Female	Total	Male	Female	Male	Female
At birth	74.8	72.0	78.8	65.2	73.5	10.36	10.02	7.80	20.04	16.09
1	74.6	71.7	78.4	65.5	73.7	.72	.76	.57	1.16	.96
2	73.6	70.8	77.5	64.6	72.8	.55	.55	.44	.94	.79
3	72.7	69.8	76.5	63.6	71.9	.43	.42	.34	.76	.64
4	71.7	68.8	75.5	62.7	70.9	.35	.34	.27	.62	.52
5	70.7	67.8	74.6	61.7	69.9	.29	.30	.22	.51	.43
6	69.8	66.9	73.6	60.7	69.0	.26	.28	.19	.43	.35
7	68.8	65.9	72.6	59.8	68.0	.23	.26	.17	.37	.29
8	67.8	64.9	71.6	58.8	67.0	.21	.23	.15	.33	.25
9	66.8	63.9	70.6	57.8	66.0	.19	.20	.14	.30	.22
10	65.8	62.9	69.6	56.8	65.0	.17	.18	.13	.30	.20
11	64.8	61.9	68.6	55.8	64.1	.18	.19	.14	.32	.20
12	63.8	61.0	67.7	54.9	63.1	.23	.27	.17	.40	.22
13	62.9	60.0	66.7	53.9	62.1	.34	.43	.23	.52	.25
14	61.9	59.0	65.7	52.9	61.1	.47	.64	.30	.69	.30
15	60.9	58.0	64.7	52.0	60.1	.63	.88	.39	.88	.36
16	59.9	57.1	63.7	51.0	59.1	.78	1.10	.46	1.08	.43
17	59.0	56.1	62.8	50.1	58.2	.90	1.29	.52	1.30	.49
18	58.0	55.2	61.8	49.1	57.2	.99	1.42	.54	1.54	.55
19	57.1	54.3	60.8	48.2	56.2	1.04	1.50	.53	1.80	.60

Table 11-10. Life Expectancy Tables (Continued)

Age in 1986 (years)	Expectation of Life in Years					Expected Deaths per 1,000 Alive at Specified Age[1]				
		White		Black			White		Black	
	Total	Male	Female	Male	Female	Total	Male	Female	Male	Female
20	56.2	53.4	59.9	47.3	55.3	1.09	1.58	.52	2.07	.66
21	55.2	52.5	58.9	46.4	54.3	1.15	1.66	.52	2.35	.73
22	54.3	51.5	57.9	45.5	53.3	1.18	1.70	.51	2.58	.79
23	53.3	50.6	56.9	44.6	52.4	1.20	1.69	.51	2.74	.86
24	52.4	49.7	56.0	43.7	51.4	1.19	1.66	.52	2.87	.93
25	51.5	48.8	55.0	42.8	50.5	1.18	1.60	.52	2.98	1.00
26	50.5	47.9	54.0	42.0	49.5	1.17	1.55	.53	3.12	1.07
27	49.6	47.0	53.1	41.1	48.6	1.18	1.53	.54	3.28	1.17
28	48.7	46.0	52.1	40.2	47.6	1.21	1.56	.55	3.48	1.28
29	47.7	45.1	51.1	39.4	46.7	1.27	1.62	.57	3.72	1.40
30	46.8	44.2	50.1	38.5	45.7	1.33	1.69	.60	3.98	1.55
31	45.8	43.2	49.2	37.7	44.8	1.39	1.76	.63	4.23	1.69
32	44.9	42.3	48.2	36.8	43.9	1.45	1.82	.67	4.49	1.82
33	44.0	41.4	47.2	36.0	43.0	1.51	1.87	.71	4.75	1.91
34	43.0	40.5	46.3	35.2	42.1	1.56	1.90	.75	5.00	1.99
35	42.1	39.5	45.3	34.3	41.1	1.61	1.95	.79	5.27	2.07
36	41.2	38.6	44.3	33.5	40.2	1.69	2.02	.85	5.55	2.17
37	40.2	37.7	43.4	32.7	39.3	1.78	2.11	.93	5.88	2.32
38	39.3	36.8	42.4	31.9	38.4	1.90	2.22	1.03	6.25	2.53
39	38.4	35.9	41.5	31.1	37.5	2.04	2.37	1.14	6.65	2.79

Table 11–10. Life Expectancy Tables (*Continued*)

Age in 1986 (years)	Expectation of Life in Years					Expected Deaths per 1,000 Alive at Specified Age[1]				
		White		Black			White		Black	
	Total	Male	Female	Male	Female	Total	Male	Female	Male	Female
40	37.4	34.9	40.5	30.3	36.6	2.20	2.54	1.27	7.11	3.09
41	36.5	34.0	39.6	29.5	35.7	2.38	2.73	1.42	7.58	3.40
42	35.6	33.1	38.6	28.7	34.8	2.57	2.95	1.57	8.02	3.68
43	34.7	32.2	37.7	28.0	34.0	2.77	3.18	1.71	8.40	3.94
44	33.8	31.3	36.7	27.2	33.1	2.98	3.43	1.86	8.75	4.18
45	32.9	30.4	35.8	26.4	32.2	3.22	3.72	2.03	9.10	4.42
46	32.0	29.5	34.9	25.7	31.4	3.50	4.05	2.22	9.52	4.71
47	31.1	28.7	33.9	24.9	30.5	3.82	4.44	2.45	10.11	5.08
48	30.2	27.8	33.0	24.1	29.7	4.21	4.90	2.72	10.92	5.56
49	29.4	26.9	32.1	23.4	28.8	4.67	5.42	3.04	11.91	6.14
50	28.5	26.1	31.2	22.7	28.0	5.17	6.00	3.39	13.03	6.78
51	27.6	25.2	30.3	22.0	27.2	5.70	6.64	3.77	14.17	7.45
52	26.8	24.4	29.4	21.3	26.4	6.27	7.35	4.15	15.25	8.08
53	26.0	23.6	28.6	20.6	25.6	6.85	8.14	4.53	16.21	8.65
54	25.1	22.7	27.7	19.9	24.8	7.46	9.01	4.93	17.09	9.19
55	24.3	21.9	26.8	19.3	24.0	8.10	9.94	5.35	17.96	9.70
56	23.5	21.2	26.0	18.6	23.3	8.82	10.94	5.83	18.95	10.31
57	22.7	20.4	25.1	18.0	22.5	9.64	12.06	6.39	20.24	11.17
58	21.9	19.6	24.3	17.3	21.8	10.60	13.30	7.07	21.94	12.35
59	21.2	18.9	23.4	16.7	21.0	11.68	14.65	7.85	23.97	13.78

Table 11-10. Life Expectancy Tables (Continued)

Age in 1986 (years)	Expectation of Life in Years					Expected Deaths per 1,000 Alive at Specified Age[1]				
		White		Black			White		Black	
	Total	Male	Female	Male	Female	Total	Male	Female	Male	Female
60	20.4	18.2	22.6	16.1	20.3	12.87	16.14	8.70	26.24	15.39
61	19.7	17.5	21.8	15.5	19.6	14.11	17.70	9.61	28.54	16.99
62	18.9	16.8	21.0	15.0	19.0	15.36	19.31	10.53	30.68	18.40
63	18.2	16.1	20.2	14.4	18.3	16.58	20.92	11.46	32.52	19.49
64	17.5	15.4	19.5	13.9	17.7	17.82	22.57	12.40	34.13	20.35
65	16.8	14.8	18.7	13.4	17.0	19.10	24.28	13.41	35.69	21.15
70	13.6	11.7	15.1	10.8	13.9	29.01	37.82	20.93	49.25	29.85
75	10.7	9.1	11.8	8.7	11.1	43.45	57.82	32.69	68.36	42.47
80	8.1	6.9	8.8	6.8	8.5	66.00	87.57	52.87	97.05	64.22
85 and over	6.0	5.1	6.4	5.5	6.7	1,000.00	1,000.00	1,000.00	1,000.00	1,000.00

[1]Based on the proportion of the cohort who are alive at the beginning of an indicated age interval who will die before reaching the end of that interval. For example, out of every 1,000 people alive and exactly 50 years old at the beginning of the period, between 5 and 6 (5.17) will die before reaching their 51st birthdays.

Source: U.S. National Center for Health Statistics, *Vital Statistics of the United States,* annual.

person the advantages of independent living, long-term security, and affordable nursing home care. However, the financial stability of many continuous care communities is shaky, and, therefore, prior to signing up, it is important to thoroughly evaluate the financial strength of the community.

LIFE EXPECTANCY TABLES

Table 11-10 shows the expectation of life and expected deaths, by gender, race, and age. Life expectancy tables can help you plan for sufficient funding of your retirement resources in order to support you and your dependents for the rest of your life. Of course, these tables are only a rough approximation, and many specialists now suggest using a life expectancy of 85 to 90 years old for people who are nearing retirement age and who are in reasonably good health.

12

Estate Planning

Effective estate planning should be uncomplicated, while achieving several worthwhile objectives, including:

Minimizing the problems and expenses of probate; to avoid potential family conflicts, where possible.

Providing your spouse with as much responsibility and flexibility in estate management as desired, consistent with potential tax savings.

Providing for the conservation of your estate and its effective management following death of either or both spouses.

Minimizing taxes at time of death as well as income taxes after death.

Avoid leaving the children "too much too soon."

Providing for adequate liquidity to cover taxes and other expenses at death without the necessity of forced sale of assets.

Providing for estate management in event of incapacity of either spouse.

Coordinating your personal estate plan with all business arrangements, if applicable.

Organizing all important papers affecting your estate plan in a spot known to all family members and reviewing them at least annually.

Informing family members about the overall estate plan.

Yet, many of us fail to complete even the most basic estate planning documents. While it's no fun contemplating our own mortality, it is a tremendous relief to organize your estate. Chances are, your personal records will also be better organized if you get your estate in order. Beyond the basics of a will, there are several more sophisticated estate planning techniques including durable power of attorney or living trust, living will, and letter of instructions; and you don't have to be Rockefeller to take advantage of many of them.

The 1990s will witness an unprecedented transfer of wealth through inheritances as these who took advantage of the post-World War II economic boom die and pass on their wealth to children and grandchildren. This, combined with a higher savings rate and a general trend toward increasing affluence among middle- and upper-class families, will mean that many families will find themselves with rather large estates that require more than passing estate planning attention. Even those people who have taken the time to prepare estate planning documents may find that their estate has outgrown them. Unfortunately, many will not realize this, and even those who do may be reticent to devote the additional time and expense necessary to assure that their estates have been properly planned.

Finally, Congress is beginning to pay more attention to the estate and gift tax as a means of raising additional revenue. There's a good chance that changes in the estate and gift tax laws will occur in the 1990s, and any changes do not bode well even for moderately affluent families. According to many experts, the tightening of the estate and gift tax laws will probably not affect many of the estate plans already in effect. This is all the more reason to attend to important estate planning matters sooner rather than later.

ESSENTIAL ESTATE PLANNING DOCUMENTS

Estate planning need not be complicated to be effective. A simple estate plan will save legal fees and unnecessary delays and ensure that your estate is distributed in accordance with your wishes. It may also have some positive effects while you are still alive. Unless you want to leave your family in chaos after your demise, take the following minimum steps to provide your loved ones, and yourself, some peace of mind. Single people need to plan their estate as well because it is highly unlikely that your estate will be distributed in accordance with your wishes upon your demise. For example, many single people want to leave at least a portion of their estate to charity, yet if they die intestate (without a will), the charity will never see any of that money.

Minimum Estate Planning Needs

A minimum estate plan usually consists of four documents.

Valid and Up-To-Date Will. Everyone knows the importance of preparing and maintaining a will, yet the vast majority of adults do not have wills. Your will should specify exactly how your estate is to be divided. It should be drawn up by an experienced attorney. Intestate estates incur higher than necessary legal fees and unnecessary delays. Still worse, a judge, rather than you, will decide how your estate is to be distributed. Changing your will to reflect changes in your personal circumstances (possibly including moving to another state) or changes in state and federal laws is also essential, and often overlooked. Writing a will is simple, but it's not foolproof.

An experienced lawyer can help you draw up a will to specify exactly how you want your estate divided. Of course, your will does not prevent you from doing whatever you like with your property while you're still alive.

Durable Power of Attorney. The second essential estate planning document will become indispensable if you ever become incapacitated (through accident, illness, or age) and unable to handle your financial affairs. If this happens, your right to manage your own money may be revoked by a court order and a guardian will be appointed. It is possible that the court will not appoint the guardian that you would have chosen, and the difficulties in securing court approval of the guardian's actions will create undue red tape and confusion. The simplest way to protect personal assets and ensure that they will continue to be managed as you see fit is to appoint a guardian for yourself through a durable power of attorney.

Assigning a durable power of attorney ensures that if you ever become unable to manage your own financial and personal affairs, someone that you trust will act on your behalf. A power of attorney may be either special, applying to only certain situations, or general, giving the attorney-in-fact virtually limitless control over the principal (the person who created the arrangement). General powers of attorney should be avoided; they are dangerous, subject to abuse, and usually unnecessary. A power of attorney may also be either indefinite or for a specific length of time. No matter how it is assigned, it may be cancelled at any time, and it terminates immediately upon the death of the principal.

An alternative to a durable power of attorney is a living trust. Living trusts may be preferable to a durable power of attorney in some states, and may provide other estate planning advantages as well. Check with an attorney who can objectively advise you on the efficacy of living trusts.

Living Will. You may be aware of the dilemmas surrounding terminally ill patients and the importance of trying to accommodate the patient's wishes. If you are concerned about these matters, you should consider drafting a so-called living will, informing family members and physicians that under certain circumstances you do not wish to be kept alive by artificial means. Living wills are legally recognized in most states, and even where they are not, experts suggest that preparing one anyway can be very helpful if the need to make these difficult decisions arises.

Letter of Instructions. A letter of instructions is not as crucial as other essential estate planning documents, but you will be doing your heirs a big favor by preparing one. A letter of instructions is an informal document (you don't need an attorney to prepare it) that gives your survivors information concerning important financial and personal matters. Although it does not carry the legal weight of a will, the letter of instructions is very important because it clarifies any further requests to be carried out upon death and provides essential financial information, thus relieving the surviving family members of needless worry and speculation.

Obviously, your survivors will benefit if you prepare a letter of instructions, but you will too; a well-prepared letter of instructions is a great way to organize your records. Be sure to keep it up-to-date since the information contained herein is likely to change. Finally, make sure your heirs know where the letter is.

The four documents described above are the essential components of a basic estate plan. You may well be able to benefit from other estate planning techniques, including trusts, gifts to relatives, and selecting the appropriate form of property ownership. As with most estate planning matters, experienced legal assistance is necessary.

ESTATE PLANNING TECHNIQUES

While you probably understand the need to have certain basic estate planning documents, including a will, you may not be familiar with various estate planning techniques that can help you in the here and now as well as benefit your heirs in the hereafter.

Property Ownership Designations

Joint ownership of property is common, particularly among married couples, and it can be advantageous from an estate planning standpoint if the estate is fairly small. But jointly held property is not desirable in many instances; in fact it is possible that the property may be subject to estate taxation *twice* in the case of property held jointly with nonspouses. Also, the surviving spouse can ignore the decedent's wishes as to the ultimate disposition of the property. Where property is held jointly with a nonspouse (or severance of joint tenancy between nonspouses) gift taxes can result. The best person to advise you on this, as well as other important estate planning matters, is an attorney. Ideally, the attorney should have considerable experience in estate planning.

Lifetime Gifts

As you probably know, the annual gift tax exclusion allows you to give up to $10,000 per year per person in gifts, as well as direct payments of tuition to educational institutions and of medical expenses. While gifts to children and grandchildren are a convenient way for high net worth families to reduce the size of their taxable estate during their lifetimes, you should be cautioned against being so generous that you end up jeopardizing your own financial well-being. Also, be particularly wary of giving money to children with the expectation that they will pay it back. Finally, the common practice of the elderly of giving money to relatives so that they can qualify for Medicaid in the event they have to go to a nursing home is full of pitfalls.

Disposition of Family Businesses

Owners of closely held businesses face particularly thorny estate planning problems. Although Congress is considering changing the legislation somewhat, current tax rules (known as anti-estate-freeze provisions) are particularly burdensome on family businesses. Therefore, careful planning is necessary to assure that the business can continue operating successfully without family rancor should the owner die. An additional estate planning consideration involves the eventual sale of the business during the owner's lifetime, whether to family members or outsiders. There are a variety of mechanisms for dealing with these problems including buy–sell agreements, installment sales of company stock, private annuities, life insurance trusts, and employee stock ownership plans.

Selection of an Executor

Many people unknowingly select an inappropriate estate executor. While close relatives are the natural choice for many people and it usually works out well, sometimes it does not. The following list of reasons why it may not work out can guide you in making sure you select an appropriate executor:

Inexperience (particularly with complicated estates)

Lack of time or inclination to devote to proper estate administration

Inability to get along with relatives

Conflict of interests between executor and other beneficiaries

Estate Liquidity

Many people fail to consider the fact that their survivors will need access to cash immediately after death. Liquidity needs may include:

Funeral expenses and expenses of final illness

Federal estate taxes and state death taxes

Federal and state income taxes

Probate and administration expenses

Payment of maturing debts

Maintenance and welfare of the family

Payment of specific cash bequests

Funds to continue running a family business

These needs must be estimated, and your estate and personal financial planning should provide your survivors with timely access to sufficient resources to meet these needs.

Multistate Property Ownership

More and more people divide their time between two states and/or own property in more than one state. Those in this situation need to be particularly careful as to establishing primary residence in one state. Even so, there may still be problems where property is located in more than one state since each state may attempt to collect death taxes on the property. Sometimes, a living trust can alleviate these problems. Expert legal advice is necessary under any circumstances.

Trusts

Whether they are established during your lifetime (living trusts) or take effect upon your death (testamentary trusts), trusts can provide a great deal of flexibility in how you want your estate handled and distributed. For example, many people are very uncomfortable with the thought that their spouses and children will receive their shares of the estate with no strings attached. However, a simple will (and most adults don't even have one) does just that. Some trusts have the added advantage of saving taxes and/or protecting your estate from creditors. One of the most commonly overlooked estate tax saving trust arrangements are marital trusts that are designed to make maximum use of the unified credit. The section entitled "Trust Summary" describes many commonly used trusts.

CHARITABLE REMAINDER INTEREST SUMMARY

Table 12-1 illustrates the characteristics and benefits of various types of charitable remainder interests. These programs have a number of tax-saving benefits for charitably inclined donors. First, there is a partial charitable income tax deduction for the value of the cash, securities, or property that is donated. Second, you (and, if you choose, other beneficiaries) receive a lifetime income from the charity. Finally, the amount you contribute to the charity is removed from your estate which can reduce estate taxes. Many people are beginning to take advantage of these arrangements. To find out more details,

Table 12–1. Characteristics and Benefits of Charitable Remainder Interests

	Type of Charitable Remainder Interest					
	Gift Annuity	Deferred Gift Annuity	Pooled Income Fund	Net Income Unitrust	Basic Unitrust	Annuity Trust
Types of Gifts:						
Cash or unappreciated securities	Yes	Yes	Yes	Yes	Yes	Yes
Appreciated securities	Yes	Yes	Yes	Yes	Yes	Yes
Real property	Yes	Yes	In special cases	Yes	In special cases	In special cases
Annual Income	Fixed	Fixed	Variable	Variable	Variable	Fixed
Taxes[1]:						
Charitable deduction	Yes	Yes	Yes	Yes	Yes	Yes
Annual income	Partly tax-free	Partly tax-free	Fully taxable	May be either	May be either	May be either
Initial capital gains	Partially taxable	Partially taxable	Usually tax-free	Usually tax-free	Usually tax-free	Usually tax-free
Management of Property Donated[2]:	Not held in trust	Not held in trust	Commingled	Separate	Separate	Separate

[1]Gift taxes can generally be precluded in all cases and estate taxes are eliminated except when one of the beneficiaries is a nonspouse.
[2]Some donors prefer that the assets donated be managed separately.

contact your favorite charity. They will be more than happy to explain the features of the various alternative programs summarized in this table.

TRUST SUMMARY

Trusts are usually thought of as being appropriate only for the very wealthy. Yet, trusts can play an important role in the lifetime and estate planning for people of more modest financial circumstances. This section highlights the many different kinds of trusts as well as the many ways a trust might be appropriate for you.

Trusts That Can Protect an Estate

A **minor's testamentary trust** is created in a will for the purpose of protecting your children's inheritance. The trustee of this trust handles its assets for the children's benefit. This prevents poor management of their inheritance by an incompetent guardian. Also, a minor's testamentary trust can establish limits and control of your heirs' access to their inheritance until they reach the age that you feel they are mature enough to handle the entire sum wisely.

A **testamentary discretionary spendthrift trust** is also created in a will. This type of trust provides security for a disabled beneficiary. It supplements government assistance by allowing for the trustee to distribute income from the fund to the disabled beneficiary. If he or she is unable to handle this money, it is given to his guardian to spend in the best interest of the beneficiary.

A **revocable living trust** is a trust into which you put your assets while you are alive. A will only affects property that is in your name at the time of your death. So, if your state is probate-unfriendly, this type of trust can be used effectively to avoid the publicity, delay, and expense involved with the probate process. The advantages of a revocable living trust include the following:

You can act as the trustee

You can keep some or all of the income it produces

You can alter its provisions

You can terminate the trust at any time

It avoids interruption of your family's income when the settlor dies or becomes disabled

It allows for an operating business to continue uninterrupted

It relieves the settlor of the burdens of investment management

It requires less accounting, administration, and judicial supervision than a testamentary trust

In some states, a revocable living trust places property beyond the reach of the settlor's creditors

After the death of the settlor, the trust can remain intact to benefit the heirs, or the trust can be dissolved and the property distributed, according to your instructions, by the successor trustee named in the trust agreement.

Income produced by a revocable living trust is taxable but, once the settlor has died, it becomes an irrevocable trust. The beneficiaries are therefore entitled to any of the tax savings that an irrevocable trust provides. In general, however, there are no immediate income tax or first generation estate tax advantages provided by a revocable living trust. Also, the cost of operating this type of trust may be high.

A **revocable standby trust** is established to take over the settlor's asset management when he or she becomes unable to do so. These circumstances could include a long trip or a serious physical or mental disability. A standby trust helps to avoid long legal incompetency proceedings. This type of trust is not created to save taxes. A standby trust is usually revocable, however, if the settlor becomes permanently disabled or incapacitated, there may be a provision included in the trust that makes it irrevocable.

Despite the fact that there are now laws to prevent parents from sheltering money from taxes by putting it in their children's names, there are still reasons to open an **irrevocable 2503(c) trust**. When you establish this trust you are giving up control of the trust property and the power to change the trust agreement, thus, the trust's assets are no longer a part of your taxable estate. With an irrevocable 2503(c) trust, you may restrict the beneficiary from obtaining the trust's income and principal until he or she reaches the age of 21 or even older if the beneficiary fails to claim the assets within 30 to 90 days of turning 21. There may also be some income tax reduction possibilities with a 2503(c) trust.

An **irrevocable Crummey trust** has essentially the same income and estate tax benefits as the irrevocable 2503(c) trust. However, one major difference is that the Crummey trust does not have to terminate when your child turns 21. This trust enables you to take advantage of the $10,000 dollar annual gift-tax exclusion by giving your beneficiary what are called Crummy powers. This means the beneficiary is allowed to withdraw a portion of the trust's principal each year. Despite these advantages, there can often be large legal and accounting fees associated with both the irrevocable Crummey trust and the irrevocable 2503(c) trust, so a considerable amount of money must be placed in the trust in order to make it cost-effective.

Trusts That Can Reduce Estate Taxes

Even married couples whose estates are less than $1 million can take advantage of certain trust arrangements that can end up saving the next generation well over $100,000 in federal estate taxes. These unified credit trusts are set up to hold that portion of the estate that is exempt from tax upon the death of the first spouse by reason of the $600,000 unified credit. The unified credit trust is designed to exempt the assets placed in the trust from estate taxation upon the death of the second spouse. In most cases to accomplish this, the choice will be between a power of appointment trust or a qualified terminable interest property (QTIP) trust.

The most distinctive characteristic of a **general power of appointment trust** is that it gives the surviving spouse the power to name (usually in a will) the ultimate beneficiary of the trust's assets, that is, a general power of appointment. If the surviving spouse fails to name a beneficiary of the assets, they will go to the beneficiary named by the spouse who died first. Two other essentials for setting up a general power of appointment trust are that it must give the surviving spouse life income interest in the trust property and it must give the trustee or surviving spouse the power to withdraw and use the trust principal for certain purposes. A common provision included in the trust states that the general power of appointment is exercisable only by will. This avoids having the capital gains of the trust taxable to the surviving spouse. If the spouse fails to execute the power of appointment, the trust's assets are included in his or her taxable estate.

A **qualified terminable interest property trust** is a way to ensure that life income interest given to your spouse will qualify for the marital deduction. However, the settlor of the QTIP may name the ultimate beneficiary of the trust himself. In order for this life income interest to qualify for the marital deduction there are certain requirements. First, the executor of the will must choose to have the interest from the trust treated as a QTIP. Also, the surviving spouse must be entitled to all of the income the trust produces, payable at least once a year. In addition, no one, including the surviving spouse, can have the power to distribute property to anyone but the spouse. Also, the QTIP interest in property that is not placed in trust must provide the surviving spouse with the rights to that income which ensures that it satisfies the rules of a marital deduction trust.

In order to avoid incurring estate taxes on life insurance proceeds, you can place your policies in an **irrevocable life insurance trust**. By doing this, you prevent your heirs from having to raise money to pay taxes on the money they received from your life insurance. On the other hand, when you set up a life insurance trust, you must give up all ownership rights. This includes the ability to borrow against the policies and to change the beneficiaries. Also, if you die within 3 years of setting up the trust, your insurance will be included in your taxable estate anyway.

A **grantor retained income trust** (GRIT) is an irrevocable trust in which you place property. You then receive all of the trust's income for up to 10 years. Neither you nor your spouse is allowed to be the trustee and, when the trust terminates, beneficiaries whom you choose receive all of the property. The tax savings comes from the value of the remainder interest (calculated by the IRS). If the trust's remainder interest is under the $600,000 dollar maximum, then there is no estate or gift tax and the money will pass to the beneficiaries tax-free.

When you set up a **charitable remainder trust,** you place your property in an irrevocable trust, the income from which is distributed to any number of beneficiaries who are selected by the settlor of the trust, including the settlor himself or herself. This trust includes the provision that when the last income recipient dies, the property in the trust is to be given to a qualified charity for unrestricted use. One tax saving benefit that a charitable remainder trust provides is an income tax deduction for the settlor based on the value of the property that the charity will ultimately receive. Another tax saving benefit is that the settlor's estate will not include the value of the property in the trust and, therefore, will not be taxed on it. Finally, the transfer of the income from settlor to the trust's beneficiaries may result in income tax savings.

A **charitable lead trust** is an irrevocable trust into which the settlor places property with the provision that the income from the property is to be given to a qualified charity. However, a charitable lead trust also includes the provision that on the occasion of the settlor's death, the property is to be given to any number of specified beneficiaries, typically family members. From the time the trust begins operation, the value of the property in the trust is no longer included in the settlor's taxable estate, but there is no immediate income tax deduction granted to the settlor upon the opening of the trust. At the expense of a lower cash flow, the transfer of income from the settlor to the charity can provide a significant estate tax savings.

PREPARING A LETTER OF INSTRUCTIONS

A letter of instructions is an informal document that gives your survivors information concerning important financial and personal matters. It should be accessible to your survivors immediately after your death. Since a letter of instructions is not a legal document like a will, you have a lot more leeway in both the language and content. Your letter is a good place to put personal wishes and final comments, but your heirs will be very grateful if you include some more useful information. This section suggests information that can be included in your letter of instructions. In addition, preparing a letter of instructions is a good way to start getting your records in order. Make sure your loved ones know where you store this document.

First Things to Do

Acquaintances and organizations to be called, including Social Security, the bank, your employer

Arrangements to be made with funeral home

Lawyer's name and telephone

Newspapers to receive obituary information

Location of insurance policies

Cemetary and Funeral

Details of your wishes and any arrangements you have made

Facts for Funeral Director

Vital statistics, including your full name, residence, marital status, spouse's name, date of birth, birthplace, father and mother's names and birthplaces, length of residence in state and in United States, military records/history, Social Security number, occupation, and life insurance information

Information for Death Certificate and Filing for Benefits

Citizen of, race, marital status, name of next of kin (other than spouse), relationship, address, and birthplace

Expected Death Benefits

Information about any potential death benefits from your employer (including life insurance, profit sharing, pension plan, or accident insurance), life insurance companies, Social Security, the Veterans Administration, or any other source

Special Wishes

Anything you want them to know

Personal Effects

A list of who is to receive certain personal effects

Personal Papers

Locations of important personal documents, including your will, birth and baptismal certificates, communion and confirmation certificates, diplomas, marriage certificate, military records, naturalization papers, and any others (for example, adoption, divorce)

Safe-Deposit Box

(State law may require the bank to seal the deceased's box as soon as notified of his death, even if the box is jointly owned.)

Location and number of box and key and an inventory of contents

Post Office Box

Location and number of box and key (or combination)

Income Tax Returns

Location of all previous returns
Location of your estimated tax file
Tax preparer's name

Loans Outstanding

Information for loans other than mortgages, including bank name and address, name on loan, account number, monthly payment, location of papers and payment book, collateral, and information on any life insurance on the loan

Debts Owed to the Estate

Debtor, description, terms, balance, location of documents, and comments on loan status/discharge

Social Security

Full name, Social Security number, and the location of Social Security cards

Life Insurance

Policy numbers and amounts, location of policy, whose life is insured, insurer's name and address, kind of policy, beneficiaries, issue and maturity date, payment options, and any special facts

Veteran's Administration

If you are a veteran, give information on collecting benefits from local Veteran's Administration office

Other Insurance

If any other insurance benefits or policies are in force (including accident, homeowners/renters, automobile, disability, medical, personal or professional liability), give insurer's name and address, policy number, beneficiary, coverage, location of policy, term, how acquired (if through employer or other group), agent

Investments

Stocks: Company, name on certificates, number of shares, certificate numbers, purchase price and date, and location of certificates

Bonds/notes/bills: Issuer, issued to, face amount, bond number, purchase price and date, maturity date, and location of certificates

Mutual funds: Company, name on account, number of shares or units, and location of statements and certificates

Other investments: For each investment, list amount invested, to whom issued, maturity date, issuer, and other applicable data, and location of certificates and other vital papers

Household Contents

List of contents with name of owners, form of ownership, and location of documents, inventory, and appraisals

Automobiles

For each car: Year, make, model, color, identification number, title in name(s) of, and location of title and registration

Important Warranties, Receipts

Location and description

Doctors' Names, Addresses, and Telephone Numbers

Including dentist, children's pediatrician, and children's dentist

Checking Accounts

Name of bank, name on account, account number, and location of passbook (or receipt) for all accounts

Credit Cards

For each card: Company (including telephone and address), name on card, number, and location of card

House, Condo, or Co-op

About the home: In whose name, address, legal description, other descriptions needed, lawyer at closing, and locations of statement of closing, policy of title insurance, deed, and land survey

About the mortgage: Held by, amount of original mortgage, date taken out, amount owed now, method of payment, and location of payment book, if any (or payment statements)

About life insurance on mortgage: Policy number, location of policy, and annual amount

About property taxes: Amount and location of receipts

About the cost of house: Initial buying price, purchase closing fee, other buying costs (real estate agent, legal, taxes), and home improvements

About improvements: What each consisted of, cost, date, and location of bills

For renters: Lease location and expiration date

Funeral Preferences

Specify whether or not you would like to have any of the following done: Donate organs, autopsy if requested, simple arrangements, embalming, public viewing, least expensive burial or cremation container, or immediate disposition. Remains should be: Donated (details of arrangements made), cremated (and the ashes: scattered, buried at), disposed of as follows (details), or buried (at)

Specify which of the following services should be performed: Memorial (after disposition), funeral (before disposition), or graveside to be held at: church, mortuary, or other

Table 12–2. Income Tax of Estates and Trusts For Tax Years
Beginning in 1990

If Taxable Income is:			Of the
Over	But Not Over	The Tax is:	Amount Over
$ 0	$ 5,450	15%	$ 0
5,450	14,150	$ 817.50 + 28%	5,450
14,150	28,320	3,253.50 + 33%	14,150
28,320	—	7,929.60 + 28%	28,320

Specify where memorial gifts should be given or whether or not to omit flowers

If prearrangements have been made with a mortuary, give details

Signature and Date

FEDERAL ESTATE TAX RATES

The following tables present federal estate tax rates for taxable years beginning 1990. Table 12-2 applies to income tax of estates and trusts for 1990. Note that the income tax brackets are adjusted for inflation each year. Table 12-3 shows the estate and gift tax rates applicable to the transfer of property from one person to another. This tax applies whether there is a gift made during the transferor's lifetime or upon the transferor's death.

Transfer Tax Rate Schedules

Note that each decedent is entitled to a $192,800 unified credit against transfer taxes which, in effect, means that the estate of decedents who did not make major gifts during their lifetime (in excess to the $10,000 annual gift tax exclusion) does not incur federal estate taxes on the first $600,000 of estate value. Such an estate may, however, incur state death taxes.

Table 12–3. Unified Transfer Tax Rate Schedules for Decedents Dying and Gifts Made

1988–1992

Amount		Tentative Tax		
Over	But Not Over	Tax + Percentage		On Excess Over
$ 0	$ 10,000	$ 0	18%	$ 0
10,000	20,000	1,800	20	10,000
20,000	40,000	3,800	22	20,000
40,000	60,000	8,200	24	40,000
60,000	80,000	13,000	26	60,000
80,000	100,000	18,200	28	80,000
100,000	150,000	23,800	30	100,000
150,000	250,000	38,800	32	150,000
250,000	500,000	70,800	34	250,000
500,000	750,000	155,800	37	500,000
750,000	1,000,000	248,300	39	750,000
1,000,000	1,250,000	345,800	41	1,000,000
1,250,000	1,500,000	448,300	43	1,250,000
1,500,000	2,000,000	555,800	45	1,500,000
2,000,000	2,500,000	780,800	49	2,000,000
2,500,000	3,000,000	1,025,800	53	2,500,000
3,000,000	10,000,000	1,290,800	55	3,000,000
10,000,000	21,040,000	5,140,800	60	10,000,000
21,040,000		11,764,800	55	21,040,000

1993 and Thereafter

Amount		Tentative Tax		
Over	But Not Over	Tax + Percentage		On Excess Over
$ 0	$ 10,000	$ 0	18%	$ 0
10,000	20,000	1,800	20	10,000
20,000	40,000	3,800	22	20,000
40,000	60,000	8,200	24	40,000
60,000	80,000	13,000	26	60,000
80,000	100,000	18,200	28	80,000
100,000	150,000	23,800	30	100,000
150,000	250,000	38,800	32	150,000
250,000	500,000	70,800	34	250,000
500,000	750,000	155,800	37	500,000
750,000	1,000,000	248,300	39	750,000
1,000,000	1,250,000	345,800	41	1,000,000
1,250,000	1,500,000	448,300	43	1,250,000
1,500,000	2,000,000	555,800	45	1,500,000
2,000,000	2,500,000	780,800	49	2,000,000
2,500,000	10,000,000	1,025,800	50	2,500,000
10,000,000	18,340,000	4,775,800	55	10,000,000
18,340,000		9,362,800	50	18,340,000

Table 12–4. Federal Estate and Gift Publications
and Tax Return Forms

Publications

Publication Number	Title
448	Federal Estate and Gift Taxes
525	Taxable and Nontaxable Income
559	Tax Information for Survivors, Executors and Administrators
721	Comprehensive Tax Guide to U.S. Civil Service Retirement Benefits
904	Interrelated Computations for Estate and Gift Taxes

Estate and Gift Tax Return Forms

Form	Title
706	U.S. Estate and Generation-Skipping Transfer Tax Return
706-A	U.S. Additional Estate Tax Return
706-B	Generation-Skipping Transfer Tax Return
706CE	Certification of Payment of Foreign Death Tax
706NA	Federal Estate (and Generation-Skipping Transfer) Tax Return for Estate of Nonresident Alien
709	U.S. Gift (and Generation-Skipping Transfer) Tax Return
709-A	U.S. Short Form Gift Tax Return
712	Life Insurance Statement
1041	U.S. Fiduciary Income Tax Return
4351	Interest Computation—Estate Tax Deficiency on Installment Basis
4768	Application for Extension of Time to File U.S. Estate Tax Return and/or Pay Estate Tax
4808	Computation of Credit for Gift Tax (No Credit Allowed for Gifts Made after 12/31/76)
6180	Line adjustment—Estate Tax

FEDERAL ESTATE AND GIFT PUBLICATIONS AND TAX RETURN FORMS

Table 12-4 is a list of federal estate and gift publications and commonly used tax return forms, all of which are available at no cost from the Internal Revenue Service. The publications can be very helpful in handling the many complexities of settling the estate of a loved one, although legal and estate tax preparation assistance will probably be needed as well. The forms and publications may be ordered by calling the IRS; check your local phone listings.

13

Industry Forecasts

This chapter contains the outlook of 57 major industries through the mid-1990s. It is divided into 2 sections. The first consists of an index of all industries surveyed, including an indication of the 5-year outlook for each—positive, neutral, or negative. The second section consists of brief forecasts for each industry, including important developments.

Industry forecasts can be quite useful in making an investment decision. All other things being equal, you are well-advised to prefer investments in companies that participate in industries whose outlook is positive and to avoid companies in lackluster industries. You may also find these forecasts useful in your business and occupational planning.

Be forewarned, however, that industry outlooks are subject to change on fairly short notice. For example, the Iraqi crisis in the latter half of 1990 caused serious tremors in the petroleum markets. In turn, the short-term outlook for many industries that rely directly or indirectly on petroleum products changed almost overnight.

INDEX

Industry Outlooks (↑ = Positive; ↔ = Neutral or Mixed; ↓ = Negative)

Household Appliances ↑
Household Furniture ↔
Insurance
    Brokerage Services ↑
    Life ↔
    Property/Casualty ↓
Machine Tools ↓
Management, Consulting, and Public Relations Services ↑
Motion Pictures ↑
Music ↔
Mutual Funds ↑
Oil Field Machinery ↑
Paper and Paperboard Mills ↑
Pulp Mills ↑
Passenger Cars ↔
Petroleum Refining ↔
Pharmaceutical Preparations ↔
Publishing
    Books ↔
    Newspapers ↔
    Magazines ↔
Rubber Products ↓
Retailing ↔
Semiconductors and Related Devices ↑
Semiconductor Manufacturing Equipment ↔
Steel Mill Products ↓
Telephone and Telegraph Equipment ↔
Travel Services ↑
Transportation
    Trucking ↑
    Railroad (Passenger) ↑
    Water (Deep Sea Foreign Transportation) ↔

INDUSTRIAL FORECASTS

Aerospace/Defense

The aerospace industry includes companies involved in the production and shipment of aircraft and aircraft engines and parts, as well as space exploration and defense equipment.

In the early 1990s, the U.S. military aircraft sector should contribute once again to industry growth, although this will be tempered somewhat by a continued decline in defense spending. Because of the long lead times involved in the production of military aircraft, signs of expansion will appear first in the aircraft equipment sectors. Into the mid-1990s, the projected compound annual rates of growth for the individual aerospace sectors are as follows: aircraft, 1.8 percent; aircraft engines and engine parts, 3.0 percent; aircraft equipment, 2.9 percent; guided missiles and space vehicles, 6.5 percent; missile and space propulsion units, 6.5 percent; and missile and space vehicle equipment, 6.3 percent. The combined value of aerospace shipments is forecast to climb at a compound annual rate of 3.4 percent.

Airlines

The airline industry's profits and losses track periods of growth and recession in the nation's economy. However, a general upward spiral in passenger fares, coupled with reductions in public convenience, could lead to the reintroduction of federal oversight, reducing the industry's freedom and placing a damper on the performance of some firms. The emerging shortage of qualified cockpit crews and the lagging expansion of the airways system could also have a significant negative impact if these problems are not addressed immediately. Failure to expand the infrastructure to match increases in the demand for air services can only stifle growth in capacity and bring higher prices for the services that are available. Aggressive independent regionals will probably find success by developing nonstop service between second-tier markets while price-matching the majors.

Apparel

The industry will face both challenges and opportunities in the years ahead. The overriding challenge stems from the intensely competitive environment within the U.S. apparel industry and the need to anticipate how best to attract the interest of today's sophisticated consumers. Anticipated demographic changes will provide new opportunities; the fastest population growth is expected in the 35 to 54 age group, which typically has rising income and high consumption rates and is therefore a key element in the growth of demand for apparel. Manufacturers whose strategies best integrate the elements of manufacturing costs, technology, marketing, and flexibility will meet with the greatest success.

Banks and Savings & Loans

Commercial Banking. Bad real estate loans have plagued many of the superregionals, and this trend is expected to continue in the near term. Weak loan demand could also have a negative impact.

On the other hand, new technologies could help the industry expand later in the decade. The evolution of electronic technology in the form of electronic funds transfer (EFT) will continue to affect every aspect of the financial services industry. Bank customer use of EFT is mainly concentrated on automated teller machines (ATMs), but point-of-sale (POS) technology is the natural outgrowth of these systems. Such technology permits retail customers to pay for goods and services by using a computerized method to debit their bank accounts. Closer cooperation among commercial banks, other depository institutions, and retail merchants will be required in order to achieve uniform standards, lower cost to customers, and improved security in these potentially popular systems. Home banking might also grow, especially if tied in to other services such as bill paying, financial planning services, home shopping, airline reservations, electronic mail, and educational and entertainment programs.

Savings Institutions. An industry dedicated to housing finance may no longer be necessary because mortgage banking companies can originate residential mortgages, and secondary mortgage market investors will ultimately fund them. Indeed, there has been a decline in both the proportion of mortgage loans originated and held (including mortgage-backed securities) by savings institutions. On the other hand, savings institutions that have specialized in residential mortgage lending are very profitable and highly solvent. They have a comparative advantage in the origination and holding of mortgage loans, and the secondary mortgage market may not be big enough to fill the void should they cease to exist.

Biotechnology

During the early 1990s, some of the 80-odd biotechnology-derived drugs and vaccines now in research and testing may be approved. The market value of new biotechnology-derived products could reach several billion dollars, and by the early twenty-first century, the market could be worth $15 billion to $40 billion. Improved livestock could appear on the market by the late 1990s, biosensors by the year 2000, and genetically engineered plants and microorganisms by the mid-1990s. The potential sales of these products will vary widely, depending on their effectiveness, quality, safety, and uses, as well as on competitive factors.

Chemicals

Agricultural. After the 10 percent increase in 1989, U.S. consumption of nitrogen fertilizer should return to its former sluggish growth rate of about 1 percent per year. Investment in additional U.S. capacity is not likely, so imports will probably rise. The rate of increase in U.S. consumption of phosphate fertilizers should return to 1 to 2 percent per year. Even though U.S. exports should continue to absorb about 50 percent of production through the early 1990s, the U.S. share of the world market is expected to diminish because of Morocco's comparative advantage in world trade. Long-term growth of the U.S. pesticides industry will require improvement in domestic and world agricultural productivity, surviving consolidation into competitive multinationals, and attracting investment despite the lack of international constraints on violators of intellectual property rights.

Inorganic. Through the early 1990s, the inorganic chemicals industry is expected to grow at the modest rate of 2 percent a year. Demand for these products is tied directly to the progress of the economy as a whole and particularly to that of the housing, automobile, fertilizer, and pulp and paper industries. Diversification into the production of specialty and high-grade chemicals with higher value added will continue, but at a slow pace. Imports of inorganic chemicals will resume their decline. If the value of the dollar remains relatively low, export levels will stabilize and gradually increase over time as foreign demand expands.

Computers

Professional Services. If the national economy remains strong and foreign sources of revenue continue to increase, this industry sector should achieve average annual growth rates in current-dollar revenues exceeding 17 percent into the mid-1990s—total revenues approaching $70 billion. Computer training and consulting will continue to gain market shares. Acquisition and use of computers by those who are marginally computer literate will increase and will continue to reconfigure the professional services market. Providers of computer professional services have a very bright future.

Workstations. Dramatic improvements in the price and performance of workstations should continue during the early 1990s and spur demand for these systems. By the mid-1990s, entry-level workstations will have the power of some of today's mainframes, for under $2,000. At the high end, graphics supercomputers could have 5 times the scalar performance of the most powerful mainframes currently available and the vector processing capabilities of today's midrange supercomputers. But if U.S. suppliers are to keep their leadership in the world market intact, they must maintain their technological edge over foreign competitors, particularly the Japanese.

Software. Software sales are expected to overtake hardware revenues as users increasingly seek added value for their installed hardware bases. The U.S. software industry should continue to attract investment capital and new entrants, maintaining an annual growth rate in revenues of between 20 and 25 percent through the early 1990s. By then the industry should command at least $50 billion in annual revenues. The worldwide software market should then exceed $130 billion. On the downside, U.S. firms may be forced to trade their software secrets for key components manufactured abroad and thus lose their major international competitive advantage.

Personal Computers. The brisk rate of growth in personal computers will continue as peripherals, software, and networks are developed to take advantage of the availability of faster, more powerful chips. Long-term growth should be in the range of 6 to 10 percent annually. Sales of 16-bit computers will begin to decline in favor of more powerful 32-bit machines. The less saturated small business and home markets for personal computers should grow faster than the corporate market.

Construction

Machinery. Today's machines have a faster work cycle than older equipment. In the long run, contractors will require fewer machines to do the same amount of work. In the shorter term, say, into the mid-1990s, product shipments will parallel GNP movement. Increases or decreases in building construction, surface mining activities, and public works funding will determine growth levels. Through effective worldwide distribution and service, product improvements, and a reputation for quality products, the U.S. industry will remain a leader in sales of construction machinery.

Nonresidential. Given the macroeconomic forecast for continued economic growth and fairly stable interest rates, the expected correction in private nonresidential construction could be relatively mild. Shopping center construction will rebound fairly quickly, whereas office construction will probably be the last category to recover. Industrial construction will gain for most of the early 1990s, especially if the trade deficit continues to drop. The reduction in hospital construction that was caused by cost-containment initiatives is largely over, and spending for this purpose will resume its long-term uptrend. Electric utility construction will probably increase during the early 1990s. The renovation market is likely to be stronger than the new construction market during the next 5 years.

Residential. Declining home ownership in the 1980s probably represents affordability difficulties rather than declining consumer preference for housing, pointing to strong pent-up demand for housing in the 1990s. Nonetheless, homebuilding is expected to grow more slowly than the overall economy through the mid-1990s, while expenditures for home improvement and repair are expected to remain strong throughout the 1990s as the housing stock ages.

Public Works. Public works construction will continue to increase modestly during the early 1990s, given the macroeconomic forecast of continued economic growth and fairly stable interest rates. During this period, it may be possible to provide substantial federal funds for construction through innovative financing techniques, increased user fees, or diversion of spending from nonconstruction programs. Maintenance and repair spending will probably increase faster than new construction spending, however, as the stock of infrastructure steadily becomes older and larger.

Consumer Electronics

Shipments of consumer electronics are expected to decline at an estimated annual rate of 0.2 percent into the mid-1990s. For U.S. companies in this field, the outlook is not promising, except in niche areas such as large screen television sets and high-quality loudspeakers. Import, export, and domestic production decisions in the consumer electronics field will be made more and more by foreign-owned companies, unless new forces enter the market in such areas of advanced technology as high-definition television and recordable compact discs. Yet prospects are dim that any such advances will be transformed into domestically designed and produced goods, since the United States is no longer a supplier of many components vital to the production of electronics items. Research and development may also be constrained now that the largest forces in the market are controlled by interests outside the United States.

Electric Components Other Than Semiconductors

This huge, multibillion dollar industry provides the fundamental building blocks for computers, cars, industrial components, and consumer products. The outlook for the industry over the next few years is mixed. Although demand for electronic components (particularly from the computer and telecommunications sectors) should continue to be strong, demand from the consumer electronic sector could weaken.

Exports of electronic components by U.S. companies has increased dramatically in recent years, particularly in Southeast Asia and Europe. While this bodes well for the industry, competition from Japan will continue to affect both domestic growth and the trade picture.

Electric Power Generating Equipment

The United States must add generating capacity beginning in the mid-1990s. The timing and nature of the equipment orders for new plants remain uncertain. If established utilities add the capacity, the regulatory environment in most states dictates delay of actions until the latest possible date. Then, many utilities could add gas turbine capacity for later expansion by adding waste heat boilers and steam turbine generators. Should natural gas or oil become expensive, utilities could add coal gasification facilities. The timing of each step must closely match the utilities' load growth, thus reducing political and economic risk of surplus capacity. This scenario favors an integrated gasification combined cycle system using gas turbines, waste heat boilers, and small steam turbines; not the larger, super-critical boilers and turbines receiving consideration a few years ago. Independent power producers will add some portion of the nation's future base-load capacity. Enterprises that do not see electricity sales as their primary source of income will choose smaller, less sophisticated systems and equipment. Meanwhile, the long-term prospects for nuclear steam supply systems will remain dim due to environmental concerns.

Environmental Services

Years ago, residential and industrial waste was routinely poured into the air and water. Now, thanks to increased government regulation and public awareness of the environmental hazards caused by pollution, such waste must be collected and treated in order to minimize damage to the environment. This creates greater opportunities for companies involved in the treatment, collection, and disposal of residential and industrial waste. Although the rising cost of regulatory compliance has forced some smaller companies out of business, the growing need for pollution control is a strong indicator that there will be growth among the larger waste management companies over the next 5 years.

Food, Beverages, and Tobacco

Eating, drinking, and smoking never go out of style, and companies involved in these pursuits should fare reasonably well during the next 5 years. Even though consumption of red meat will continue to decline, the meat industry will continue to improve profitability through product innovations, the closing of inefficient plants, and increasing exports. Seafood, which became a staple in many American diets during the 1980s, will continue to gain consumer acceptance. Companies involved in the production of processed fruits, vegetables, and packaged meals will grow both domestically and internationally.

Nonalcoholic beverage producers will also prosper, thanks to continued domestic and foreign consumer demand for cold, sweet, fizzy soft drinks. On the other hand, producers of alcoholic beverages face a tough road ahead as consumers lower their consumption of alcohol in response to health and social concerns. Restrictions on advertising, labeling, and promotion of alcoholic beverages, as well as the possibility of increases in excise taxes, could also hamper the industry.

The tobacco industry will continue to be plagued with lower domestic demand, thanks to the widely known health risks of cigarettes, and the increasing number of lawsuits being brought by relatives of deceased smokers. However, growing exports, particularly to recently opened Far Eastern markets, will permit production levels to be maintained or increased for the next few years.

Equipment Leasing

The growth of equipment leasing will depend ultimately on the level and composition of investment in equipment. The effects of tax reform and trends in the economy will be the primary determinants of the direction of investment. Active lease markets should continue to develop and grow around transportation, medical, communications, and high-technology equipment. The leasing industry will move toward products that embody a comprehensive range of financing, accounting, servicing, and risk-sharing characteristics. Operating leases will grow in use in relation to other types of leasing. The entry of banks into the operating lease market can only enhance its growth. Local and regional finance companies will focus on small-ticket leasing for local equipment markets. Meanwhile, the international leasing market is developing rapidly and should provide increasing opportunities for U.S. leassors.

Health Care

Hospitals. Health care expenditures will rise at an average annual rate of 11 to 13 percent into the mid-1990s. Hospitals will undoubtedly increase their fees to make up for past losses. Managed health care organizations will also increase their premiums to continue to provide quality care. The health care situation, meanwhile, will continue to change as more managed care organizations enter the market, hospitals and nursing homes affiliate with one another, and other companies enter the home care business. Hospitals will have to develop more aggressive marketing strategies to compete with the growing number of managed care organizations. A number of nonprofit health care organizations needing corporate reorganization may end up becoming for-profit subsidiaries. The proliferation of for-profit enterprises in the health care industry may weaken the professional bond between patient and physician.

Surgical and Medical Instruments. Into the mid-1990s, industry shipments of medical and surgical instruments are forecast to increase about 7 percent annually (in 1982 dollars). Alternate care markets should top $1 billion, as half of surgical procedures currently being performed in inpatient settings can be done at freestanding surgical centers. For inpatient markets, manufacturers will seek to establish long-term contracts with buyer groups. They may focus on higher margin products to relieve some of the price pressures of the high-volume, low-profit commodities.

Surgical Appliances and Supplies. Industry shipments of surgical appliances and supplies are projected to rise at an annual constant dollar rate of 8.5 percent into the mid-1990s. The changing health care environment will strongly affect this medical equipment industry. Alternate site facilities, spearheaded by immediate care and ambulatory care centers, will continue to grow as a source for primary care at the expense of the traditional doctor's office and hospital emergency room. Orthopedic supplies and basic patient care items will benefit most from this change.

X-ray and Electromedical Equipment. Into the mid-1990s, industry shipments of X-ray and electromedical equipment are projected to grow at a compound annual rate of 6 percent. Development of capital-intensive equipment will require high outlays for research and development as companies increasingly draw on technology of their high-tech industries such as semiconductors, information processing, and computer software. Hospital demand for high-tech equipment will remain strong, and expanding foreign markets will result in increased exports of X-ray and electromedical equipment. Diagnostic procedures performed outside the hospital should further stimulate demand for X-ray and related products.

Home Entertainment

The home video industry should continue to grow. Revenues from rentals and sales of videocassettes should increase at an annual average rate of 12 to 15 percent, with sales leading. Meanwhile, cable television is expected to be in over 60 percent of U.S. TV households by the mid-1990s, with total cable revenues growing at an average annual rate of 8 percent up to that time. Advertising revenues should rise as cable television's share of the viewing audience increases. In the future, the cable industry's ability to sustain growth and capture a larger share of the television market will depend on how well it can compete with broadcast television and videocassettes.

Hotels and Motels

The lodging industry will remain fiercely competitive. The trend toward diversification in types of accommodations offered by a single hotel chain is expected to continue, although somewhat more slowly because of the slowdown in hotel construction. Projects that would rely heavily on tax advantages available in the past will no longer be feasible. Most growth is expected to occur in all-suite properties and economy properties with limited public space. Resorts and spas will keep growing, as will the conventions and meetings market and foreign tourism (hurting those without worldwide access to computer reservation systems). The number of companies that dominate the lodging business is going to shrink as the pace of mergers and acquisitions quickens. As the labor force shrinks, the industry will automate more of its operations and place greater emphasis on the hiring, training, and retention of employees. Since senior citizens constitute a fast-growing segment of the population, hotels are expected to launch more programs aimed at them.

Household Appliances

The long-term prospects for the appliance industry are good. The number of households will grow at the rate of 1.2 percent, which is less than in recent years, but the baby boom generation will be reaching its peak income years in the 1990s. This generation, the first in which both spouses in the majority of families were employed, has been more interested in time-saving appliances than older generations. Shipments of household appliances are expected to increase at a compound annual rate of 1 percent into the mid-1990s.

Household Furniture

Furniture shipments are expected to increase 0.5 percent annually into the mid-1990s, after adjustment for inflation. If the dollar continues to increase in value on foreign exchange markets, imports could become a serious problem for the industry. The demographic outlook, however, is favorable for the furniture industry. With the aging of the baby boom generation, total spending for furniture by adults 35 and over will increase at a rate of about 2.5 percent a year, while total spending by adults under 35 will remain level. If the industry wants to tap the full potential of the high end of the market, it must improve the accessibility and speed of delivery of its products to the consumer.

Insurance

Brokerage Services. Future prospects for the insurance brokerage business are generally good. The prospect of reductions in premium rates enacted by primary insurers in the face of increased competition will affect revenue and profits for the industry during the next few years. Some consolidation among the smaller brokers will occur as larger companies aggressively seek business, thereby putting competitive pressure on smaller firms. Corporations that are currently not in the insurance business will, depending on legal constraints, look with great interest at the possibility of entering or investing in the insurance brokerage industry. Major brokers are also revaluating their markets and are expanding into what traditionally were insurance agency areas, with a new emphasis on personal lines, mass marketing, and international brokerage services. Forthcoming liberalization of rules and regulations in the European community could provide new opportunities for U.S. brokers. Brokers will continue to push for fixed fees and work to reduce costs to position themselves against downswings in the U.S. insurance industry.

Life Insurance. Life insurance companies will continue to expand the range of insurance products and design new channels of distribution. Joint ventures with other financial services industries for distribution of life insurance products will continue to grow. The life insurance industry will become increasingly global as U.S. life insurers greatly expand their presence in overseas markets and foreign life insurers establish more subsidiaries in the United States. Meanwhile, the challenge of dealing with AIDS will become more acute as the number of actual cases of AIDS substantially increases. Future profitability of life insurance companies could be severely affected as they pay out on policies currently in force on individuals who have or will acquire AIDS-related diseases.

Property/Casualty. The property/casualty industry will probably face increased competition through the 1990s. The banking industry will continue its efforts to obtain expanded insurance powers, and the controversy over comingling banking and insurance activities will retain its high profile during that period. Most financial services analysts expect that banks will be permitted to engage in insurance activities and that insurance companies, including property-casualty insurers, will be allowed to engage in certain banking activities. The consensus remains, however, that strict guidelines will be required to prevent the mingling of assets and liabilities of insurance companies and banks within the same corporate structure.

Machine Tools

The U.S. machine tool industry will grow at an annual real rate of only about 2 percent into the mid-1990s. This assumes that the dollar exchange rate will remain stable at or near the current rate. Any substantial upward adjustment will spark an abnormal reduction in demand through reduced foreign orders, upsetting recent gains made by manufacturers. But through joint ventures and foreign investments, U.S. manufacturers can supply their domestic customers with a broader range of products, hold down prices, and gain influence overseas. Above all the machine tool industry's future will depend on its ability to stay on the technological edge.

Management, Consulting, and Public Relations Services

Management, consulting, and public relations will continue to be expanding industries and should be able to maintain significant growth into the next decade. Increased use of high-technology equipment and systems will boost productivity. The foreign market will keep growing at a rapid pace, although U.S. firms will face increased competition from European and Asian companies.

Motion Pictures

Motion picture theaters seem to be competing successfully with the home video revolution and should remain a major source of entertainment revenue worldwide. With production starts continuing at high levels and ticket prices edging up, box office receipts are expected to grow at an annual average rate of 3 percent through the early 1990s. To remain successful, however, the industry must hold down increases in production costs while maintaining the high-quality product that attracts the public to movie theaters.

Music

Revenues of the prerecorded music industry are expected to grow at an average annual rate of about 6 percent through the early 1990s. Technological developments promise to provide better quality and contribute to industry growth in the long term. On the other hand, some observers believe that the growing number of formats (e.g., digital audio tapes and recorders and recordable, erasable compact disks) may confuse consumers and restrain sales of hardware and recordings. The influence of new technology is hard to predict.

Mutual Funds

The proportion of personal savings held in mutual funds should continue to increase during the next few years. An increasing number of shareholders, both institutional and household, will open mutual fund accounts. Investment companies, aided by advances in technology, will offer greater diversity in funds, ranging from general growth or income funds to funds with highly specialized portfolios aimed at select groups of investors. Other channels of distribution will continue to emerge and will reach more potential shareholders. Changes in the regulatory environment will influence the growth of mutual funds: If banks and other depository institutions are allowed by law to sponsor and sell shares in them, competition will intensify. Mutual funds will probably not settle into a precise market niche during the foreseeable future, but the industry will grow at a healthy rate.

Oil Field Machinery

Into the mid-1990s, the U.S. oil field machinery industry will grow at an annual real rate of about 3.2 percent, assuming that oil prices will remain stable or trend upward slightly above $15 a barrel. Below that price many oil companies will curtail oil field activities and close many marginal wells. On the upside, many U.S. petroleum companies will be under pressure to undertake more exploratory drilling in order to replenish depleted reserves. Also, many foreign countries will be promoting joint ventures and licensing agreements with U.S. oil field equipment manufacturers (or other foreign suppliers) in order to import technology. Both of these developments will improve the market for oil field machinery.

Paper and Paperboard Mills

Longer-term demand paper and board prospects remain positive, if not exciting, with the latest studies foreseeing the long-term growth rate for paper and board consumption averaging between 2.6 and 2.9 percent worldwide. Unless burdened by a very strong dollar, U.S. producers are cost competitive worldwide and can be expected to maintain their share of the anticipated world market growth. Paper and board mill managers have shown their willingness to cull out antiquated mills, upgrade old equipment and to accept and invest in new proven technology, thereby maintaining the industry's front-ranking world position. The accelerated capital expenditures in recent years would indicate that this position will be maintained.

Pulp Mills

The U.S. market pulp industry should continue its recent success, with the quantity of pulp shipments increasing at a 3 percent annual rate of growth though the early 1990s. Several key economic variables, including higher U.S. and foreign pulp and paper demand, a relatively low-valued U.S. dollar vis-á-vis other foreign supplier currencies, moderating producer pulp inventories, and high operating rates for U.S. pulp suppliers, will have a positive effect on U.S. suppliers' profitability during this period. The U.S. pulp industry, which will face increased competition from overseas low-cost producers and suppliers, must and will continue to make technological improvements in its pulp-making and bleaching processes to improve cost and energy efficiency.

Passenger Cars

The industry can expect further, but slow, growth as long as the economy expands. Competitive pressure from new entrant countries and from new U.S. manufacturers will continue to grow for the foreseeable future, possibly forcing industry restructuring. The increasingly competitive environment will continue to exert pressure on firms to cut costs, improve quality, and identify and exploit market niches. The growing demand for larger and more spacious vehicles suggests that the traditional domestic manufacturers may be able to recover some of the market share lost to the subcompact and compact segments. However, U.S. dominance in this segment will be threatened to a degree by the imminent introduction of large, luxury Japanese cars. This challenge, perhaps the greatest U.S. automakers have ever faced, will determine the nature of the auto market in North America well into the next century.

Petroleum Refining

Although the oil price outlook for the next 5 years is highly uncertain, the average price of petroleum products, measured in constant dollars, is projected to increase at an average annual rate of 1.5 percent through the early 1990s. During the same period, consumption of petroleum products is expected to grow at an average rate of just over 1 percent a year. Approximately half of the growth is projected to occur in the industrial end-use sector, 30 percent in electric utilities, and 20 percent in transportation. Refiners will continue to face challenges with regard to product mix, increasing environmental constraints, declining quality of crude oil, and access to crude oil supplies as U.S. production of crude oil continues to decline. Total imports of crude oil and refined products will grow at an average annual rate of 9 percent in the early 1990s.

Pharmaceutical Preparations

The value of pharmaceutical shipments is projected to increase 2 to 3 percent a year in constant dollars into the mid-1990s. The generic market could expand by $6.5 billion during this period due to patent expirations, and the demand for nonprescription drugs could grow to $12 billion due to increased availability and better-informed patients. More research and development, with emphasis on causes instead of symptoms and more effective delivery systems, is planned during the next few years. In the meantime, the volume of inert ingredients required for pharmaceutical preparation is growing at 5 percent a year.

Publishing

Books. Growth of book publishers' shipments into the mid-1990s should average 4 percent annually. Steady gains in the U.S. reading population, higher levels of income and educational attainment, and increased funds for schools and libraries will expand book sales. Publishers' output should be aided by changes in technology, improved distribution patterns, and new product developments. More widespread use of low-cost desktop publishing and electronic editing systems should increase U.S. title output, and improvements in computer ordering systems, linking publishers, wholesalers, and retailers, will make more efficient distribution of these titles to bookstores possible. Publishers will make increased use of tapes, computer discs, and other media as alternatives to printing on paper.

Newspapers. Newspaper industry receipts are expected to grow at a yearly rate of 2 to 3 percent in constant dollars into the mid-1990s. Classified advertising is likely to show more moderate growth during the next few weeks because real estate and employment advertising are unlikely to show vigorous growth. Newspapers should benefit from a larger share of national advertising into the mid-1990s by providing national advertisers with greater standardization in ad purchasing and national ad rates more in line with local rates. Daily newspaper circulation is not expected to show significant growth during this period, although weeklies, daily suburban papers, and some large metropolitan papers will continue to make gains in the range of 1 to 2 percent a year. Sunday circulation will continue to record higher growth than daily circulation.

Magazines. If the economy grows at a steady rate of just over 3 percent into the mid-1990s, as forecast, magazine industry revenues should grow at an average yearly rate of 2 to 3 percent after adjustment for inflation. During this period, magazine publishers will focus on providing advertisers with high-quality marketing demographics to demonstrate the advantages of advertising in their magazines. While a great deal of the growth in the magazine industry will come from special interest magazines, some of them are likely to become victims of shakeouts caused by saturation of these special market niches. Cable television could become a significant threat to magazines in the next few years because it targets the same audience as they do. As the domestic market for magazine titles becomes more crowded, magazine publishers may look for more opportunities to sell their products or engage in joint ventures and licensing arrangements abroad.

Rubber Products

Demand for tires should grow at a 1 to 2 percent annual rate over the next several years. Import competition will be a major long-term factor for the rubber and plastics footwear industry, with possible changes in the countries of origin as production shifts to the lowest cost producers. The future of the hose and belt industry depends on the needs of the machinery using sectors. Product shipments of hose are projected to grow about 2 percent annually (in constant dollars) over the next 5 years, shipments of flat belts about 1.5 percent, and V-belts about 2.5 percent. Assuming modest expansion in motor vehicle production, the rubber product industry will most likely grow at an estimated annual rate of 1.5 percent. Fabricated rubber products, still highly dependent on demand from the motor vehicle industry, face a future marked by international competition and declining demand resulting from substitution of plastics for rubber. The compounding of plastics with rubber and other materials to create hybrid materials is likely to spur growth in the plastics industry, as will gains in reinforced plastic products.

Retailing

Along with the manufacturing sector, U.S. retailers are undergoing a quiet reorganization of their physical premises and marketing objectives to use capital and manpower more efficiently and to meet consumer requirements. Retailers are trying new means of distribution, including warehouse-type stores and hypermarkets and are employing cable television and computer-assisted technology to sell merchandise. Where nonretailers perceive that different management could improve net profits, they will not hesitate to acquire retailers. Well-managed firms that offer the public a choice of upscale merchandise or good quality wares at a discount price will prosper. With an increasing amount of disposable income available to more Americans, enterprising retailers should be richly rewarded at the cash register.

Semiconductors and Related Devices

U.S. product shipments of semiconductor devices should grow at an average annual rate of 12 percent through the early 1990s. This growth will be driven by the further expansion of semiconductor-based products. Worldwide demand for semiconductors in the automotive sector, a largely untapped market, is expected to increase substantially. The U.S. industry will continue to be strong in design technology, while product lifetimes will shorten, requiring increased innovation and product development at lower cost. While no immediate large-scale displacement of semiconductors is expected, superconductors could be of great importance by the turn of the century.

Semiconductor Manufacturing Equipment

The early 1990s will be a period of intense competition in the semiconductor manufacturing equipment industry, with no firm expected to remain a leader for very long. U.S. equipment vendors will probably regain lost market shares, however, as the industry matures and communications with the device industry improve. Although financial problems have assailed certain U.S. producers of microlithography equipment during the last few years (giving added impetus to the efforts of foreign equipment vendors to gain market shares), strategic joint ventures and acquisitions will serve to rationalize certain segments of the U.S. equipment industry and will provide leading technology companies with the support that will enable them to compete more effectively.

Steel Mill Products

This highly cyclical industry will certainly be adversely affected by any future economic downturn. Unfunded pension plans are a serious problem for the integrated sector, likely to be aggravated in a recession, since plants may be closed and employees laid off. Structural changes in the economy, more efficient uses of steel, substitution of other materials for steel, the downsizing of automobiles, and the deterioration in the balance of trade in steel-intensive products have contributed to a downward trend in steel consumption in the past decade (with the exception of stainless steel). Steelmakers are responding with aggressive and practical programs to retain or recapture their traditional markets, such as the automotive, construction, container, and appliance industries. But existing surplus steelmaking capacity and developments in the international steel industry are likely to maintain pressure on domestic manufacturers.

Telephone and Telegraph Equipment

Overall, telephone and telegraph equipment industry shipments are expected to grow slowly but steadily during the early 1990s at an annual rate of 3 percent (in constant dollars). Shipments of customer premises equipment are forecast to increase marginally during that period. During the same period, employment in the telecommunications equipment industry is expected to decline slightly. Low-technology products and technologically outdated equipment will decline; data communications equipment, integrated voice data workstations, and protocol converters will experience fairly strong growth rates. Local service providers will stress their abilities to meet customers' needs for low-cost, enhanced services available through simultaneous voice/data transmission capabilities. Increased competition for limited product and service markets will reduce profitability of companies and lead to acquisitions and mergers among companies specializing in similar product areas.

Travel Services

Demand for travel services will continue to grow at rates close to or above the rate of GNP growth. If the dollar continues to weaken, the growth rate could be even higher as Americans and foreign visitors spend more money traveling in the United States. The industry will continue to be restructured, but the changes are not likely to impede growth in consumer demand significantly. This growth in travel will be sustained by real increases in discretionary income and long-term demographic changes. An increasingly competitive environment will see companies trying to create specific niches. Financially stronger companies will take over their competitors; weak companies will disappear. Cooperative advertising will grow. Small- and medium-size travel agencies and airlines will have difficulty competing with the large, more diverse firms. In the airline industry, the few carriers that will eventually survive may create an oligopolistic environment wherein they might exert more control over pricing, scheduling, and flight frequencies.

Transportation

Trucking. The eagerness of carriers of all types to invest in new, more efficient equipment—and their ability to acquire ready financing—strongly suggests widespread confidence in the medium- to long-term future for intercity trucking, at least for efficient carriers. The carriers are reportedly seeking equipment with low operating costs that can be converted to meet changing demands, for example, tractors that can be reconfigured to haul double or triple trailers or to operate at differing cruising speeds. Meanwhile, wages and working conditions for nonunion labor are likely to continue improving as the demand for their services continues to grow faster than the supply of drivers willing to take such jobs. Efforts to improve truckers' image and working conditions, as well as to improve driver training opportunities, may offset some of the labor shortage.

Railroad (Passenger)

Amtrak ridership has the potential to grow by 4 to 5 percent a year through the early 1990s. Ridership is highly sensitive to economic activity and airline fares, however, so year-to-year fluctuations are likely to occur. Travel times and reliability of service in the Northeast should continue to improve as the railroad realizes the benefits of long-term improvements in plant and equipment. Amtrak will also maintain its program of tight control over costs in response to the scarcity of federal funds and other pressures on the operating budget.

Water (Deep Sea Foreign Transportation)

The projections for continued trade growth suggest stable or improving conditions for U.S.-flag foreign trade operations. Overtonnaging in world shipping will persist, however, because of the long life of shipping assets. The profitability of the U.S.-flag tanker fleet is not expected to show substantial improvement as long as this is the case.

14

The Economy

After a decade that witnessed unparalleled growth, worsening economic conditions at the beginning of the 1990s have caused many to wonder if all of the prosperity of the 1980s will be undone. The crisis with Iraq commencing in the summer of 1990 brought to a head many negative influences on an economy that, if not already in a recession, was flirting with one. In fact, many areas of the country were beginning to feel the effects of a slowdown and the emerging view, at least by the fall of 1990, was that the economy was likely to get worse before it got better.

Economic uncertainty scares the daylights out of most people, largely because they don't know what to expect. Stories of travail abound, and many of us lie awake at night wondering when economic calamity will befall our families. The only thing that can be said with certainty about economic downturns is that they are certain to occur. Once we have emerged from the current one, we should all keep in mind that it will happen again.

Most of what people do to maintain their family finances on a strong footing and improve their personal financial circumstances is helping them prepare for less robust economic climates. Put more succinctly, nothing can beat some money in the bank to weather economic storms. The possibility of temporary unemployment, while always unpleasant, is much easier to deal with if one has accumulated a nice nest egg rather than lived hand-to-mouth. Conservative spending habits, adequate savings, and relatively little or no indebtedness are perhaps the best ways to handle whatever a recession can inflict upon you.

The next decade will likely not be a repeat of the prosperity of the 1980s. Pervasive uncertainty about future economic conditions often causes investors to head for the hills. Many make wholesale changes in their portfolios, often preferring cash equivalent investments. Successful long-term investors (particularly those who have been through a few recessions in the past) prefer to maintain a steady course through all economic conditions. Investors who make major shifts in their portfolios in response to short-term market and economic vacillations almost always do the wrong thing. They are often selling when they should be buying and vice versa. Most often the best thing to do in the face of uncertainty is nothing, because if you have a well-balanced, diversified investment portfolio and other personal financial planning matters continue to be dealt with effectively, you will prosper under any economic conditions.

HOW TO INTERPRET ECONOMIC INDICATORS

Most people hear economists and commentators talking about the latest economic indicators, but they don't understand what these indicators are telling us. This section briefly summarizes what some of the more commonly used indicators mean.

Three-Month Treasury Bill Rate. This is the interest rate paid to buyers of U.S. Treasury bills (at auction) and best predicts the direction that the interest rates will take. It is published every Tuesday after the weekly auction on Monday. Because it is quoted every week, trends may be hard to spot.

Wage Settlements. The results of major wage contracts can indicate the magnitude of the rise in the cost of goods and services. Lower annual salary increase agreements usually mean lower inflation. These figures appear in news stories of major labor settlements.

Payroll Employment. This figure—the number of employees on company payrolls—is issued on the first Friday of each month in most major newspapers. It not only reflects the employment situation but also best predicts future consumer spending patterns, which depend heavily on employment.

The Dollar Index. This indicates future interest rates and corporate profits and shows the value of the dollar against a group of foreign currencies compiled by Morgan Guaranty Trust. It is published Monday through Friday in some newspapers. Because it is issued so frequently, minor fluctuations should be ignored.

Inventory-to-Sales Ratio. This is a crude, but useful, measure of the extent to which the demand for goods is satisfied, and thus indicates sales patterns that affect corporate profits. It consists of the dollar value of business inventory nationwide divided by sales and is issued near the tenth working day of each month by the Census Bureau. When the economy is flagging, this ratio may be a high as 1.5:1, as inventories build up and sales slow. A 1.3:1 ratio is balanced by experts' opinion, as businesses like to keep a little extra inventory on hand. This indicator should be scrutinized, because changes of a quarter of a point are usually important.

The Standard and Poor's (S&P) 500-Stock Index. The stock market predicts general economic recoveries as no other indicator can, but, as the joke goes, it has also predicted 9 out of the last 5 recessions. The S&P 500-Stock Index is quoted daily in most newspapers and best predicts the economy's future prospects, because it reflects many more stocks than other stock averages.

THE EFFECT OF INFLATION ON THE PURCHASING POWER OF THE DOLLAR

Table 14-1 shows the erosion in the purchasing power of the dollar from 1950 to 1988, based on indexes measuring the levels of consumer prices and producer prices. This is a good illustration of the

Table 14-1. Purchasing Power of the U.S. Dollar: 1950–1988

Year	Annual Average as Measured By—		Year	Annual Average as Measured By—		Year	Annual Average as Measured By—	
	Producer prices	Consumer prices		Producer prices	Consumer prices		Producer prices	Consumer prices
1950	$3.546	$4.151	1963	$2.994	$3.265	1976	$1.645	$1.757
1951	3.247	3.846	1964	2.985	3.220	1977	1.546	1.649
1952	3.268	3.765	1965	2.933	3.166	1978	1.433	1.532
1953	3.300	3.735	1966	2.841	3.080	1979	1.289	1.380
1954	3.289	3.717	1967	2.809	2.993	1980	1.136	1.215
1955	3.279	3.732	1968	2.732	2.873	1981	1.041	1.098
1956	3.195	3.678	1969	2.632	2.726	1982	1.000	1.035
1957	3.077	3.549	1970	2.545	2.574	1983	.984	1.003
1958	3.012	3.457	1971	2.469	2.466	1984	.964	.961
1959	3.021	3.427	1972	2.392	2.391	1985	.955	.928
1960	2.994	3.373	1973	2.193	2.251	1986	.969	.913
1961	2.994	3.340	1974	1.901	2.029	1987	.949	.880
1962	2.985	3.304	1975	1.718	1.859	1988	.926	.846

Source: U.S. Bureau of Labor Statistics. Monthly data in U.S. Bureau of Economic Analysis, *Survey of Current Business.*

Table 14–2. Annual Percentage Changes for the Consumer Price Index: 1965–1989

Year	Change in Consumer Prices, All Items	Period	Average Annual Change
1965	1.6	1960–1965	1.3%
1966	2.9	1965–1970	4.3
1967	3.1	1970–1975	6.8
1968	4.2	1975–1980	8.9
1969	5.5	1980–1985	5.5
		1980–1986	4.9
1970	5.7	1980–1987	4.7
1971	4.4	1980–1988	4.7
1972	3.2	1980–1989	4.7
1973	6.2	1985–1989	3.6
1974	11.0		
1975	9.1		
1976	5.8		
1977	6.5		
1978	7.6		
1979	11.3		
1980	13.5		
1981	10.3		
1982	6.2		
1983	3.2		
1984	4.3		
1985	3.6		
1986	1.9		
1987	3.7		
1988	4.1		
1989	4.8		

Source: U.S. Bureau of Labor Statistics, Monthly Labor Review

Table 14–3. Expenditures of American Households

		Percent of Income Spent		
Category	Overall	$15,000– $30,000	$30,000– $50,000	$50,000– $150,000
Taxes:				
Federal income	12%	7%	11%	15%
Social Security*	7	7	8	7
State and local	7	6	6	7
Housing:				
Mortgage or rent	10	11	11	9
Other housing costs†	11	13	12	11
Food and groceries	14	20	15	10
Transportation**	9	12	10	7
Vacation, recreation	5	5	4	5
Health care insurance‡	4	5	4	3
Clothing	3	3	3	3
Savings and investments*	8	5	8	12
Other	11	6	8	13

*Estimated

†Includes utilities, furnishings, home improvements, and insurance

**Includes auto insurance

††Includes life, health, and disability insurance

impact of inflation. Note that while inflation today may be somewhat high by historical standards, it is much lower than it was during the mid- to late-1970s.

ANNUAL CHANGES IN THE CONSUMER PRICE INDEX

Table 14-2 shows the annual percentage changes for the Consumer Price Index from 1965 through 1989. Overall, inflation has been trending higher since the 1950s, and experts recommend that for purposes of projecting inflation into the future, an annual rate of 4 to 5 percent is a reasonable assumption, except for college costs which are expected to increase at a 6 to 7 percent annual rate.

Table 14-4. Federal Information Centers

State/City	Address	Telephone
Alabama		
Birmingham	75 Spring St. SW, Atlanta, GA 30303	205/322-8591
Mobile		205/438-1421
Alaska		
Anchorage	Box 33, 701 C St., 99513	907/271-3650
Arizona		
Phoenix	880 Front St., San Diego, CA 92188	602/261-3313
Arkansas		
Little Rock	819 Taylor St., Forth Worth, TX 76102	501/378-6177
California		
Los Angeles	300 N. Los Angeles St., 90012	213/894-3800
Sacramento	1825 Bell, 95825	916/978-4010
San Diego	880 Front St., 92188	619/557-6030
San Francisco	Box 36082, 450 Golden Gate Ave., 94102	415/556-6600
Santa Ana	880 Front St., San Diego 92188	714/836-2386
Colorado		
Colorado Springs	1961 Stout St., P.O. Drawer 3526, Denver 80294	719/471-9491
Denver		719/544-9523
Pueblo		719/544-9523
Connecticut	Rm. 2-110, 26 Federal Plaza, New York, NY 10278	
Hartford		203/527-2617
New Haven		203/624-4720

Table 14-4. Federal Information Centers (*Continued*)

State/City	Address	Telephone
Florida		
Ft. Lauderdale	Rm. 105, 144 1st Ave. S., St. Petersburg 37701	305/522-8531
Jacksonville		904/354-4756
Miami		305/536-4155
Orlando		407/422-1800
St. Petersburg		813/893-3495
Tampa		813/229-7911
West Palm Beach		813/229-7911
Georgia		
Atlanta	75 Spring St. SW., 30303	404/331-6891
Hawaii		
Honolulu	Box 50091, 300 Ala Moana Blvd., 96850	808/541-1365
Illinois		
Chicago	33d Floor, 230 S. Dearborn St., 60604	312/353-4242
Indiana	Rm. 7411, 550 Main St., Cincinnati, OH 45202	
Gary		219/883-4110
Indianapolis		317/269-7373
Iowa	215 N. 17th St., Omaha, NE 68102	800/532-1556
Kansas	Rm. 529, 210 N. Tucker Blvd., St. Louis, MO 63101	800/432-2934
Kentucky		
Louisville	Rm. 7411, 550 Main St., Cincinnati, OH 45202	502/582-6261
Louisiana		
New Orleans	515 Rusk Ave., Houston, TX 77002	504/589-6696

Table 14-4. Federal Information Centers (*Continued*)

State/City	Address	Telephone
Maryland		
Baltimore	Rm. 1337, 9th and Market Sts., Philadelphia, PA 19107	301/962-4980
Massachusetts		
Boston	Rm. 216, 10 Causeway St., 02222	617/565-8121
Michigan		
Detroit	Rm. M-25, 477 Michigan Ave., Detroit, 48226	313/226-7016
Grand Rapids		616/451-2628
Minnesota		
Minneapolis	33d Fl., 230 S. Dearborn St., Chicago, IL 60604	612/349-3333
Missouri		
St. Louis	Rm. 529, 210 N. Tucker Blvd., St. Louis 63101	314/425-4106
From elsewhere in		
Missouri		800/392-7711
Nebraska		
Omaha	215 N. 17th St., Omaha 68102	402/221-3353
From elsewhere in		
Nebraska		800/642-8383
New Jersey		
Northern NJ	Rm. 2-110, 26 Federal Plaza, New York, NY 10278	
Southern NJ	Rm. 1337, 9th and Market Sts., Philadelphia, PA 19107	
Newark		201/645-3600
Trenton		609/396-4400
New Mexico		
Albuquerque	819 Taylor St., Fort Worth, TX 67102	505/766-3091

293

Table 14-4. Federal Information Centers (*Continued*)

State/City	Address	Telephone
New York		
Albany		518/463-4421
Buffalo	111 W. Huron, 14202	716/846-4010
New York	Rm. 2-110, 26 Federal Plaza, 10278	212/264-4464
Rochester		716/546-5075
Syracuse		315/476-8545
North Carolina		
Charlotte	75 Spring St. SW., Atlanta, GA 30303	704/376-3600
Ohio	Rm. 7411, 550 Main St., Cincinnati 45202	
Akron		216/375-5638
Cincinnati		513/684-2801
Cleveland		216/522-4040
Columbus		614/221-1014
Dayton		513/223-7377
Toledo		419/241-3223
Oklahoma		
Oklahoma City	819 Taylor St., Forth Worth, TX 76102	405/231-4868
Tulsa		918/584-4193
Oregon		
Portland	Box 18, 1220 SW. 3d Ave. 97204	918/584-4193
Pennsylvania	Rm. 1337, 9th and Market Sts., Philadelphia 19107	215/597-7042
Philadelphia		412/644-3456
Pittsburgh		

Table 14-4. Federal Information Centers (*Continued*)

State/City	Address	Telephone
Rhode Island		
Providence	Rm. 216, 10 Causeway St., Boston, MA 02222	401/331-5565
Tennessee	75 Spring St. SW., Atlanta, GA 30303	
Chattanooga		615/265-8231
Memphis		901/521-3265
Nashville		615/242-5064
Texas		
Austin	515 Rusk Ave., Houston 77002	512/472-5494
Dallas	819 Taylor St., Forth Worth 76102	214/767-8585
Forth Worth	819 Taylor St. 76102	817/334-3624
Houston	515 Rusk Ave 77002	713/229-2552
San Antonio	515 Rusk Ave., Houston 77002	512/224-4471
Utah		
Salt Lake City	1961 Stout St., P.O. Drawer 3526, Denver, CO 80294	801/524-5353
Virginia	Rm. 1337, 9th and Market Sts., Philadelphia, PA 19107	
Norfolk		804/441-3101
Richmond		804/643-4926
Roanoke		703/982-8591
Washington	Box 18, 1220 SW. 3d Ave., Portland, OR 97204	
Seattle		206/442-0570
Tacoma		206/383-7970
Wisconsin		
Milwaukee	33d Fl., 230 S. Dearborn St., Chicago, IL 60604	414/271-2273

HOW AMERICANS SPEND THEIR MONEY

Table 14-3 is a reprint of a survey of the expenditures of American households conducted by Consumer Reports. *It is important for everyone to periodically summarize how they are spending their money. If you have already done so, you might want to compare your spending patterns with these averages.*

FEDERAL INFORMATION CENTERS

Federal Information Centers can eliminate the maze of referrals that people often experience in contacting the federal government. They are clearinghouses for information about the federal government. Persons with questions about a government program or agency and who are unsure of which office can help may call or write to their nearest center (see Table 14.1).

15

Financial Tables

This chapter contains the following financial tables that will assist you in your financial planning.

Mortgage Amortization Table. Shows monthly mortgage payments under varying interest rates and mortgage durations.

Compound Interest Table. Allows you to calculate increases in investments at varying rates of return or increases in living costs at varying inflation rates.

Present Value Table. Shows the erosion in purchasing power caused by inflation and allows you to calculate how much you need to deposit today to accumulate a certain amount in the future.

Accumulated Values of Monthly Savings. Reveals how much a regular monthly savings program will accumulate over a period of time.

Savings Withdrawal Table. Shows how long savings will last at a specified level of periodic withdrawals.

MORTGAGE AMORTIZATION TABLES

Table 15-1 shows the percent of the principal amount of a loan needed each year to pay off the loan when the actual payments are monthly and are paid in arrears. Divide the percent or the result by 12 to get the level monthly payment that includes both interest and principal. If payments are made in advance, rather than in arrears, the payment amount will be slightly smaller than the amounts derived from this table.

EXAMPLE: The annual amount needed to pay off a $75,000, 10 percent, 30-year mortgage if payments are made monthly and in arrears is $7,905 (factor of 10.54% times $75,000). The monthly payment, therefore, is $658.75 ($7,905 id divided by 12 months). If the loan is to be paid off over 15 years, rather than 30 years, the annual payment is $9,675 (factor of 12.90 percent times $75,000) and the monthly payment is $806.25 ($9,675 divided by 12 months). In other words, by paying $147.50 more per month ($806.25 minus $658.75) the mortgage will be paid off in 15 years rather than 30 years.

COMPOUND INTEREST TABLE

Table 15-2 shows how much a current amount will increase in the future at an assumed rate of appreciation or inflation. It can also be used to estimate future living expenses.

EXAMPLE 1: An investor has $25,000 set aside for educating her 3-year-old child and wants to estimate what it will amount to in 15 years when the child enters college, assuming an 8 percent annual rate of return on the investment. The factor for 8 percent and 15 years is 3.1722, so the estimated future value of the $25,000 is $79,305 ($25,000 times 3.1722).

EXAMPLE 2: A couple, both age 45, is concerned about how much income they will need to meet living expenses when they retire at age 65. They estimate that if they retired today, they would need about $35,000 per year, but they know that $35,000 will not buy as much in the future because inflation erodes the value of the dollar. How much income will they need at age 65 to have the same purchasing power that $35,000 has today, assuming a 4 percent annual rate of inflation? Since they plan to retire in 20 years, the compound interest factor over

Table 15–1. Mortgage Amortization

Interest Rate	10 yr	15 yr	20 yr	25 yr	30 yr
8.00	14.56	11.47	10.04	9.27	8.81
8.25	14.72	11.65	10.23	9.47	9.02
8.50	14.88	11.82	10.42	9.67	9.23
8.75	15.04	12.00	10.61	9.87	9.45
9.00	15.21	12.18	10.80	10.08	9.66
9.25	15.37	12.36	11.00	10.28	9.88
9.50	15.53	12.54	11.19	10.49	10.10
9.75	15.70	12.72	11.39	10.70	10.31
10.00	15.86	12.90	11.59	10.91	10.54
10.25	16.03	13.08	11.78	11.12	10.76
10.50	16.20	13.27	11.99	11.34	10.98
10.75	16.37	13.46	12.19	11.55	11.21
11.00	16.54	13.64	12.39	11.77	11.43
11.25	16.71	13.83	12.60	11.98	11.66
11.50	16.88	14.02	12.80	12.20	11.89
11.75	17.05	14.21	13.01	12.42	12.12
12.00	17.22	14.41	13.22	12.64	12.35
12.25	17.40	14.60	13.43	12.87	12.58
12.50	17.57	14.80	13.64	13.09	12.81
12.75	17.75	14.99	13.85	13.31	13.05
13.00	17.92	15.19	14.06	13.54	13.28
13.25	18.10	15.39	14.28	13.77	13.51
13.50	18.28	15.58	14.49	13.99	13.75
13.75	18.46	15.78	14.71	14.22	13.99
14.00	18.64	15.99	14.93	14.45	14.22
14.25	18.82	16.19	15.15	14.68	14.46
14.50	19.00	16.39	15.36	14.91	14.70
14.75	19.18	16.60	15.59	15.14	14.94
15.00	19.37	16.80	15.81	15.37	15.18

Table 15–2. Rate of Appreciation or Inflation

Number of Periods	2%	3%	4%	5%	6%	7%	8%	9%	10%	11%	12%	13%	14%	15%
1	1.0200	1.0300	1.0400	1.0500	1.0600	1.0700	1.0800	1.0900	1.1000	1.1100	1.1200	1.1300	1.1400	1.1500
2	1.0404	1.0609	1.0816	1.1025	1.1236	1.1449	1.1664	1.1881	1.2100	1.2321	1.2544	1.2769	1.2996	1.3225
3	1.0612	1.0927	1.1249	1.1576	1.1910	1.2250	1.2597	1.2950	1.3310	1.3676	1.4049	1.4429	1.4815	1.5209
4	1.0824	1.1255	1.1699	1.2155	1.2625	1.3108	1.3605	1.4116	1.4641	1.5181	1.5735	1.6305	1.6890	1.7490
5	1.1041	1.1593	1.2167	1.2763	1.3382	1.4026	1.4693	1.5386	1.6105	1.6851	1.7623	1.8424	1.9254	2.0114
6	1.1262	1.1941	1.2653	1.3401	1.4185	1.5007	1.5869	1.6771	1.7716	1.8704	1.9738	2.0820	2.1950	2.3131
7	1.1487	1.2299	1.3159	1.4071	1.5036	1.6058	1.7138	1.8280	1.9487	2.0762	2.2107	2.3526	2.5023	2.6600
8	1.1717	1.2668	1.3686	1.4775	1.5938	1.7182	1.8509	1.9926	2.1436	2.3045	2.4760	2.6584	2.8526	3.0590
9	1.1951	1.3048	1.4233	1.5513	1.6895	1.8385	1.9990	2.1719	2.3579	2.5580	2.7731	3.0040	3.2519	3.5179
10	1.2190	1.3439	1.4802	1.6289	1.7908	1.9672	2.1589	2.3674	2.5937	2.8394	3.1058	3.3946	3.7072	4.0456
15	1.3459	1.5580	1.8009	2.0789	2.3966	2.7590	3.1722	3.6425	4.1772	4.7846	5.4736	6.2543	7.1379	8.1371
20	1.4859	1.8061	2.1911	2.6533	3.2071	3.8697	4.6610	5.6044	6.7275	8.0623	9.6463	11.5231	13.7435	16.3665
25	1.6406	2.0938	2.6658	3.3864	4.2919	5.4274	6.8485	8.6231	10.8347	13.5855	17.0001	21.2305	26.4619	32.9190
30	1.8114	2.4273	3.2434	4.3219	5.7435	7.6123	10.0627	13.2677	17.4494	22.8923	29.9599	39.1159	50.9502	66.2118
35	1.9999	2.8139	3.9461	5.5160	7.6861	10.6766	14.7853	20.4140	28.1024	38.5749	52.7996	72.0685	98.1002	133.1755
40	2.2080	3.2620	4.8010	7.0400	10.2857	14.9745	21.7245	31.4094	45.2593	63.0009	93.0510	132.7816	188.8835	267.8635

20 years at 4 percent is 2.1911. Therefore, they will need $76,688 at age 65 ($35,000 times 2.1911) to be able to meet living expenses that are the equivalent of $35,000 today.

PRESENT VALUE TABLE

Table 15-3 can be used to estimate the erosion in purchasing power caused by inflation and to calculate how much you need to deposit today to accumulate a certain amount in the future.

EXAMPLE 1: A couple just retired and, in addition to Social Security and personal investment income, will receive a fixed annuity of $12,000 per year. They are interested in knowing how much the purchasing power of this annuity will erode 15 years from now if their cost of living rises by 3 percent per year. The present value factor for 15 years at a 3 percent rate is .6419. Therefore, their $12,000 annual annuity will have a purchasing power of $7,703 in 15 years ($12,000 times .6419) if their cost of living increases at a 3 percent annual rate.

EXAMPLE 2: A couple would like to set aside enough money today so that they will have $60,000 in a college fund in 9 years. They estimate that they can earn 10 percent on this college fund. The present value factor for 9 years at 10 percent interest is .4241. Therefore, they will need to set aside $25,446 now ($60,000 times .4241) in order to have $60,000 available to meet college costs 9 years from now assuming a 10 percent annual return.

WHAT $100 DEPOSITED MONTHLY WILL GROW TO IN A GIVEN NUMBER OF YEARS

The miracle of compounding is quite evident from Table 15-4. It shows what a monthly deposit of $100 grows to over a period of years. Compounding is monthly and deposits are assumed to have been made at the beginning of the month.

EXAMPLE: A newlywed couple wants to save some money on a monthly basis and is interested in what they can accumulate over 30 years, assuming they can earn 9 ½ percent on their savings. As the table shows, they will have $204,913 in savings after 30 years, based on a 9 ½ percent annual return. If they can manage to save $150 per

Table 15–3. Present Value and Future Accumulation

Number of Periods	2%	3%	4%	5%	6%	7%	8%	9%	10%	11%	12%	13%	14%	15%
1	.9804	.9709	.9615	.9524	.9434	.9346	.9259	.9174	.9091	.9009	.8929	.8850	.8772	.8696
2	.9612	.9426	.9246	.9070	.8900	.8734	.8573	.8417	.8264	.8116	.7972	.7831	.7695	.7561
3	.9423	.9151	.8890	.8638	.8396	.8163	.7938	.7722	.7513	.7312	.7118	.6931	.6750	.6575
4	.9238	.8885	.8548	.8227	.7921	.7629	.7350	.7084	.6830	.6587	.6355	.6133	.5921	.5718
5	.9057	.8626	.8219	.7835	.7473	.7130	.6806	.6499	.6209	.5935	.5674	.5428	.5194	.4972
6	.8880	.8375	.7903	.7462	.7050	.6663	.6302	.5963	.5645	.5346	.5066	.4803	.4556	.4323
7	.8706	.8131	.7599	.7107	.6651	.6227	.5835	.5470	.5132	.4817	.4523	.4251	.3996	.3759
8	.8535	.7894	.7307	.6768	.6274	.5820	.5403	.5019	.4665	.4339	.4039	.3762	.3506	.3269
9	.8368	.7664	.7026	.6446	.5919	.5439	.5002	.4604	.4241	.3909	.3606	.3329	.3075	.2843
10	.8203	.7441	.6756	.6139	.5584	.5083	.4632	.4224	.3855	.3522	.3220	.2946	.2697	.2472
15	.7430	.6419	.5553	.4810	.4173	.3624	.3152	.2745	.2394	.2090	.1827	.1599	.1401	.1229
20	.6730	.5537	.4564	.3769	.3118	.2584	.2145	.1784	.1486	.1240	.1037	.0868	.0728	.0611
25	.6095	.4776	.3751	.2953	.2330	.1842	.1460	.1160	.0923	.0736	.0588	.0471	.0378	.0304
30	.5521	.4120	.3083	.2314	.1741	.1314	.0994	.0754	.0573	.0437	.0334	.0256	.0196	.0151
35	.5000	.3554	.2534	.1813	.1301	.0937	.0676	.0490	.0356	.0259	.0189	.0139	.0102	.0075
40	.4529	.3066	.2083	.1420	.0972	.0668	.0460	.0318	.0221	.0154	.0107	.0075	.0053	.0037

Table 15–4. Growth of a $100 Monthly Deposit

Interest Rate	5 Years	10 Years	15 Years	20 Years	25 Years	30 Years	35 Years	40 Years
5%	$6,829	$15,593	$26,840	$41,275	$ 59,799	$ 83,573	$114,083	$153,238
5½	6,920	16,024	28,002	43,762	64,498	91,780	127,675	174,902
6	7,012	16,470	29,227	46,435	69,646	100,954	143,183	200,145
6½	7,106	16,932	30,519	49,308	75,289	111,217	160,898	229,599
7	7,201	17,409	31,881	52,397	81,480	122,709	181,156	264,012
7½	7,298	17,904	33,318	55,719	88,274	135,587	204,345	304,272
8	7,397	18,417	34,835	59,295	95,737	150,030	230,918	351,428
8½	7,497	18,947	36,435	63,144	103,937	166,240	261,395	406,726
9	7,599	19,497	38,124	67,290	112,953	184,447	296,385	471,643
9½	7,703	20,066	39,908	71,756	122,872	204,913	336,590	547,933
10	7,808	20,655	41,792	76,570	133,789	227,933	382,828	637,678

303

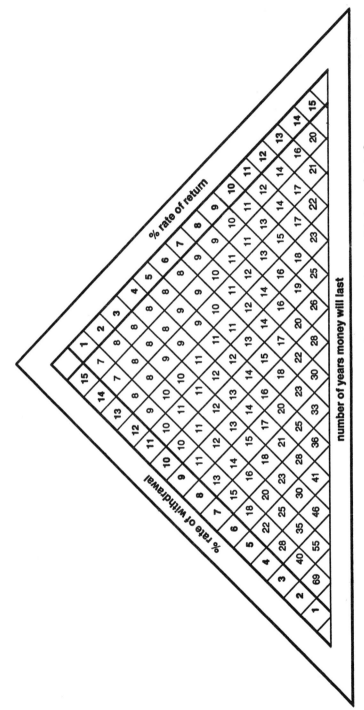

Figure 15-1. How long will money last at a given withdrawal rate?

month over the same period, they will have accumulated $307,369 ($204,913 times 1.5)

NUMBER OF YEARS MONEY WILL LAST
AT A GIVEN WITHDRAWAL RATE

Figure 15-1 shows the number of years that a nest egg will last at a given annual rate of withdrawal. Retirees are often concerned about how long their money will last. If you withdraw money at an annual rate that is less than its rate of return, you will never run out of money. For example, if you take 5 percent of your invested funds out each year, but it is growing at a rate of 8 percent, you will never invade principal. On the other hand, if you take 10 percent out each year from a nest egg that is earning 8 percent, as the following table shows, you will run out of money in 20 years. This can be determined by looking at the box where the 10 percent rate of withdrawal column intersects with the 8 percent rate of return column.

16

Worksheets and Checklists

PERSONAL INVESTMENT SUMMARY

The worksheet in Figure 16-1 can be used to facilitate the process of summarizing your investment portfolio.

PERSONAL INVESTMENT EVALUATION CHECKLIST

The checklist in Figure 16-2 can help guide you in evaluating your current investments and investing wisely in the future.

FINANCIAL PLANNING CHECKUP

The checklist in Figure 16-3 will help you identify matters in all areas of personal financial planning that may require further attention. If a particular question does not apply to you, leave it unanswered.

Figure 16-1. Personal Investment Summary

Date at which market values are indicated: _____

Description	Number of Shares or Face Value	Date Acquired	Original Cost	Current Market Value	Estimated Annual Interest or Dividend
1. Cash equivalent investments:					
Money market funds and accounts			$	$	$
Savings Accounts					
CDs					

Figure 16–1. Personal Investment Summary (*Continued*)

Date at which market values are indicated: _____

Description	Number of Shares or Face Value	Date Acquired	Original Cost	Current Market Value	Estimated Annual Interest or Dividend
Other cash equivalent investments					
Total cash equivalent investments			$ ____	$ ____	$ ____
2. Fixed-income investments:					
U.S. government securities					
U.S. government securities funds					
Mortgage-backed securities					
Mortgage-backed securities funds					

Figure 16-1. Personal Investment Summary (*Continued*)

Date at which market values are indicated: _____

Description	Number of Shares or Face Value	Date Acquired	Original Cost	Current Market Value	Estimated Annual Interest or Dividend
Corporate bonds	____ ____	____	____	____	____
	____ ____	____	____	____	____
Corporate bond funds	____ ____	____	____	____	____
	____ ____	____	____	____	____
Municipal bonds	____ ____	____	____	____	____
	____ ____	____	____	____	____
Municipal bond funds	____ ____	____	____	____	____
	____ ____	____	____	____	____

Figure 10.1 Personal Investment Summary (Continued)

Date at which market values are indicated: _____

Description	Number of Shares or Face Value	Date Acquired	Original Cost	Current Market Value	Estimated Annual Interest or Dividend
Other fixed-income investments					
Total fixed-income investments			$	$	$
3. Equity Investments:					
Common stock in publicly traded companies			$	$	$
Stock mutual funds					
Precious metals and precious metal funds					
Other equity investments					
Total equity investments			$	$	$

Figure 16-1. Personal Investment Summary (Continued)

Date at which market values are indicated: _____

Description	Number of Shares or Face Value	Date Acquired	Original Cost	Current Market Value	Estimated Annual Interest or Dividend
4. Real estate investments:					
Undeveloped land	_____	_____	$ _____	$ _____	$ _____
	_____	_____	_____	_____	_____
Directly owned, income-producing real estate	_____	_____	_____	_____	_____
	_____	_____	_____	_____	_____
Real estate limited partnerships	_____	_____	_____	_____	_____
	_____	_____	_____	_____	_____
Total real estate investments			$ _____	$ _____	$ _____
5. Interests in privately held businesses:					
	_____	_____	_____	$ _____	$ _____
	_____	_____	_____	_____	_____
Total interests in privately held businesses			$ _____	$ _____	$ _____
Grand total investments			$ _____	$ _____	$ _____

Figure 16-2. Evaluation of Personal Investments

	Current Status	
	I Need To Do This	I Have Done This (Or I Don't Need To)
1. Establish short- and long-term investment objectives. Review them periodically to keep them up to date.	☐	☐
2. Familiarize yourself with the variety of commonly used investment securities. Learn about the current investment climate.	☐	☐
3. Determine an allocation for your investments among stock, interest-earning securities, and real estate that is appropriate for your age and position.	☐	☐
4. Summarize your current investments, including any retirement plan investments.	☐	☐
5. Determine how your investments are currently allocated among the three investment categories.	☐	☐
6. Redeploy your investments to achieve the allocation you want. Keep a portion of your portfolio sufficiently liquid to provide for unanticipated emergencies.	☐	☐
7. Build up your investment portfolio by saving regularly. Formulate an explicit program for doing this.	☐	☐
8. Coordinate your investing with other areas of financial planning, particularly taxes and estate planning.	☐	☐
9. Develop a buy and hold strategy. Stick to it.	☐	☐
10. Maximize portfolio diversification by including mutual fund investments in your portfolio.	☐	☐
11. Never invest in real estate (or anything else) for solely tax-motivated reasons. Evaluate a contemplated real estate investment by its economic merit.	☐	☐

PERSONAL RECORD KEEPING ORGANIZER

Figure 16-4 serves two purposes. First, you can indicate next to each item where that particular item is now located. Second, you can organize your personal records by consolidating your documents into the three files noted in the figure.

PERSONAL BUDGET PLANNER

Individuals and families should prepare budgets just like businesses. Figure 16-5 can be used either to record your past cash receipts and cash disbursements and/or to budget future receipts and disbursements. You may want to use the first column to record your past receipts and disbursements, the second column to list your budget over the next month, quarter, or year, and the third column to compare your actual future receipts and disbursements against your budget in the second column. If you budget over a period of less than one year, be sure to take into consideration those expenses that you pay less frequently than monthly, such as insurance, vacations, and tuition. You should be setting aside an amount each month that will eventually cover those large bills.

Indicate at the top of each column whether the amounts in that column are actual or estimated past figures or budgeted future figures. Also indicate the time period in each column, e.g., "March 1991" or "Year 1990."

Figure 16-3. Financial Planning Checklist

	Yes	No or Not Sure
Planning and Record Keeping		
1. Have you established realistic short-term financial goals?	☐	☐
2. Have you established realistic long-term financial goals?	☐	☐
3. Have you developed a satisfactory record keeping system that is simple enough to use yet comprehensive enough to be useful?	☐	☐
4. Do you use a safe-deposit box for storage of valuable papers and possessions?	☐	☐
5. Do you maintain an up-to-date inventory of the contents of the safe-deposit box?	☐	☐
6. Have you prepared a comprehensive and up-to-date inventory of household furnishings and possessions?	☐	☐
7. Do you prepare a personal balance sheet periodically?	☐	☐
8. Have you prepared a household budget listing expected income and expenses?	☐	☐
9. Do you have sufficient cash reserves to avoid being financially strapped periodically because of unexpected expenses or large annual bills?	☐	☐
Insurance		
1. Have you obtained sufficient life insurance to prevent your dependents from suffering financial hardship in the event of death?	☐	☐

Figure 16-3. Financial Planning Checklist (*Continued*)

	Yes	No or Not Sure
2. Has your spouse obtained sufficient life insurance to meet the financial needs of dependents in the event of death?	☐	☐
3. Have you determined the most appropriate form of life insurance to meet those needs?	☐	☐
4. Does the entire family have comprehensive and continuous health insurance coverage?	☐	☐
5. Have any elderly members of the family acquired Medicare gap insurance and considered acquiring long-term care insurance?	☐	☐
6. Do you have adequate long-term disability insurance coverage (equivalent to at least 60% of salary)?	☐ ☐	☐ ☐
7. Does your spouse have adequate long-term disability insurance coverage?	☐	☐
8. Do both spouses' disability policies provide benefits as long as they are prevented from gainful employment in their "usual and customary" occupation?	☐ ☐	☐ ☐
9. Do your disability policies cover both illness and accident?	☐	☐
10. Do you have adequate homeowner's or renter's insurance?	☐	☐
11. Does your homeowner's or renter's policy provide replacement cost coverage for the home?	☐	☐

Figure 16–3. Financial Planning Checklist (*Continued*)

	Yes	No or Not Sure
12. Does your homeowner's or renter's policy provide replacement cost coverage for the contents of the home?	☐	☐
13. Have you obtained additional insurance protection for jewelry, silverware, safe-deposit box contents, or other valuables?	☐	☐
14. Do you have adequate personal liability (umbrella) insurance coverage?	☐	☐
15. If your profession warrants it, do you have adequate professional liability insurance coverage?	☐	☐
16. Does your spouse have adequate professional liability insurance coverage, if applicable?	☐	☐
Borrowing and Credit		
1. Have you established your credit through borrowing for worthwhile purposes?	☐	☐
2. If you have a home equity loan, are you paying off the principal on a regular basis?	☐	☐
3. Are you confident that you will have sufficient resources to fund your children's education?	☐	☐
4. Are you aware of your personal credit rating as reported by the national credit bureaus?	☐	☐
5. If you have an automobile loan, will it be paid off well in advance of your acquiring another automobile?	☐	☐

Figure 16–3. Financial Planning Checklist (*Continued*)

	Yes	No or Not Sure
Savings and Investments		
1. Do you save through payroll withholding or other regular savings programs?	☐	☐
2. Have you established an emergency fund of liquid savings equal to at least three months' salary?	☐	☐
3. Is more than two-thirds of your total portfolio invested in the stock market?	☐	☐
4. Is more than two-thirds of your total portfolio invested in savings instruments (e.g., savings accounts, certificates of deposit, bonds, government securities)?	☐	☐
5. Do you have appropriate investment objectives?	☐	☐
6. Are your investments appropriate for your age, wealth, and family status as well as for your investment objectives?	☐	☐
7. Do you review the investment portfolio regularly?	☐	☐
8. Are your investments appropriate in terms of risk?	☐	☐
9. Do you participate in your employer's stock purchase and/or thrift plans?	☐	☐
10. Is your investment portfolio appropriately diversified?	☐	☐
11. If you expect to receive a substantial inheritance, have you considered how to invest and manage it?	☐	☐

Figure 16-3. Financial Planning Checklist (*Continued*)

	Yes	No or Not Sure
Real Estate		
1. If you don't own a home or condominium, do you plan to buy one in the future?	☐	☐
2. If you are contemplating future real estate investments, either directly owned or through limited partnerships, do you understand the risks associated with them?	☐	☐
3. Are your real estate investments appropriate to your financial circumstances?	☐	☐
Tax Planning		
1. Are you well-informed about tax-saving techniques and current tax law?	☐	☐
2. Do you keep a notebook handy to record miscellaneous tax-deductible expenses?	☐	☐
3. Do you maintain adequate tax records?	☐	☐
4. Are you familiar with tax-advantaged investments?	☐	☐
Retirement Planning		
1. Do you make regular contributions to an Individual Retirement Account?	☐	☐
2. If you have any income from self-employment, do you contribute to a Keogh Plan or Simplified Employee Pension (SEP)?	☐	☐
3. Are you currently enrolled in a company pension plan?	☐	☐
4. Do you participate in an employer-sponsored salary reduction [401-(k)] plan?	☐	☐
5. If you are contemplating early retirement, are you preparing for the increased financial requirements of such an action?	☐	☐

Figure 16-3. Financial Planning Checklist (*Continued*)

	Yes	No or Not Sure
6. Will your estimated retirement income be sufficient to meet your retirement expenses?	☐	☐
7. Are you taking action now to assure financial security by retirement age?	☐	☐
8. If you are nearing retirement age, have you evaluated your investment portfolio mix in light of retirement income needs?	☐	☐
9. If you are nearing retirement age, have you decided where to live during retirement?	☐	☐
10. If you are nearing retirement age, have you discussed expected pension benefits with a company representative?	☐	☐
11. Have you requested from the Social Security Administration a record of your earnings and an estimate of your retirement benefits?	☐	☐
Estate Planning		
1. Do you have a valid will?	☐	☐
2. Do you review your will periodically to assure that it still conforms to your wishes?	☐	☐
3. Does your spouse also have a valid and current will?	☐	☐
4. Have you prepared a letter of instructions?	☐	☐
5. Has your spouse prepared a letter of instructions?	☐	☐

Figure 16–3. Financial Planning Checklist (*Continued*)

	Yes	No or Not Sure
6. Have you discussed both the location and the contents of the will and letter of instructions with your family?	☐	☐
7. Have you appointed a financial guardian for any dependent children?	☐	☐
8. Have you appointed a personal guardian for any dependent children?	☐	☐
9. Have you established an adult guardianship arrangement (durable power of attorney, living trust) in the event that either spouse becomes disabled or mentally incapacitated?	☐	☐
10. Is the manner in which you own property (single ownership, joint ownership) consistent with effective estate planning?	☐	☐
11. Have you evaluated the estate planning and estate tax implications of owning business or real estate interests in more than one state?	☐	☐
12. Have you evaluated the impact of possible long-term uninsured hospitalization during retirement?	☐	☐

Figure 16–4. Personal Record Keeping Organizer

I. Items for Storage in a Safe-Deposit Box

Personal
1. Family birth certificates   _____
2. Family death certificates   _____
3. Marriage certificate   _____
4. Citizenship papers   _____
5. Adoption papers   _____
6. Veteran's papers   _____
7. Social Security verification   _____

Ownership
1. Bonds and certificates   _____
2. Deeds   _____
3. Automobile titles   _____
4. Household inventories
5. Home ownership records (e.g. blueprints,   _____
   deeds, surveys, capital addition records,
   yearly records)
6. Copies of trust documents   _____

Obligation/Contract
1. Contracts   _____
2. Copies of insurance policies   _____
3. IOUs   _____
4. Retirement and pension plan documents

Copies of Estate-Planning Documents
1. Wills   _____
2. Living wills   _____
3. Trusts   _____
4. Letters of instruction   _____
5. Guardianship arrangements   _____

II. Items for Storage in Home Active File

Current Income/Expense Documents
1. Unpaid bills   _____
2. Current bank statements   _____
3. Current broker's statements   _____
4. Current cancelled checks and money order   _____
   receipts
5. Credit card information   _____

Contractual Documents
1. Loan statements and payment books   _____
2. Appliance manuals and warranties   _____
   (including date and place of purchase)

Figure 16-4. Personal Record Keeping Organizer *(Continued)*

3. Insurance policies   _____
   Home
   Life   _____
   Automobile   _____
   Personal liability   _____
   Health and medical   _____
   Other: _____   _____
4. Receipts for expensive items not yet paid for   _____

Personal
1. Employment records   _____
2. Health and benefits information   _____
3. Family health records   _____
4. Copies of wills   _____
5. Copies of letters of instruction   _____
6. Education information   _____
7. Cemetery records   _____
8. Important telephone numbers   _____
9. Inventory and spare key to safe-deposit box   _____
10. Receipts for items under warranty   _____
11. Receipts for expensive items   _____

Tax
1. Tax receipts   _____
2. Paid bill receipts (with deductible receipts   _____
   filed separately to facilitate tax preparation
   and possibly reduce taxes)
3. Brokerage transaction advices   _____
4. Income tax working papers   _____
5. Credit statements   _____
6. Income and expense records for rental   _____
   properties
7. Medical, dental, and drug expenses   _____
8. Records of business expenses

III. Items for Storage in Home Inactive File
1. Prior tax returns   _____
2. Home improvement records   _____
3. Brokerage advices (prior to three most recent   _____
   years)
4. Family health records (prior to three most   _____
   recent years)
5. Proof that major debts or other major   _____
   contracts have been met
6. Cancelled checks (prior to three most recent   _____
   years)

Figure 16–5. Personal Budget Planner

Indicate if actual or budget: ——— ——— ———
Indicate the time period: ——— ——— ———

Cash Receipts
1. Gross salary $——— $——— $———
2. Interest ——— ——— ———
3. Dividends ——— ——— ———
4. Bonuses/profit sharing ——— ——— ———
5. Alimony/child support received ——— ——— ———
6. Distributions from partnerships ——— ——— ———
7. Income from outside businesses ——— ——— ———
8. Trust distributions ——— ——— ———
9. Pension ——— ——— ———
10. Social Security ——— ——— ———
11. Gifts ——— ——— ———
12. Proceeds from sale of investments ——— ——— ———
13. Other
   -——————————— ——— ——— ———
   -——————————— ——— ——— ———
   -——————————— ——— ——— ———
14. Total cash receipts $——— $——— $———

Cash Disbursements
1. Housing (rent/mortgage) $——— $——— $———
2. Food ——— ——— ———
3. Household maintenance ——— ——— ———
4. Utilities and telephone ——— ——— ———
5. Clothing ——— ——— ———
6. Personal care ——— ——— ———
7. Medical and dental care ——— ——— ———
8. Automobile/transportation ——— ——— ———
9. Childcare expenses ——— ——— ———
10. Entertainment ——— ——— ———
11. Vacation(s) ——— ——— ———
12. Gifts ——— ——— ———
13. Contributions ——— ——— ———
14. Insurance ——— ——— ———
15. Miscellaneous out-of-pocket expenses ——— ——— ———
16. Furniture ——— ——— ———
17. Home improvements ——— ——— ———
18. Real estate taxes ——— ——— ———

Figure 16–5. Personal Budget Planner *(Continued)*

19. Loan payments
20. Credit card payments
21. Alimony/child support payments
22. Tuition/educational expenses
23. Business and professional expenses
24. Savings/investments
25. Income and Social Security taxes
26. Other

    -_____
    -_____
    -_____

27. Total cash disbursements $_____ $_____ $_____

Excess (Shortfall) of Cash Receipts
Over Cash Disbursements $_____ $_____ $_____

STATEMENT OF PERSONAL ASSETS AND LIABILITIES

Figure 16-6 can be used to summarize your assets and liabilities. Three columns are included so that you can periodically monitor your progress. This statement should be prepared at least once per year and many people prepare it more frequently.

SUMMARY OF PERSONAL INSURANCE COVERAGE

Figure 16-7 can assist you in summarizing your insurance policies and evaluating the adequacy of your insurance coverage.

COLLEGE EDUCATION FUNDING WORKSHEET

Figure 16-8 can be used to estimate how much you will need to save each year in order to fund future college expenses. The college education cost forecaster projects average college education costs for a 4-year public or private school education for children who are now

Figure 16–6. Statement of Personal Assets and Liabilities

	19___	19___	19___
Assets			
1. Cash in checking and brokerage accounts	$	$	$
2. Money market funds and accounts			
3. Fixed-income investments			
Savings accounts			
CDs			
Government securities and funds			
Mortgage-backed securities and funds			
Corporate bonds and bond funds			
Municipal bonds and bond funds			
Other fixed-income investments			
4. Stock investments			
Common stock in publicly traded companies			
Stock mutual funds			
Other stock investments			
5. Real estate investments			
Undeveloped land			
Directly owned, income-producing real estate			
Real estate limited partnerships			
6. Ownership interest in private business			
7. Cash value of life insurance policies			
8. Retirement-oriented assets			
Individual retirement accounts			
Salary reduction 401(k) plans			

Figure 16-6. Statement of Personal Assets and Liabilities *(Continued)*

	19___	19___	19___	19___
Keogh or simplified employee pension plans	$	$	$	$
Vested interest in corporate pension and profit-sharing plans				
Employee thrift and stock purchase plans				
Tax-deferred annuities				
Other retirement-oriented assets				
9. Personal assets				
Personal residence(s)				
Automobile(s)				
Jewelry				
Personal property				
10. Other assets				
_____				
_____				
11. Total assets	$	$	$	$
Liabilities				
1. Credit cards and charge accounts	$	$	$	$
2. Income taxes payable				
3. Miscellaneous accounts payable				
4. Bank loans				
5. Policy loans on life insurance policies				
6. Automobile loans				

Figure 16–6. Statement of Personal Assets and Liabilities (*Continued*)

	19___	19___	19___
7. Student loans	___	___	___
8. Mortgages on personal residence	___	___	___
9. Mortgages on investment real estate	___	___	___
10. Broker's margin loans	___	___	___
11. Limited partnership debt	___	___	___
12. Other liabilities	___	___	___
	___	___	___
	___	___	___
13. Total liabilities	$___	$___	$___
14. Net worth (total assets less total liabilities)	$___	$___	$___

Note: Assets should be listed at their current market values. Be realistic in valuing those assets that require an estimate of market value such as your home and personal property.

Figure 16-7. Personal Insurance Coverage

Type of Insurance	Annual Cost	Dollar Amount of Protection	Coverage is Adequate	Coverage is Inadequate or Unsure	Cash Surrender Value
Life, health, and annuities					
Life					
Term (or group)	$____	$____			
Whole life	____	____	☐	☐	____
Universal	____	____	☐	☐	____
Variable	____	____	☐	☐	____
Endowment	____	____	☐	☐	____
Health and accident	____	____	☐	☐	
Disability	____	____	☐	☐	
Annuities	____	____	☐	☐	____
Property					
Homeowner's	____	____	☐	☐	
Household goods and personal effects floater	____	____	☐	☐	
Renter's	____	____	☐	☐	
Safe-deposit box	____	____	☐	☐	
Flood insurance	____	____	☐	☐	
Automobile					
Bodily injury liability	____	____	☐	☐	
Property damage liability	____	____	☐	☐	
Medical payments	____	____	☐	☐	
Comprehensive	____	____	☐	☐	
Collision	____	____	☐	☐	
Uninsured motorists	____	____	☐	☐	
Motorcycle, boat, airplane	____	____	☐	☐	
Other					
Farm owner's	____	____	☐	☐	
Extended personal liability (umbrella)	____	____	☐	☐	

Figure 16–8. College Education Funding Worksheet

College Education Cost Forecaster
The following table projects current average 4-year education costs compiled by the College Board, assuming a 6% annual increase in costs. These figures can be used as a guide in estimating the costs of college for your child or children.

Year Entering	Public School	Private School	Selective Private School
1991	$24,405	$ 62,104	$ 87,690
1992	25,870	65,831	92,951
1993	27,422	69,780	98,528
1994	29,067	73,967	104,440
1995	30,811	78,405	110,706
1996	32,660	83,110	117,348
1997	34,620	88,096	124,389
1998	36,697	93,382	131,853
1999	38,899	98,985	139,764
2000	41,232	104,923	148,150
2001	43,706	111,219	157,039
2002	46,329	117,893	166,461
2003	49,109	124,966	176,449
2004	52,055	132,464	187,036
2005	55,178	140,412	198,258
2006	58,489	148,837	210,153
2007	61,998	157,767	222,762
2008	65,718	167,233	236,127
2009	69,661	177,267	250,295
2010	73,841	187,903	265,313

College Education Savings Estimator
Name of Child _____ _____ _____   **Total**

1. Total estimated college costs
   (from above) $____ $____ $____ $_____
2. Amount of savings currently
   available for college[1] $____ $____ $____
3. Multiplied by appreciation
   factor (from table)[2]   ×____ ×____ ×____
4. Equals estimated amount of
   current savings available at
   college age (line 2 times
   line 3) $____ $____ $____
5. Estimated amount of costs
   remaining to be funded
   (line 1 minus line 4) $____ $____ $____
6. Adjustments[3] $____ $____ $____ $____
7. Equals amount that you wish
   to accumulate by college age
   (line 5 plus/minus line 6) $____ $____ $____ $____
8. Multiplied by accumulation
   factor from table[4]   ×____ ×____ ×____

Figure 16–8. College Education Funding Worksheet (*Continued*)

9. Equals the amount to be
   saved each year to meet
   future college costs[5] $_____ $_____ $_____ $_____

Appreciation Factor For Line 3

Year Child Enters College	Factor	Year Child Enters College	Factor
1991	1.07	2001	2.11
1992	1.15	2002	2.25
1993	1.23	2003	2.41
1994	1.31	2004	2.58
1995	1.40	2005	2.76
1996	1.50	2006	2.94
1997	1.60	2007	3.15
1998	1.72	2008	3.37
1999	1.84	2009	3.61
2000	1.97	2010	3.87

Accumulation Factor Table for Line 8

Year Child Enters College	Factor	Year Child Enters College	Factor
1991	.483	2001	.056
1992	.311	2002	.050
1993	.225	2003	.044
1994	.174	2004	.040
1995	.140	2005	.036
1996	.116	2006	.032
1997	.097	2007	.027
1998	.083	2008	.027
1999	.072	2009	.024
2000	.063	2010	.022

[1]Indicate on line 2 any savings you now have that are earmarked to pay education costs. Many parents with more than one child simply divide these savings equally among the children unless the savings or investment accounts are in a specified child's name.

[2]The appreciation factor on Line 3 is provided in the above table. It recognizes the future increase in value of the savings or investments that you presently have earmarked for college costs. The factor assumes a 7 percent annual increase in value.

[3]Many parents will want to make adjustments in Line 6 to the estimated amount of college costs to be funded. Reductions might be appropriate in situations where financial aid can reasonably be anticipated or where the child will be expected to contribute to college costs through summer or school-year income. Additions to the estimated costs to be funded will be appropriate if, for example, the parent expects the child to go to a college that is more expensive than the average. Selective private colleges, in particular, may be considerably more expensive than the averages provided on this worksheet.

[4]The accumulation factor to be entered on Line 2 is provided in the above table. Multiplying this factor by the amount of money that you wish to accumulate by college age will show the amount of money that you would need to save each year to accumulate the necessary funds. An annual return of 7 percent is assumed.

[5]Parents are often dismayed by the amount of money that they would have to save each year to meet future college costs (Line 9). Don't be discouraged, however. The important thing to do is to begin a regular savings program even if it's only a portion of the amount indicated. Remember also that the annual amount to be saved assumes level payment. Even if you can afford to save only a portion of the amount indicated on Line 9, you will still be able to accumulate a nest egg that will go a long way toward easing the financial burden of your children's education. It is often more realistic for parents to gradually increase the amount of money they set aside each year.

between 1 and 17 years old. The college education savings forecaster calculates how much you will have to save to meet those costs.

RETIREMENT PLANNING TIMETABLE

It's never too early to plan for retirement. To prepare for a financially comfortable retirement, you need to take action throughout your working years. The following timetable describes important steps to take at various ages to help you on your way.

During All Working Years

1. Make sure you always have adequate and continuous insurance coverage.
2. Consider the ramifications on future pension benefits of any contemplated job change. Job hopping can curtail pension benefits severely.
3. Roll over any vested pension benefits received as a result of a job change into an IRA or other tax-deferred retirement plan.

Before Age 40

1. Contribute regularly to an IRA or other retirement-earmarked savings fund.
2. Purchase a home so that by the time you retire your housing costs will be under control.
3. Discuss the fine points of the pension plan with your company's benefits officer.

Ages 40–49

1. Periodically check with Social Security by requesting and filing form SSA-7004. You will receive a "Personal Earnings and Benefit Estimate Statement" to verify that your wages are being properly credited to your account and to prepare retirement income projections.

2. Analyze personal assets, and work out a plan for funding an adequate retirement income.
3. Actively manage your IRA and other retirement funds with appropriate emphasis on capital gains-oriented investments.
4. Make a will, and review it every 3 years or when moving to another state. Discuss other estate planning techniques with an experienced estate planning attorney.

Ages 50–59

1. Continue to request your Social Security "Personal Earnings and Benefit Estimate Statement" periodically.
2. Review your status with your company's pension plan regularly.
3. Revise your retirement income and expense projections, taking inflation into consideration.
4. Confirm the beneficiary designations on life insurance policies.
5. Start gradually shifting some of your IRA and other retirement-earmarked funds into lower risk investments with more emphasis on yield.
6. Join the American Association of Retired Persons to take advantage of the may sources of information and help that they offer. The address is:
AARP
1909 K St., N.W.
Washington, DC 20049

Ages 60–64

1. If you are contemplating an early retirement, discuss the advantages and disadvantages with your employer's personnel office and the Social Security office.
2. Collect the documents necessary to process Social Security benefits:-
Both spouses' Social Security cards
- Proof of both spouses' ages
- Marriage certificate
- Copy of latest income tax withholding statement (W-2)

3. Before taking any major actions, such as selling a house, weigh the merits of waiting until age 65 when many special breaks are available to the elderly or retired.

4. Determine the status and duration of ongoing financial commitments such as mortgages and loans.

5. Prepare detailed cash flow projections from estimated year of retirement until age 90, taking inflation into consideration.

6. Practice living for a month under the planned retirement income.

7. Consider different retirement locations. If a location other than the present home is chosen, try living there for a while before making the move.

Right Before Retirement

1. Establish what your retirement income will be, and estimate as closely as possible what your retirement costs of living will be.

2. Have your employer's personnel officer determine exactly what your pension benefits will be, what company or bank will send the pension, and when the first check (or lump sum distribution) will arrive; what can be done about accumulated vacation time; whether there are any special annuity benefits; and whether supplemental or hospital insurance is available.

3. Register with the Social Security Administration at least three months before retirement.

4. Inquire about possible entitlements to partial pensions from past jobs.

RETIREMENT EXPENSE AND RESOURCES FORECASTER

Figure 16-9 can be used to approximate the amount of annual retirement income that will allow you to maintain your preretirement standard of living. First, the approximate income necessary to main-

Figure 16–9. Amount of Annual Retirement Income Needed to Maintain Preretirement Standard of Living

Current gross annual income[1]	$_____
Minus amount of annual savings[2]	(_____)
Subtotal (the amount you spend currently)	_____
Multiplied by 75%[3]	× .75
Equals approximate annual cost (in current dollars) of maintaining your current standard of living if you were retiring this year	$_____
Multiplied by inflation factor (Refer to inflation factor table below)[4]	× _____
Equals approximate annual cost (in future dollars) of maintaining your current standard of living when you retire	$_____

Inflation Factor Table

Number of Years Until Retirement	Factor
5	1.2
10	1.6
15	1.9
20	2.4
25	3.0
30	3.7
35	4.7
40	5.8

[1]"Current gross annual income" includes all income from all sources.

[2]"Annual savings" includes, in addition to the usual sources of savings, reinvested dividends and capital gains, and any contributions to retirement plans that are taken from your annual income.

[3]The 75% multiplier is a general rule of thumb that says, in essence, that a retiree can maintain his/her preretirement standard of living by spending roughly 75% of his/her preretirement income. Of course, individual circumstances may dictate a higher or lower percentage. Ideally, you should prepare a retirement budget that details expected expenses. You may find a multiplier less than 75% in some circumstances (e.g., low housing costs due to paid-off mortgage) or, in other circumstances, a higher multiplier (e.g., extensive travel plans).

[4]In order to project retirement expenses to retirement age, current dollar living expenses must be multiplied by a factor to account for inflationary increases. The inflation factor table can be used for that purpose. The assumed long-term inflation rate is 4.5%.

Figure 16–10. Pension and Social Security Forecast-Savings and Investments Needed

	Current Dollars	Times Inflation Factor(1)	Future (Retirement Age) Dollars
1. Estimated annual living expenses at retirement age[1]			$_____
2. Annual pension income (projection at retirement age available from employer)[2]	$____ ×	____ =	_____
3. Plus annual Social Security benefits (projection at retirement age available from Social Security Administration)[3]	$____ ×	____ =	_____
4. Subtotal projected pension and Social Security income (add lines 2 and 3)			_____
5. Shortfall (if expenses are greater than income) that must be funded out of personal savings/investments (subtract line 4 from line 1)			_____
6. Multiplied by 17[4]			_____ × 1?
7. Equals amount of savings/investments in future dollars that need to be accumulated by retirement age to fund retirement[5]			$_____

[1]Use Inflation Factor Table from Figure 16–9 for the appropriate calculation.

[2]Employers usually provide pension plan projections at retirement age, expressed in cur dollars. If so, the amount should be multiplied by an inflation factor to approximate benefi future dollars.

[3]Social Security estimates are expressed in current dollars and therefore they shoul adjusted for inflation similar to footnote 2 above.

[4]As a general rule of thumb, for every $1,000 of annual income you will need to fun retirement age, you will need to have at least $17,000 in savings/investments in order to keep up inflation. If you plan to retire before age 62, use a factor of 20, rather than 17.

[5]You may be dismayed by the magnitude of the amount of personal resources that you need to fund your retirement, which can easily exceed $1,000,000 for younger persons and/or pe with minimal pension benefits. Nevertheless, good savings habits combined with the powe compounding can usually close the gap between current resources and eventual needs.

Figure 16-11. Annual Amount of Savings Required to Meet Retirement Objectives

1. Amount of savings/investments in future dollars that need to be accumulated by retirement age to fund retirement (from Figure 16–10)	\$_____
2. Minus resources that are currently available for retirement purposes[1]	\$_____
3. Multiplied by appreciation factor (refer to annual appreciation factor table below)[2]	× _____
4. Equals estimated future value of retirement resources that are currently available (Multiply Line 2 by Line 3)	(_____)
5. Retirement funds needed by retirement age (Subtract Line 4 from Line 1)	_____
6. Multiplied by annual savings factor (Refer to annual savings factor table below)[3]	× _____
7. Equals savings needed over the next year (Multiply Line 5 by Line 6)[4]	\$_____

Appreciation Factor Table		Annual Savings Factor Table	
Number of Years Until Retirement	Factor	Number of Years Until Retirement	Factor
5	1.4	5	.1513
10	2.1	10	.0558
15	3.0	15	.0274
20	4.2	20	.0151
25	6.1	25	.0088
30	8.8	30	.0054
35	12.6	35	.0034
40	18.0	40	.0022

[1]Resources that are currently available typically include the current value of all of your investment-related assets that are not expected to be used before retirement. Don't include the value of your home unless you expect to sell it to raise money for retirement. Don't include any vested pension benefits if you have already factored them in on Line 2 of Figure 16–10.

[2]The appreciation factor is used to estimate what your currently available retirement resources will be worth when you retire. The appreciation factor assumes a 7½ percent after-tax rate of appreciation.

[3]The annual savings factor computes the amount you will need to save during the next year in order to begin accumulating the retirement fund needed by retirement age as indicated on Line 5. The annual savings factor assumes a 7½ percent after-tax rate of return.

[4]The annual savings needed to accumulate your retirement nest egg assumes that you will increase the amount of money you save by 5 percent each year until retirement.

Figure 16–12. Estate Planning Review Checklist

	Yes	No	N/
1. Have you clearly articulated your wishes regarding the ultimate disposition of your estate?	☐	☐	☐
2. Do you have an up-to-date will that is consistent with your personal wishes and individual circumstances?	☐	☐	☐
3. Has an appropriate executor been named? (Your spouse or children may not be the best choice for executor.)	☐	☐	☐
4. Have you prepared an up-to-date letter of instructions?	☐	☐	☐
5. Have you provided an appropriate adult guardianship arrangement (such as a durable power of attorney or living trust) in the event you should become incompetent?	☐	☐	☐
6. Have you designated personal and financial guardians for children and other dependents?	☐	☐	☐
7. Have you considered preparing a living will?	☐	☐	☐
8. Have you estimated the size of the taxable estate?	☐	☐	☐
9. Have provisions been made to provide adequate estate liquidity upon your death?	☐	☐	☐
10. Have you evaluated the impact of estate taxes on the estate?	☐	☐	☐
11. Are the property ownership designations (single ownership, joint ownership, etc.) pertaining to your assets appropriate from an estate planning standpoint?	☐	☐	☐
12. Married people often assume that one spouse, typically the husband, will predecease the other spouse. Have you imagined the personal and estate planning effects if the assumed order of death does not occur?	☐	☐	☐
13. Are your gifts to children or charities consistent with your financial condition and estate planning program? (Gifting programs by the elderly are sometimes too generous.)	☐	☐	☐

Figure 16–12. Estate Planning Review Checklist *(Continued)*

	Yes	No	N/A
14. Have appropriate provisions been made in your estate planning process if you own property in more than one state?	☐	☐	☐
15. Have trusts been considered as part of the estate planning process?	☐	☐	☐
16. If you have a closely held business, have provisions been made for its disposition that are consistent with estate planning requirements?	☐	☐	☐
17. Have you considered the possibility that you may incur substantial uninsured health care costs in retirement?	☐	☐	☐
18. Does the estate plan include provisions for any heirs or dependents who may have special needs?	☐	☐	☐
19. Do you have a clear understanding of what employee benefits will be paid/available upon death?	☐	☐	☐
20. Have you clearly articulated your funeral wishes for your survivors?	☐	☐	☐
21. If you have elderly parents and/or grandparents, are you aware of any gap or omission in their estate plan?	☐	☐	☐

tain current living standard in current dollars is calculated. Then, by reference to inflation tables, you can project this amount to your estimated retirement date.

Figure 16-10 can be used to forecast pension and Social Security benefits at retirement age and then approximate the total amount of savings/investments that will be needed by retirement age to cover any shortfall between Social Security/pension benefits and your total income needs.

Figure 16-11 can be used to estimate the annual amount of savings that is required to accumulate the funds necessary to meet your retirement objectives. The amount computed on Line 7 equals the *required first year savings. The annual savings should be increased by 5 percent in each succeeding year until you retire.*

ESTATE PLANNING REVIEW

Figure 16-12 can help you evaluate the adequacy of your family's overall estate planning program. Although estate planning concerns typically assume prominence for older and elderly persons, you should review the following checklist items no matter how young you are. Most of the following checklist items apply both to you and your spouse, if applicable.

Index

Take Control Over Your Financial Future

Now that you're ready to take control of your financial future, you're ready for **SMART PLANNER**. **SMART PLANNER** is an innovative approach to individual financial analysis that gives you a personalized report on your unique financial needs. Developed by Jonathan Pond, **SMART PLANNER** provides useful recommendations to help you in all the areas covered in this book, including:

- Saving
- Investing
- Real estate
- Insurance

- Retirement planning
- Record keeping
- Income taxes

- Budgeting
- Education planning
- Estate planning

Your personalized **SMART PLANNER** report will show you how to:

- Save more in order to assure financial security
- Make the right kind of investments to meet your financial goals
- Avoid making financially crippling mistakes
- Take immediate action to assure a comfortable retirement
- Assure you will be cared for if you are disabled
- Avoid having a judge decide who should inherit your estate

SMART PLANNER is:

- *Unbiased*   **SMART PLANNER** is not affiliated with any financial institution. Its analysis and recommendations are completely objective.
- *Customized*   Your report addresses your specific financial status and needs. Persons of all ages and income levels benefit from **SMART PLANNER** since each report is unique.
- *Easy to Understand*   You are assured of receiving up-to-date information in everyday language.
- *Confidential*   Information from your questionnaire and report is held in the strictest confidence.
- *Realistic*   **SMART PLANNER** provides down-to-earth recommendations, not "get rich quick" schemes.
- *Guaranteed*   If you are not completely satisfied with your **SMART PLANNER** report, your money will be refunded promptly.

IT'S EASY TO RECEIVE YOUR PERSONAL *SMART PLANNER* REPORT.

1. After ordering **SMART PLANNER**, you will receive a confidential financial planning questionnaire. The questionnaire is easy to fill out. You will not have to spend hours digging up obscure financial information and filling out confusing financial forms. In fact, most people complete the questionnaire in less than 30 minutes.
2. Send the completed questionnaire back to the data center. Your responses are then processed and your individualized report is prepared.
3. Your personalized **SMART PLANNER** report is sent to you by first-class mail within two weeks. The report presents a comprehensive and objective review of your financial situation in all areas of personal finance. Age, family status, and income information provided in the questionnaire allow **SMART PLANNER** to tailor the report to your unique financial needs.

Every bit of valuable information in your 20 to 25 page report pertains to you and you alone. Plus, it comes with a list of *recommendations* in order of importance so you will know exactly which items are most essential to your financial security and *work sheets* so that you can start to take action to improve your financial status.

ORDER *SMART PLANNER* TODAY

When you're ready to order **SMART PLANNER**, send a check for $39.95 to

SMART PLANNER
9 Galen Street
Watertown, MA 02172

or call 1 (800) 448-8112 with your MasterCard or VISA ready. Massachusetts residents add 5% sales tax for a total of $41.95.